PENGUIN BOOKS

BLINK

Author, journalist, cultural commentator and intellectual adventurer, Malcolm Gladwell was born in 1963 in England to a Jamaican mother and an English mathematician father. He grew up in Canada and graduated with a degree in history from the University of Toronto in 1984. From 1987 to 1996, he was a reporter for the *Washington Post*, first as a science writer and then as New York City bureau chief. Since 1996, he has been a staff writer for the *New Yorker* magazine. His curiosity and breadth of interests are shown in *New Yorker* articles ranging over a wide array of subjects including early childhood development and the flu, not to mention hair dye, shopping and what it takes to be cool. His phenomenal bestseller *The Tipping Point* captured the world's attention with its theory that a curiously small change can have unforeseen effects, and the phrase has become part of our language, used by writers, politicians and business people everywhere to describe cultural trends and strange phenomena.

T0313562

ALSO BY MALCOLM GLADWELL

The Tipping Point

Outliers

What the Dog Saw

Blink

The Power of Thinking Without Thinking

Malcolm Gladwell

PENGUIN BOOKS

PENGUIN BOOKS

Published by the Penguin Group
Penguin Books Ltd, 80 Strand, London WC2R ORL, England
Penguin Group (USA) Inc., 375 Hudson Street, New York, New York 10014, USA
Penguin Group (Canada), 90 Eglinton Avenue East, Suite 700, Toronto, Ontario, Canada M4P 2Y3
(a division of Pearson Penguin Canada Inc.)
Penguin Ireland, 25 St Stephen's Green, Dublin 2, Ireland (a division of Penguin Books Ltd)
Penguin Group (Australia), 250 Camberwell Road, Camberwell, Victoria 3124, Australia
(a division of Pearson Australia Group Pty Ltd)
Penguin Books India Pvt Ltd, 11 Community Centre, Panchsheel Park, New Delhi – 110 017, India
Penguin Group (NZ), 67 Apollo Drive, Rosedale, North Shore 0632, New Zealand
(a division of Pearson New Zealand Ltd)
Penguin Books (South Africa) (Pty) Ltd, 24 Sturdee Avenue, Rosebank, Johannesburg 2196, South Africa

Penguin Books Ltd, Registered Offices: 80 Strand, London WC2R ORL, England

www.penguin.com

First published in the United States of America by Little, Brown and Company 2005
First published in Great Britain by Allen Lane 2005
Published in Penguin Books 2006

080

Photographs in chapter 3 by Brooke Williams

The author is grateful for permission to use the following previously copyrighted material:
Mark Sullivan, *Our Times: The United States 1900–1925*, vol. 6, *The Twenties*
(New York: Charles Scribner's Sons, 1935), 16; Dick Morris, *Behind the Oval Office*
(Los Angeles: Renaissance Books, 1999), 46–47; and David Klinger, *Into the Kill Zone:
A Cop's Eye View of Deadly Force* (San Francisco: Jossey-Bass, 2004).

Printed in England by Clays Ltd, Elcograf S.p.A

978-0-141-01459-3

www.greenpenguin.co.uk

To my parents,
Joyce and Graham Gladwell

Contents

BLINK

Introduction
The Statue That Didn't
Look Right

In September of 1983, an art dealer by the name of Gianfranco Becchina approached the J. Paul Getty Museum in California. He had in his possession, he said, a marble statue dating from the sixth century BC. It was what is known as a kouros — a sculpture of a nude male youth standing with his left leg forward and his arms at his sides. There are only about two hundred kouroi in existence, and most have been recovered badly damaged or in fragments from grave sites or archeological digs. But this one was almost perfectly preserved. It stood close to seven feet tall. It had a kind of light-colored glow that set it apart from other ancient works. It was an extraordinary find. Becchina's asking price was just under $10 million.

The Getty moved cautiously. It took the kouros on loan and began a thorough investigation. Was the statue consistent with other known kouroi? The answer appeared to be yes. The style of the sculpture seemed reminiscent of the Anavyssos kouros in the National Archaeological Museum of Athens, meaning that it seemed to fit with a particular time and place. Where and when had the statue been found? No one knew precisely, but Becchina gave the Getty's legal department a sheaf of documents relating to its more recent history. The kouros, the records stated, had been in the private collection of a Swiss physician named Lauffenberger since the 1930s, and he in turn had acquired it from a well-known Greek art dealer named Roussos.

A geologist from the University of California named Stanley Margolis came to the museum and spent two days examining the surface of the statue with a high-resolution stereomicroscope. He then removed a core sample measuring one centimeter in diameter and two centimeters in length from just below the right knee and analyzed it using an electron microscope, electron microprobe, mass spectrometry, X-ray diffraction, and X-ray fluorescence. The statue was made of dolomite marble from the ancient Cape Vathy quarry on the island of Thasos, Margolis concluded, and the surface of the statue was covered in a thin layer of calcite — which was significant, Margolis told the Getty, because dolomite can turn into calcite only over the course of hundreds, if not thousands, of years. In other words, the statue was old. It wasn't some contemporary fake.

The Getty was satisfied. Fourteen months after their investigation of the kouros began, they agreed to buy the statue. In the fall of 1986, it went on display for the first time. The *New York Times* marked the occasion with a front-page story. A few months later, the Getty's curator of antiquities, Marion True, wrote a long, glowing account of the museum's acquisition for the art journal *The Burlington Magazine*. "Now standing erect without external support, his closed hands fixed firmly to his thighs, the kouros ex-presses the confident vitality that is characteristic of the best of his brothers." True concluded triumphantly, "God or man, he embodies all the radiant energy of the adolescence of western art."

The kouros, however, had a problem. It didn't look right. The first to point this out was an Italian art histo-rian named Federico Zeri, who served on the Getty's board of trustees. When Zeri was taken down to the museum's restoration studio to see the kouros in December of 1983, he found himself staring at the sculpture's fingernails. In a way he couldn't immediately articulate, they seemed wrong to him. Evelyn Harrison was next. She was one of the world's foremost experts on Greek sculpture, and she was in Los Angeles visiting the Getty just before the museum finalized the deal with Becchina. "Arthur Hough-ton, who was then the curator, took us down to see it," Harrison remembers. "He just swished a cloth off the top of it and said, 'Well, it isn't ours yet, but it will be in a couple of weeks.' And I said, 'I'm sorry to hear that.'" What did Harrison see? She didn't know. In that very first moment, when Houghton swished off the cloth, all Harri-son had was a hunch, an instinctive sense that something was amiss. A few months later, Houghton took Thomas Hoving, the former director of the Metropolitan Museum of Art in New York, down to the Getty's conservation stu-dio to see the statue as well. Hoving always makes a note of the first word that goes through his head when he sees something new, and he'll never forget what that word was when he first saw the kouros. "It was 'fresh' — 'fresh,'" Hoving recalls. And "fresh" was not the right reaction to have to a two-thousand-year-old statue. Later, thinking back on that moment, Hoving realized why that thought had popped into his mind: "I had dug in Sicily, where we found bits and pieces of these things. They just don't come out looking like that. The kouros looked like it had been dipped in the very best caffè latte from Starbucks."

Hoving turned to Houghton. "Have you paid for this?"

Houghton, Hoving remembers, looked stunned.

"If you have, try to get your money back," Hoving said. "If you haven't, don't."

The Getty was getting worried, so they convened a special symposium on the kouros in Greece. They wrapped the statue up, shipped it to Athens, and invited the country's most senior sculpture experts. This time the chorus of dismay was even louder.

Harrison, at one point, was standing next to a man named George Despinis, the head of the Acropolis Museum in Athens. He took one look at the kouros and blanched. "Anyone who has ever seen a sculpture coming out of the ground," he said to her, "could tell that that thing has never been in the ground." Georgios Dontas, head of the Archeological Society in Athens, saw the statue and immediately felt cold. "When I saw the kouros for the first time," he said, "I felt as though there was a glass between me and the work." Dontas was followed in the symposium by Angelos Delivorrias, director of the Benaki Museum in Athens. He spoke at length on the contradiction between the style of the sculpture and the fact that the marble from which it was carved came from Thasos. Then he got to the point. Why did he think it was a fake? Because when he first laid eyes on it, he said, he felt a wave of "intuitive repulsion." By the time the symposium was over, the consensus among many of the attendees appeared to be that the kouros was not at all what it was supposed to be. The Getty, with its lawyers and scientists and months of painstaking investigation, had come to one conclusion, and some of the world's foremost experts in Greek sculpture — just by looking at the statue and sensing their own "intuitive repulsion" — had come to another. Who was right?

For a time it wasn't clear. The kouros was the kind of thing that art experts argued about at conferences. But then, bit by bit, the Getty's case began to fall apart. The letters the Getty's lawyers used to carefully trace the kouros back to the Swiss physician Lauffenberger, for instance, turned out to be fakes. One of the letters dated 1952 had a postal code on it that didn't exist until twenty years later. Another letter dated 1955 referred to a bank account that wasn't opened until 1963. Originally the conclusion of long months of research was that the Getty kouros was in the style of the Anavyssos kouros. But that, too, fell into doubt: the closer experts in Greek sculpture looked at it, the more they began to see it as a puzzling pastiche of several different styles from several different places and time periods. The young man's slender proportions looked a lot like those of the Tenea kouros, which is in a museum in Munich, and his stylized, beaded hair was a lot like that of the kouros in the Metropolitan Museum in New York. His feet, meanwhile, were, if anything, modern. The kouros it most resembled, it turned out, was a smaller, fragmentary statue that was found by a British art historian in Switzerland in 1990. The two statues were cut from similar marble and sculpted in quite similar ways.

But the Swiss kouros didn't come from ancient Greece. It came from a forger's workshop in Rome in the early 1980s. And what of the scientific analysis that said that the surface of the Getty kouros could only have aged over many hundreds or thousands of years? Well, it turns out things weren't that cut and dried. Upon further analysis, another geologist concluded that it might be possible to "age" the surface of a dolomite marble statue in a couple of months using potato mold. In the Getty's catalogue, there is a picture of the kouros, with the notation "About 530 BC, or modern forgery."

When Federico Zeri and Evelyn Harrison and Thomas Hoving and Georgios Dontas — and all the others — looked at the kouros and felt an "intuitive repulsion," they were absolutely right. In the first two seconds of looking — in a single glance — they were able to understand more about the essence of the statue than the team at the Getty was able to understand after fourteen months.

Blink is a book about those first two seconds.

1. Fast and Frugal

Imagine that I were to ask you to play a very simple gambling game. In front of you are four decks of cards — two of them red and the other two blue. Each card in those four decks either wins you a sum of money or costs you some money, and your job is to turn over cards from any of the decks, one at a time, in such a way that maximizes your winnings. What you don't know at the beginning, however, is that the red decks are a minefield. The rewards are high, but when you lose on the red cards, you lose a lot. Actually, you can win only by taking cards from the blue decks, which offer a nice steady diet of $50 payouts and modest penalties. The question is how long will it take you to figure this out?

A group of scientists at the University of Iowa did this experiment a few years ago, and what they found is that after we've turned over about fifty cards, most of us start to develop a hunch about what's going on. We don't know why we prefer the blue decks, but we're pretty sure at that point that they are a better bet. After turning over about eighty cards, most of us have figured out the game and can explain exactly why the first two decks are such a bad idea. That much is straightforward. We have some experiences. We think them through. We develop a theory. And then finally we put two and two together. That's the way learning works.

But the Iowa scientists did something else, and this is where the strange part of the experiment begins. They hooked each gambler up to a machine that measured the activity of the sweat glands below the skin in the palms of their hands. Like most of our sweat glands, those in our palms respond to stress as well as temperature — which is why we get clammy hands when we are nervous. What the Iowa scientists found is that gamblers started generating stress responses to the red decks by the tenth card, *forty* cards before they were able to say that they had a hunch about what was wrong with those two decks. More important, right around the time their palms started sweating, their behavior began to change as well. They started favoring the blue cards and taking fewer and fewer cards from the red decks. In other words, the gamblers figured the game out before they realized they had figured the game out: they began making the necessary adjustments long before they were consciously aware of what adjustments they were supposed to be making.

The Iowa experiment is just that, of course, a simple card game involving a handful of subjects and a stress detector. But it's a very powerful illustration of the way our minds work. Here is a situation where the stakes were high, where things were moving quickly, and where the participants had to make sense of a lot of new and confusing information in a very short time. What does the Iowa experiment tell us? That in those moments, our brain uses two very different strategies to make sense of the situation. The first is the one we're most familiar with. It's the conscious strategy. We think about what we've learned, and eventually we come up with an answer. This strategy is logical and definitive. But it takes us eighty cards to get there. It's slow, and it needs a lot of information. There's a second strategy, though. It operates a lot more quickly. It starts to kick in after ten cards, and it's really smart, because it picks up the problem with the red decks almost immediately. It has the drawback, however, that it operates — at least at first — entirely below the surface of consciousness. It sends its messages through weirdly indirect channels, such as the sweat glands in the palms of our hands. It's a system in which our brain reaches conclusions without immediately telling us that it's reaching conclusions.

The second strategy was the path taken by Evelyn Harrison and Thomas Hoving and the Greek scholars. They didn't weigh every conceivable strand of evidence. They considered only what could be gathered in a glance. Their thinking was what the cognitive psychologist Gerd Gigerenzer likes to call "fast and frugal." They simply took a look at that statue and some part of their brain did a series of instant calculations, and before any kind of conscious thought took place, they *felt* something, just like the sudden prickling of sweat on the palms of the gamblers. For Thomas Hoving, it was the completely inappropriate word "fresh" that suddenly popped into his head. In the case of Angelos Delivorrias, it was a wave of "intuitive repulsion." For Georgios Dontas, it was the feeling that there was a glass between him and the work. Did they know why they knew? Not at all. But they *knew*.

2. The Internal Computer

The part of our brain that leaps to conclusions like this is called the adaptive unconscious, and the study of this kind of decision making is one of the most important new fields in psychology. The adaptive unconscious is not to be confused with the unconscious described by Sigmund Freud, which was a dark and murky place filled with desires and memories and fantasies that were too disturbing for us to think about consciously. This new notion of the adaptive unconscious is thought of, instead, as a kind of giant computer that quickly and quietly processes a lot of the data we need in order to keep functioning as human beings. When you walk out into the street and suddenly realize that a truck is bearing down on you, do you have time to think through all your options? Of course not. The only way that human beings could ever have survived as a species for as long as we have is that we've developed another kind of decision-making apparatus that's capable of making very quick judgments based on very little information. As the psychologist Timothy D. Wilson writes in his book *Strangers to Ourselves:* "The mind operates most efficiently by relegating a good deal of high-level, sophisticated thinking to the unconscious, just as a modern jetliner is able to fly on automatic pilot with little or no input from the human, 'conscious' pilot. The adaptive unconscious does an excellent job of sizing up the world, warning people of danger, setting goals, and initiating action in a sophisticated and efficient manner."

Wilson says that we toggle back and forth between our conscious and unconscious modes of thinking, depending on the situation. A decision to invite a co-worker over for dinner is conscious. You think it over. You decide it will be fun. You ask him or her. The spontaneous decision to argue with that same co-worker is made unconsciously — by a different part of the brain and motivated by a different part of your personality.

Whenever we meet someone for the first time, whenever we interview someone for a job, whenever we react to a new idea, whenever we're faced with making a decision quickly and under stress, we use that second part of our brain. How long, for example, did it take you, when you were in college, to decide how good a teacher your professor was? A class? Two classes? A semester? The psychologist Nalini Ambady once gave students three ten-second videotapes of a teacher — with the sound turned off — and found they had no difficulty at all coming up with a rating of the teacher's effectiveness. Then Ambady cut the clips back to five seconds, and the ratings were the same.

They were remarkably consistent even when she showed the students just *two* seconds of videotape. Then Ambady compared those snap judgments of teacher effectiveness with evaluations of those same professors made by their students after a full semester of classes, and she found that they were also essentially the same. A person watching a silent two-second video clip of a teacher he or she has never met will reach conclusions about how good that teacher is that are very similar to those of a student who has sat in the teacher's class for an entire semester. That's the power of our adaptive unconscious.

You may have done the same thing, whether you realized it or not, when you first picked up this book. How long did you first hold it in your hands? Two seconds? And yet in that short space of time, the design of the cover, whatever associations you may have with my name, and the first few sentences about the kouros all generated an impression — a flurry of thoughts and images and preconceptions — that has fundamentally shaped the way you have read this introduction so far. Aren't you curious about what happened in those two seconds?

I think we are innately suspicious of this kind of rapid cognition. We live in a world that assumes that the quality of a decision is directly related to the time and effort that went into making it. When doctors are faced with a difficult diagnosis, they order more tests, and when we are uncertain about what we hear, we ask for a second opinion. And what do we tell our children? Haste makes waste. Look before you leap. Stop and *think*. Don't judge a book by its cover. We believe that we are always better off gathering as much information as possible and spending as much time as possible in deliberation. We really only trust conscious decision making. But there are moments, particularly in times of stress, when haste does not make waste, when our snap judgments and first impressions can offer a much better means of making sense of the world. The first task of *Blink* is to convince you of a simple fact: decisions made very quickly can be every bit as good as decisions made cautiously and deliberately.

Blink is not just a celebration of the power of the glance, however. I'm also interested in those moments when our instincts betray us. Why, for instance, if the Getty's kouros was so obviously fake — or, at least, problematic — did the museum buy it in the first place? Why didn't the experts at the Getty also have a feeling of intuitive repulsion during the fourteen months they were studying the piece? That's the great puzzle of what happened at the Getty, and the answer is that those feelings, for one reason or another, were thwarted. That is partly because the scientific data seemed so compelling. (The geologist Stanley Margolis was so convinced by his own analysis that he published a long account of his method in *Scientific American.*) But mostly it's because the Getty desperately wanted the statue to be real. It was a young museum, eager to build a world-class collection, and the kouros was such an extraordinary find that its experts were blinded to their instincts. The art historian George Ortiz was once asked by Ernst Langlotz, one of the world's foremost experts on archaic sculpture, whether he wanted to purchase a bronze statuette. Ortiz went to see the piece and was taken aback; it was, to his mind, clearly a fake, full of contradictory and slipshod elements. So why was Langlotz, who knew as much as anyone in the world about Greek statues, fooled? Ortiz's explanation is that Langlotz had bought the sculpture as a very young man, before he acquired much of his formidable expertise. "I suppose," Ortiz said, "that Langlotz fell in love with this piece; when you are a young man, you do fall in love with your first purchase, and perhaps this was his first love. Notwithstanding his unbelievable knowledge, he was obviously unable to question his first assessment."

That is not a fanciful explanation. It gets at something fundamental about the way we think. Our unconscious is a powerful force. But it's fallible. It's not the case that our internal computer always shines through, instantly decoding the "truth" of a situation. It can be thrown off, distracted, and disabled. Our instinctive reactions often have to compete with all kinds of other interests and emotions and sentiments. So, when should we trust our instincts, and when should we be wary of them? Answering that question is the second task of *Blink*. When our powers of rapid cognition go awry, they go awry for a very specific and consistent set of reasons, and those reasons can be identified and understood. It is possible to learn when to listen to that powerful onboard computer and when to be wary of it.

The third and most important task of this book is to convince you that our snap judgments and first impressions can be educated and controlled. I know that's hard to believe. Harrison and Hoving and the other art experts who looked at the Getty kouros had powerful and sophisticated reactions to the statue, but didn't they bubble up unbidden from their unconscious? Can that kind of mysterious reaction be controlled? The truth is that it can. Just as we can teach ourselves to think logically and deliberately, we can also teach ourselves to make better snap judgments. In *Blink* you'll meet doctors and generals and coaches and furniture designers and musicians and actors and car salesmen and countless others, all of whom are very good at what they do and all of whom owe their success, at least in part, to the steps they have taken to shape and manage and educate their unconscious reactions. The power of knowing, in that first two seconds, is not a gift given magically to a fortunate few. It is an ability that we can all cultivate for ourselves.

3. A Different and Better World

There are lots of books that tackle broad themes, that analyze the world from great remove. This is not one of them. *Blink* is concerned with the very smallest components of our everyday lives — the content and origin of those instantaneous impressions and conclusions that spontaneously arise whenever we meet a new person or confront a complex situation or have to make a decision under conditions of stress. When it comes to the task of understanding ourselves and our world, I think we pay too much attention to those grand themes and too little to the particulars of those fleeting moments. But what would happen if we took our instincts seriously? What if we stopped scanning the horizon with our binoculars and began instead examining our own decision making and behavior through the most powerful of microscopes? I think that would change the way wars are fought, the kinds of products we see on the shelves, the kinds of movies that get made, the way police officers are trained, the way couples are counseled, the way job interviews are conducted, and on and on. And if we were to combine all of those little changes, we would end up with a different and better world. I believe — and I hope that by the end of this book you will believe it as well — that the task of making sense of ourselves and our behavior requires that we acknowledge there can be as much value in the blink of an eye as in months of rational analysis. "I always considered scientific opinion more objective than esthetic judgments," the Getty's curator of antiquities Marion True said when the truth about the kouros finally emerged. "Now I realize I was wrong."

The Theory of Thin Slices: How a Little Bit of Knowledge Goes a Long Way

Some years ago, a young couple came to the University of Washington to visit the laboratory of a psychologist named John Gottman. They were in their twenties, blond and blue-eyed with stylishly tousled haircuts and funky glasses. Later, some of the people who worked in the lab would say they were the kind of couple that is easy to like — intelligent and attractive and funny in a droll, ironic kind of way — and that much is immediately obvious from the videotape Gottman made of their visit. The husband, whom I'll call Bill, had an endearingly playful manner. His wife, Susan, had a sharp, deadpan wit.

They were led into a small room on the second floor of the nondescript two-story building that housed Gottman's operations, and they sat down about five feet apart on two office chairs mounted on raised platforms. They both had electrodes and sensors clipped to their fingers and ears, which measured things like their heart rate, how much they were sweating, and the temperature of their skin. Under their chairs, a "jiggle-o-meter" on the platform measured how much each of them moved around. Two video cameras, one aimed at each person, recorded everything they said and did. For fifteen minutes, they were left alone with the cameras rolling, with instructions to discuss any topic from their marriage that had become a point of contention. For Bill and Sue it was their dog. They lived in a small apartment and had just gotten a very large puppy. Bill didn't like the dog; Sue did. For fifteen minutes, they discussed what they ought to do about it.

The videotape of Bill and Sue's discussion seems, at least at first, to be a random sample of a very ordinary kind of conversation that couples have all the time. No one gets angry. There are no scenes, no breakdowns, no epiphanies. "I'm just not a dog person" is how Bill starts things off, in a perfectly reasonable tone of voice. He complains a little bit — but about the dog, not about Susan. She complains, too, but there are also moments when they simply forget that they are supposed to be arguing. When the subject of whether the dog smells comes up, for example, Bill and Sue banter back and forth happily, both with a half smile on their lips.

Sue: Sweetie! She's not smelly . . .

Bill: Did you smell her today?

Sue: I smelled her. She smelled good. I petted her, and my hands didn't stink or feel oily. Your hands have never smelled oily.

Bill: Yes, sir.

Sue: I've never let my dog get oily.

Bill: Yes, sir. She's a dog.

Sue: My dog has never gotten oily. You'd better be careful.
Bill: No, you'd better be careful.
Sue: No, you'd better be careful. . . . Don't call my dog
   oily, boy.

1. The Love Lab

How much do you think can be learned about Sue and
Bill's marriage by watching that fifteen-minute videotape?
Can we tell if their relationship is healthy or unhealthy? I
suspect that most of us would say that Bill and Sue's dog
talk doesn't tell us much. It's much too short. Marriages
are buffeted by more important things, like money and sex
and children and jobs and in-laws, in constantly changing
combinations. Sometimes couples are very happy together.
Some days they fight. Sometimes they feel as though they
could almost kill each other, but then they go on vaca-
tion and come back sounding like newlyweds. In order
to "know" a couple, we feel as though we have to observe
them over many weeks and months and see them in every
state — happy, tired, angry, irritated, delighted, having a
nervous breakdown, and so on — and not just in the re-
laxed and chatty mode that Bill and Sue seemed to be in.
To make an accurate prediction about something as serious as the future of a marriage — indeed, to make a prediction of any sort — it seems that we would have to gather
a lot of information and in as many different contexts as
possible.

But John Gottman has proven that we don't have to do
that at all. Since the 1980s, Gottman has brought more than
three thousand married couples — just like Bill and Sue —

into that small room in his "love lab" near the University of Washington campus. Each couple has been videotaped, and the results have been analyzed according to something Gottman dubbed SPAFF (for specific affect), a coding system that has twenty separate categories corresponding to every conceivable emotion that a married couple might express during a conversation. Disgust, for example, is 1, contempt is 2, anger is 7, defensiveness is 10, whining is 11, sadness is 12, stonewalling is 13, neutral is 14, and so on. Gottman has taught his staff how to read every emotional nuance in people's facial expressions and how to interpret seemingly ambiguous bits of dialogue. When they watch a marriage videotape, they assign a SPAFF code to every second of the couple's interaction, so that a fifteen-minute conflict discussion ends up being translated into a row of eighteen hundred numbers — nine hundred for the husband and nine hundred for the wife. The notation "7, 7, 14, 10, 11, 11," for instance, means that in one six-second stretch, one member of the couple was briefly angry, then neutral, had a moment of defensiveness, and then began whining. Then the data from the electrodes and sensors is factored in, so that the coders know, for example, when the husband's or the wife's heart was pounding or when his or her temperature was rising or when either of them was jiggling in his or her seat, and all of that information is fed into a complex equation.

On the basis of those calculations, Gottman has proven something remarkable. If he analyzes an hour of a husband and wife talking, he can predict with 95 percent accuracy whether that couple will still be married fifteen years later. If he watches a couple for fifteen minutes, his success rate is around 90 percent. Recently, a professor who works with Gottman named Sybil Carrère, who was playing around with some of the videotapes, trying to design a new study, discovered that if they looked at only *three minutes* of a couple talking, they could still predict with fairly impressive accuracy who was going to get divorced and who was going to make it. The truth of a marriage can be understood in a much shorter time than anyone ever imagined.

John Gottman is a middle-aged man with owl-like eyes, silvery hair, and a neatly trimmed beard. He is short and very charming, and when he talks about something that excites him — which is nearly all the time — his eyes light up and open even wider. During the Vietnam War, he was a conscientious objector, and there is still something of the '60s hippie about him, like the Mao cap he sometimes wears over his braided yarmulke. He is a psychologist by training, but he also studied mathematics at MIT, and the rigor and precision of mathematics clearly moves him as much as anything else. When I met Gottman, he had just published his most ambitious book, a dense five-hundred-page treatise called *The Mathematics of Divorce,* and he attempted to give me a sense of his argument, scribbling equations and impromptu graphs on a paper napkin until my head began to swim.

Gottman may seem to be an odd example in a book about the thoughts and decisions that bubble up from our unconscious. There's nothing instinctive about his approach. He's not making snap judgments. He's sitting down with his computer and painstakingly analyzing videotapes, second by second. His work is a classic example of conscious and deliberate thinking. But Gottman, it turns out, can teach us a great deal about a critical part of rapid cognition known as thin-slicing. "Thin-slicing" refers to the ability of our unconscious to find patterns in situations and behavior based on very narrow slices of experience. When Evelyn Harrison looked at the kouros and blurted out, "I'm sorry to hear that," she was thin-slicing; so were the Iowa gamblers when they had a stress reaction to the red decks after just ten cards.

Thin-slicing is part of what makes the unconscious so dazzling. But it's also what we find most problematic about rapid cognition. How is it possible to gather the necessary information for a sophisticated judgment in such a short time? The answer is that when our unconscious engages in thin-slicing, what we are doing is an automated, accelerated unconscious version of what Gottman does with his videotapes and equations. Can a marriage really be understood in one sitting? Yes it can, and so can lots of other seemingly complex situations. What Gottman has done is to show us how.

2. Marriage and Morse Code

I watched the videotape of Bill and Sue with Amber Tabares, a graduate student in Gottman's lab who is a trained SPAFF coder. We sat in the same room that Bill and Sue used, watching their interaction on a monitor. The conversation began with Bill. He liked their old dog, he said. He just didn't like their new dog. He didn't speak angrily or with any hostility. It seemed like he genuinely just wanted to explain his feelings.

If we listened closely, Tabares pointed out, it was clear that Bill was being very defensive. In the language of SPAFF, he was cross-complaining and engaging in "yes-but" tactics — appearing to agree but then taking it back. Bill was coded as defensive, as it turned out, for forty of the first sixty-six seconds of their conversation. As for Sue, while Bill was talking, on more than one occasion she rolled her eyes very quickly, which is a classic sign of contempt. Bill then began to talk about his objection to the pen where the dog lives. Sue replied by closing her eyes and then assuming a patronizing lecturing voice. Bill went on to say that he didn't want a fence in the living room. Sue said, "I don't want to argue about that," and rolled her eyes — another indication of contempt. "Look at that," Tabares said. "More contempt. We've barely started and we've seen him be defensive for almost the whole time, and she has rolled her eyes several times."

At no time as the conversation continued did either of them show any overt signs of hostility. Only subtle things popped up for a second or two, prompting Tabares to stop the tape and point them out. Some couples, when they fight, *fight*. But these two were a lot less obvious. Bill complained that the dog cut into their social life, since they always had to come home early for fear of what the dog might do to their apartment. Sue responded that that wasn't true, arguing, "If she's going to chew anything, she's going to do it in the first fifteen minutes that we're gone." Bill seemed to agree with that. He nodded lightly and said, "Yeah, I know," and then added, "I'm not saying it's rational. I just don't want to have a dog."

Tabares pointed at the videotape. "He started out with 'Yeah, I know.' But it's a yes-but. Even though he started to validate her, he went on to say that he didn't like the dog. He's really being defensive. I kept thinking, He's so nice. He's doing all this validation. But then I realized he was doing the yes-but. It's easy to be fooled by them."

Bill went on: "I'm getting way better. You've got to admit it. I'm better this week than last week, and the week before and the week before."

Tabares jumped in again. "In one study, we were watching newlyweds, and what often happened with the couples who ended up in divorce is that when one partner would ask for credit, the other spouse wouldn't give it. And with the happier couples, the spouse would hear it and say, 'You're right.' That stood out. When you nod and say 'uh-huh' or 'yeah,' you are doing that as a sign of support, and here she never does it, not once in the entire session, which none of us had realized until we did the coding.

"It's weird," she went on. "You don't get the sense that they are an unhappy couple when they come in. And when they were finished, they were instructed to watch their own discussion, and they thought the whole thing was hilarious. They seem fine, in a way. But I don't know. They haven't been married that long. They're still in the glowy phase. But the fact is that she's completely inflexible. They are arguing about dogs, but it's really about how whenever they have a disagreement, she's completely inflexible. It's one of those things that could cause a lot of long-term harm. I wonder if they'll hit the seven-year wall. Is there enough positive emotion there? Because what seems positive isn't actually positive at all."

What was Tabares looking for in the couple? On a technical level, she was measuring the amount of positive and negative emotion, because one of Gottman's findings is that for a marriage to survive, the ratio of positive to negative emotion in a given encounter has to be at least five to one. On a simpler level, though, what Tabares was looking for in that short discussion was a pattern in Bill and Sue's marriage, because a central argument in Gottman's work is that all marriages have a distinctive pattern, a kind of marital DNA, that surfaces in any kind of meaningful interaction. This is why Gottman asks couples to tell the story of how they met, because he has found that when a husband and wife recount the most important episode in their relationship, that pattern shows up right away.

"It's so easy to tell," Gottman says. "I just looked at this tape yesterday. The woman says, 'We met at a ski weekend, and he was there with a bunch of his friends, and I kind of liked him and we made a date to be together. But then he drank too much, and he went home and went to sleep, and I was waiting for him for three hours. I woke him up, and I said I don't appreciate being treated this way. You're really not a nice person. And he said, yeah, hey, I really had a lot to drink.'" There was a troubling pattern in their first interaction, and the sad truth was that that pattern persisted throughout their relationship. "It's not that hard," Gottman went on. "When I first started doing these interviews, I thought maybe we were getting these people on a crappy day. But the prediction levels are just so high, and if you do it again, you get the same pattern over and over again."

One way to understand what Gottman is saying about marriages is to use the analogy of what people in the world of Morse code call a fist. Morse code is made up of dots and dashes, each of which has its own prescribed length. But no one ever replicates those prescribed lengths perfectly. When operators send a message — particularly using the old manual machines known as the straight key or the bug — they vary the spacing or stretch out the dots and dashes or combine dots and dashes and spaces in a particular rhythm. Morse code is like speech. Everyone has a different voice.

In the Second World War, the British assembled thousands of so-called interceptors — mostly women — whose job it was to tune in every day and night to the radio broadcasts of the various divisions of the German military. The Germans were, of course, broadcasting in code, so — at least in the early part of the war — the British couldn't understand *what* was being said. But that didn't necessarily matter, because before long, just by listening to the cadence of the transmission, the interceptors began to pick up on the individual fists of the German operators, and by doing so, they knew something nearly as important, which was *who* was doing the sending. "If you listened to the same call signs over a certain period, you would begin to recognize that there were, say, three or four different operators in that unit, working on a shift system, each with his own characteristics," says Nigel West, a British military historian. "And invariably, quite apart from the text, there would be the preambles, and the illicit exchanges. How are you today? How's the girlfriend? What's the weather like in Munich? So you fill out a little card, on which you write down all that kind of information, and pretty soon you have a kind of relationship with that person."

The interceptors came up with descriptions of the fists and styles of the operators they were following. They assigned them names and assembled elaborate profiles of their personalities. After they identified the person who was sending the message, the interceptors would then locate their signal. So now they knew something more. They knew who was *where*. West goes on: "The interceptors had such a good handle on the transmitting characteristics of the German radio operators that they could literally follow them around Europe — wherever they were. That was extraordinarily valuable in constructing an order of battle, which is a diagram of what the individual military units in the field are doing and what their location is. If a particular radio operator was with a particular unit and transmitting from Florence, and then three weeks later you recognized that same operator, only this time he was in Linz, then you could assume that that particular unit had moved from northern Italy to the eastern front. Or you would know that a particular operator was with a tank repair unit and he always came up on the air every day at twelve o'clock. But now, after a big battle, he's coming up at twelve, four in the afternoon, and seven in the evening, so you can assume that unit has a lot of work going on. And in a moment of crisis, when someone very high up asks, 'Can you really be absolutely certain that this particular Luftwaffe *Fliegerkorps* [German air force squadron] is outside of Tobruk and not in Italy?' you can answer, 'Yes, that was Oscar, we are absolutely sure.'"

The key thing about fists is that they emerge naturally. Radio operators don't deliberately try to sound distinctive. They simply end up sounding distinctive, because some part of their personality appears to express itself automatically and unconsciously in the way they work the Morse code keys. The other thing about a fist is that it reveals itself in even the smallest sample of Morse code. We have to listen to only a few characters to pick out an individual's pattern. It doesn't change or disappear for stretches or show up only in certain words or phrases. That's why the British interceptors could listen to just a few bursts and say, with absolute certainty, "It's Oscar, which means that yes, his unit is now definitely outside of Tobruk." An operator's fist is stable.

What Gottman is saying is that a relationship between two people has a fist as well: a distinctive signature that arises naturally and automatically. That is why a marriage can be read and decoded so easily, because some key part of human activity — whether it is something as simple as pounding out a Morse code message or as complex as being married to someone — has an identifiable and stable pattern. Predicting divorce, like tracking Morse Code operators, is pattern recognition.

"People are in one of two states in a relationship," Gottman went on. "The first is what I call positive sentiment override, where positive emotion overrides irritability. It's like a buffer. Their spouse will do something bad, and they'll say, 'Oh, he's just in a crummy mood.' Or they can be in negative sentiment override, so that even a relatively neutral thing that a partner says gets perceived as negative. In the negative sentiment override state, people draw lasting conclusions about each other. If their spouse does something positive, it's a selfish person doing a positive thing. It's really hard to change those states, and those states determine whether when one party tries to repair things, the other party sees that as repair or hostile manipulation. For example, I'm talking with my wife, and she says, 'Will you shut up and let me finish?' In positive sentiment override, I say, 'Sorry, go ahead.' I'm not very happy, but I recognize the repair. In negative sentiment override, I say, 'To hell with you, I'm not getting a chance to finish either. You're such a bitch, you remind me of your mother.'"

As he was talking, Gottman drew a graph on a piece of paper that looked a lot like a chart of the ups and downs of the stock market over the course of a typical day. What he does, he explains, is track the ups and downs of a couple's level of positive and negative emotion, and he's found that it doesn't take very long to figure out which way the line on the graph is going. "Some go up, some go down," he says. "But once they start going down, toward negative emotion, ninety-four percent will continue going down. They start on a bad course and they can't correct it. I don't think of this as just a slice in time. It's an indication of how they view their whole relationship."

3. The Importance of Contempt

Let's dig a little deeper into the secret of Gottman's success rate. Gottman has discovered that marriages have distinctive signatures, and we can find that signature by collecting very detailed emotional information from the interaction of a couple. But there's something else that is very interesting about Gottman's system, and that is the way in which he manages to simplify the task of prediction. I hadn't realized how much of an issue this was until I tried thin-slicing couples myself. I got one of Gottman's tapes, which had on it ten three-minute clips of different couples talking. Half the couples, I was told, split up at some point in the fifteen years after their discussion was filmed. Half were still together. Could I guess which was which? I was pretty confident I could. But I was wrong. I was terrible at it. I answered five correctly, which is to say that I would have done just as well by flipping a coin.

My difficulty arose from the fact that the clips were utterly overwhelming. The husband would say something guarded. The wife would respond quietly. Some fleeting emotion would flash across her face. He would start to say something and then stop. She would scowl. He would laugh. Someone would mutter something. Someone would frown. I would rewind the tape and look at it again, and I would get still more information. I'd see a little trace of a smile, or I'd pick up on a slight change in tone. It was all too much. In my head, I was frantically trying to determine the ratios of positive emotion to negative emotion. But what counted as positive, and what counted as negative? I knew from Susan and Bill that a lot of what looked positive was actually negative. And I also knew that there were no fewer than twenty separate emotional states on the SPAFF chart. Have you ever tried to keep track of twenty different emotions simultaneously? Now, granted, I'm not a marriage counselor. But that same tape has been given to almost two hundred marital therapists, marital researchers, pastoral counselors, and graduate students in clinical psychology, as well as newlyweds, people who were recently divorced, and people who have been happily married for a long time — in other words, almost two hundred people who know a good deal more about marriage than I do — and none of them was any better than I was. The group as a whole guessed right 53.8 percent of the time, which is just above chance. The fact that there was a pattern didn't much matter. There were so many other things going on so quickly in those three minutes that we couldn't find the pattern.

Gottman, however, doesn't have this problem. He's gotten so good at thin-slicing marriages that he says he can be in a restaurant and eavesdrop on the couple one table over and get a pretty good sense of whether they need to start thinking about hiring lawyers and dividing up custody of the children. How does he do it? He has figured out that he doesn't need to pay attention to everything that happens. I was overwhelmed by the task of counting negativity, because everywhere I looked, I saw negative emotions. Gottman is far more selective. He has found that he can find out much of what he needs to know just by focusing on what he calls the Four Horsemen: defensiveness, stonewalling, criticism, and contempt. Even within the Four Horsemen, in fact, there is one emotion that he considers the most important of all: contempt. If Gottman observes one or both partners in a marriage showing contempt toward the other, he considers it the single most important sign that the marriage is in trouble.

"You would think that criticism would be the worst,"

Gottman says, "because criticism is a global condemnation of a person's character. Yet contempt is qualitatively different from criticism. With criticism I might say to my wife, 'You never listen, you are really selfish and insensitive.' Well, she's going to respond defensively to that. That's not very good for our problem solving and interaction. But if I speak from a superior plane, that's far more damaging, and contempt is any statement made from a higher level. A lot of the time it's an insult: 'You are a bitch. You're scum.' It's trying to put that person on a lower plane than you. It's hierarchical."

Gottman has found, in fact, that the presence of contempt in a marriage can even predict such things as how many colds a husband or a wife gets; in other words, having someone you love express contempt toward you is so stressful that it begins to affect the functioning of your immune system. "Contempt is closely related to disgust, and what disgust and contempt are about is completely rejecting and excluding someone from the community. The big gender difference with negative emotions is that women are more critical, and men are more likely to stonewall. We find that women start talking about a problem, the men get irritated and turn away, and the women get more critical, and it becomes a circle. But there isn't any gender difference when it comes to contempt. Not at all." Contempt is special. If you can measure contempt, then all of a sudden you don't need to know every detail of the couple's relationship.

I think that this is the way that our unconscious works. When we leap to a decision or have a hunch, our unconscious is doing what John Gottman does. It's sifting through the situation in front of us, throwing out all that is irrelevant while we zero in on what really matters. And the truth is that our unconscious is really good at this, to the point where thin-slicing often delivers a better answer than more deliberate and exhaustive ways of thinking.

4. The Secrets of the Bedroom

Imagine that you are considering me for a job. You've seen my résumé and think I have the necessary credentials. But you want to know whether I am the right fit for your organization. Am I a hard worker? Am I honest? Am I open to new ideas? In order to answer those questions about my personality, your boss gives you two options. The first is to meet with me twice a week for a year — to have lunch or dinner or go to a movie with me — to the point where you become one of my closest friends. (Your boss is quite demanding.) The second option is to drop by my house when I'm not there and spend half an hour or so looking around. Which would you choose?

The seemingly obvious answer is that you should take the first option: the thick slice. The more time you spend with me and the more information you gather, the better off you are. Right? I hope by now that you are at least a little bit skeptical of that approach. Sure enough, as the psychologist Samuel Gosling has shown, judging people's personalities is a really good example of how surprisingly effective thin-slicing can be.

Gosling began his experiment by doing a personality workup on eighty college students. For this, he used what is called the Big Five Inventory, a highly respected, multi-item questionnaire that measures people across five dimensions:

1. Extraversion. Are you sociable or retiring? Fun-loving or reserved?
2. Agreeableness. Are you trusting or suspicious? Helpful or uncooperative?
3. Conscientiousness. Are you organized or disorganized? Self-disciplined or weak willed?
4. Emotional stability. Are you worried or calm? Insecure or secure?
5. Openness to new experiences. Are you imaginative or down-to-earth? Independent or conforming?

Then Gosling had close friends of those eighty students fill out the same questionnaire.

When our friends rank us on the Big Five, Gosling wanted to know, how closely do they come to the truth? The answer is, not surprisingly, that our friends can describe us fairly accurately. They have a thick slice of experience with us, and that translates to a real sense of who we are. Then Gosling repeated the process, but this time he didn't call on close friends. He used total strangers who had never even met the students they were judging. All they saw were their dorm rooms. He gave his raters clipboards and told them they had fifteen minutes to look around and answer a series of very basic questions about the occupant of the room: On a scale of 1 to 5, does the inhabitant of this room seem to be the kind of person who is talkative? Tends to find fault with others? Does a thorough job? Is original? Is reserved? Is helpful and unselfish with others? And so on. "I was trying to study everyday impressions," Gosling says. "So I was quite careful not to tell my subjects what to do. I just said, 'Here is your questionnaire. Go into the room and drink it in.' I was just trying to look at intuitive judgment processes."

How did they do? The dorm room observers weren't nearly as good as friends in measuring extraversion. If you want to know how animated and talkative and outgoing someone is, clearly, you have to meet him or her in person. The friends also did slightly better than the dorm room visitors at accurately estimating agreeableness — how helpful and trusting someone is. I think that also makes sense. But on the remaining three traits of the Big Five, the strangers with the clipboards came out on top. They were more accurate at measuring conscientiousness, and they were much more accurate at predicting both the students' emotional stability and their openness to new experiences. On balance, then, the strangers ended up doing a much better job. What this suggests is that it is quite possible for people who have never met us and who have spent only twenty minutes thinking about us to come to a better understanding of who we are than people who have known us for years. Forget the endless "getting to know" meetings and lunches, then. If you want to get a good idea of whether I'd make a good employee, drop by my house one day and take a look around.

If you are like most people, I imagine that you find Gosling's conclusions quite incredible. But the truth is that they shouldn't be, not after the lessons of John Gottman. This is just another example of thin-slicing. The observers were looking at the students' most personal belongings, and our personal belongings contain a wealth of very telling information. Gosling says, for example, that a person's bedroom gives three kinds of clues to his or her personality. There are, first of all, identity claims, which are deliberate expressions about how we would like to be seen by the world: a framed copy of a magna cum laude degree from Harvard, for example. Then there is behavioral residue, which is defined as the inadvertent clues we leave behind: dirty laundry on the floor, for instance, or an alphabetized CD collection. Finally, there are thoughts and feelings regulators, which are changes we make to our most personal spaces to affect the way we feel when we inhabit them: a scented candle in the corner, for example, or a pile of artfully placed decorative pillows on the bed. If you see alphabetized CDs, a Harvard diploma on the wall, incense on a side table, and laundry neatly stacked in a hamper, you *know* certain aspects about that individual's personality instantly, in a way that you may not be able to grasp if all you ever do is spend time with him or her directly. Anyone who has ever scanned the bookshelves of a new girlfriend or boyfriend — or peeked inside his or her medicine cabinet — understands this implicitly: you can learn as much — or more — from one glance at a private space as you can from hours of exposure to a public face.

Just as important, though, is the information you *don't* have when you look through someone's belongings. What you avoid when you don't meet someone face-to-face are all the confusing and complicated and ultimately irrelevant pieces of information that can serve to screw up your judgment. Most of us have difficulty believing that a 275-pound football lineman could have a lively and discerning intellect. We just can't get past the stereotype of the dumb jock. But if all we saw of that person was his bookshelf or the art on his walls, we wouldn't have that same problem.

What people say about themselves can also be very confusing, for the simple reason that most of us aren't very objective about ourselves. That's why, when we measure personality, we don't just ask people point-blank what they think they are like. We give them a questionnaire, like the Big Five Inventory, carefully designed to elicit telling responses. That's also why Gottman doesn't waste any time asking husbands and wives point-blank questions about the state of their marriage. They might lie or feel awkward or, more important, they might not *know* the truth. They may be so deeply mired — or so happily ensconced — in their relationship that they have no perspective on how it works. "Couples simply aren't aware of how they sound," says Sybil Carrère. "They have this discussion, which we videotape and then play back to them. In one of the studies we did recently, we interviewed couples about what they learned from the study, and a remarkable number of them — I would say a majority of them — said they were surprised to find either what they looked like during the conflict discussion or what they communicated during the conflict discussion. We had one woman whom we thought of as extremely emotional, but she said that she had no idea that she was so emotional. She said that she thought she was stoic and gave nothing away. A lot of people are like that. They think they are more forthcoming than they actually are, or more negative than they actually are. It was only when they were watching the tape that they realized they were wrong about what they were communicating."

If couples aren't aware of how they sound, how much value can there be in asking them direct questions? Not much, and this is why Gottman has couples talk about something involving their marriage — like their pets — without being *about* their marriage. He looks closely at indirect measures of how the couple is doing: the telling traces of emotion that flit across one person's face; the hint of stress picked up in the sweat glands of the palm; a sudden surge in heart rate; a subtle tone that creeps into an exchange. Gottman comes at the issue sideways, which, he has found, can be a lot quicker and a more efficient path to the truth than coming at it head-on.

What those observers of dorm rooms were doing was simply a layperson's version of John Gottman's analysis. They were looking for the "fist" of those college students. They gave themselves fifteen minutes to drink things in and get a hunch about the person. They came at the question sideways, using the indirect evidence of the students' dorm rooms, and their decision-making process was simplified: they weren't distracted at all by the kind of confusing, irrelevant information that comes from a face-to-face encounter. They thin-sliced. And what happened? The same thing that happened with Gottman: those people with the clipboards were *really good* at making predictions.

5. Listening to Doctors

Let's take the concept of thin-slicing one step further. Imagine you work for an insurance company that sells doctors medical malpractice protection. Your boss asks you to figure out for accounting reasons who, among all the physicians covered by the company, is most likely to be sued. Once again, you are given two choices. The first is to examine the physicians' training and credentials and then analyze their records to see how many errors they've made over the past few years. The other option is to listen in on very brief snippets of conversation between each doctor and his or her patients.

By now you are expecting me to say the second option is the best one. You're right, and here's why. Believe it or not, the risk of being sued for malpractice has very little to do with how many mistakes a doctor makes. Analyses of malpractice lawsuits show that there are highly skilled doctors who get sued a lot and doctors who make lots of mistakes and never get sued. At the same time, the overwhelming number of people who suffer an injury due to the negligence of a doctor never file a malpractice suit at all. In other words, patients don't file lawsuits because they've been harmed by shoddy medical care. Patients file lawsuits because they've been harmed by shoddy medical care and *something else* happens to them.

What is that something else? It's how they were treated, on a personal level, by their doctor. What comes up again and again in malpractice cases is that patients say they were rushed or ignored or treated poorly. "People just don't sue doctors they like," is how Alice Burkin, a leading medical malpractice lawyer, puts it. "In all the years I've been in this business, I've never had a potential client walk in and say, 'I really like this doctor, and I feel terrible about doing it, but I want to sue him.' We've had people come in saying they want to sue some specialist, and we'll say, 'We don't think that doctor was negligent. We think it's your primary care doctor who was at fault.' And the client will say, 'I don't care what she did. I love her, and I'm not suing her.'"

Burkin once had a client who had a breast tumor that wasn't spotted until it had metastasized, and she wanted to sue her internist for the delayed diagnosis. In fact, it was her radiologist who was potentially at fault. But the client was adamant. She wanted to sue the internist. "In our first meeting, she told me she hated this doctor because she never took the time to talk to her and never asked about her other symptoms," Burkin said. "'She never looked at me as a whole person,' the patient told us. . . . When a patient has a bad medical result, the doctor has to take the time to explain what happened, and to answer the patient's questions — to treat him like a human being. The doctors who don't are the ones who get sued." It isn't necessary, then, to know much about how a surgeon operates in order to know his likelihood of being sued. What you need to understand is the relationship between that doctor and his patients.

Recently the medical researcher Wendy Levinson recorded hundreds of conversations between a group of physicians and their patients. Roughly half of the doctors had never been sued. The other half had been sued at least twice, and Levinson found that just on the basis of those conversations, she could find clear differences between the two groups. The surgeons who had never been sued spent more than three minutes longer with each patient than those who had been sued did (18.3 minutes versus 15 minutes).

They were more likely to make "orienting" comments, such
as "First I'll examine you, and then we will talk the problem
over" or "I will leave time for your questions" — which
help patients get a sense of what the visit is supposed to ac-
complish and when they ought to ask questions. They were
more likely to engage in active listening, saying such things
as "Go on, tell me more about that," and they were far more
likely to laugh and be funny during the visit. Interestingly,
there was no difference in the amount or quality of information they gave their patients; they didn't provide more details about medication or the patient's condition. The
difference was entirely in *how* they talked to their patients.

It's possible, in fact, to take this analysis even further.
The psychologist Nalini Ambady listened to Levinson's
tapes, zeroing in on the conversations that had been
recorded between just surgeons and their patients. For each
surgeon, she picked two patient conversations. Then, from
each conversation, she selected two ten-second clips of the
doctor talking, so her slice was a total of forty seconds. Finally, she "content-filtered" the slices, which means she removed the high-frequency sounds from speech that enable
us to recognize individual words. What's left after content-
filtering is a kind of garble that preserves intonation, pitch,
and rhythm but erases content. Using that slice — and that
slice alone — Ambady did a Gottman-style analysis. She
had judges rate the slices of garble for such qualities as
warmth, hostility, dominance, and anxiousness, and she
found that by using only those ratings, she could predict
which surgeons got sued and which ones didn't.

Ambady says that she and her colleagues were "totally
stunned by the results," and it's not hard to understand

why. The judges knew nothing about the skill level of the surgeons. They didn't know how experienced they were, what kind of training they had, or what kind of procedures they tended to do. They didn't even know *what* the doctors were saying to their patients. All they were using for their prediction was their analysis of the surgeon's tone of voice. In fact, it was even more basic than that: if the surgeon's voice was judged to sound dominant, the surgeon tended to be in the sued group. If the voice sounded less dominant and more concerned, the surgeon tended to be in the non-sued group. Could there be a thinner slice? Malpractice sounds like one of those infinitely complicated and multidimensional problems. But in the end it comes down to a matter of respect, and the simplest way that respect is communicated is through tone of voice, and the most corrosive tone of voice that a doctor can assume is a dominant tone. Did Ambady need to sample the entire history of a patient and doctor to pick up on that tone? No, because a medical consultation is a lot like one of Gottman's conflict discussions or a student's dorm room. It's one of those situations where the signature comes through loud and clear.

Next time you meet a doctor, and you sit down in his office and he starts to talk, if you have the sense that he isn't listening to you, that he's talking down to you, and that he isn't treating you with respect, *listen to that feeling*. You have thin-sliced him and found him wanting.

6. The Power of the Glance

Thin-slicing is not an exotic gift. It is a central part of what it means to be human. We thin-slice whenever we meet a new person or have to make sense of something quickly or encounter a novel situation. We thin-slice because we have to, and we come to rely on that ability because there are lots of hidden fists out there, lots of situations where careful attention to the details of a very thin slice, even for no more than a second or two, can tell us an awful lot.

It is striking, for instance, how many different professions and disciplines have a word to describe the particular gift of reading deeply into the narrowest slivers of experience. In basketball, the player who can take in and comprehend all that is happening around him or her is said to have "court sense." In the military, brilliant generals are said to possess "coup d'oeil" — which, translated from the French, means "power of the glance": the ability to immediately see and make sense of the battlefield. Napoleon had coup d'oeil. So did Patton. The ornithologist David Sibley says that in Cape May, New Jersey, he once spotted a bird in flight from two hundred yards away and knew, instantly, that it was a ruff, a rare sandpiper. He had never seen a ruff in flight before; nor was the moment long enough for him to make a careful identification. But he was able to capture what bird-watchers call the bird's "giss" — its essence — and that was enough.

"Most of bird identification is based on a sort of subjective impression — the way a bird moves and little instantaneous appearances at different angles and sequences of different appearances, and as it turns its head and as it flies and as it turns around, you see sequences of different shapes and angles," Sibley says. "All that combines to create a unique impression of a bird that can't really be taken apart and described in words. When it comes down to being in the field and looking at a bird, you don't take the time to analyze it and say it shows this, this, and this; therefore it must be this species. It's more natural and instinctive. After a lot of practice, you look at the bird, and it triggers little switches in your brain. It *looks* right. You know what it is at a glance."

The Hollywood producer Brian Grazer, who has produced many of the biggest hit movies of the past twenty years, uses almost exactly the same language to describe the first time he met the actor Tom Hanks. It was in 1983. Hanks was then a virtual unknown. All he had done was the now (justly) forgotten TV show called *Bosom Buddies*. "He came in and read for the movie *Splash*, and right there, in the moment, I can tell you just what I saw," Grazer says. In that first instant, he *knew* Hanks was special. "We read hundreds of people for that part, and other people were funnier than him. But they weren't as likable as him. I felt like I could live inside of him. I felt like his problems were problems I could relate to. You know, in order to make somebody laugh, you have to be interesting, and in order to be interesting, you have to do things that are mean. Comedy comes out of anger, and interesting comes out of angry; otherwise there is no conflict. But he was able to be mean and you forgave him, and you have to be able to forgive somebody, because at the end of the day, you still have to be with him, even after he's dumped the girl or made some choices that you don't agree with. All of this wasn't thought out in words at the time. It was an intuitive conclusion that only later I could deconstruct."

My guess is that many of you have the same impression of Tom Hanks. If I asked you what he was like, you would say that he is decent and trustworthy and down-to-earth and funny. But you don't know him. You're not friends with him. You've only seen him in the movies, playing a wide range of different characters. Nonetheless, you've managed to extract something very meaningful about him from those thin slices of experience, and that impression has a powerful effect on how you experience Tom Hanks's movies. "Everybody said that they couldn't see Tom Hanks as an astronaut," Grazer says of his decision to cast Hanks in the hit movie *Apollo 13*. "Well, I didn't know whether Tom Hanks was an astronaut. But I saw this as a movie about a spacecraft in jeopardy. And who does the world want to get back the most? Who does America want to save? Tom Hanks. We don't want to see him die. We like him too much."

If we couldn't thin-slice — if you really had to know someone for months and months to get at their true selves — then *Apollo 13* would be robbed of its drama and *Splash* would not be funny. And if we could not make sense of complicated situations in a flash, basketball would be chaotic, and bird-watchers would be helpless. Not long ago, a group of psychologists reworked the divorce prediction test that I found so overwhelming. They took a number of Gottman's couples videos and showed them to nonexperts — only this time, they provided the raters with a little help. They gave them a list of emotions to look for. They broke the tapes into thirty-second segments and allowed everyone to look at each segment twice, once to focus on the man and once to focus on the woman. And what happened? This time around, the observers' ratings predicted with better than 80 percent accuracy which marriages were going to make it. That's not quite as good as Gottman. But it's pretty impressive — and that shouldn't come as a surprise. We're old hands at thin-slicing.

The Locked Door: The Secret Life of Snap Decisions

Not long ago, one of the world's top tennis coaches, a man named Vic Braden, began to notice something strange whenever he watched a tennis match. In tennis, players are given two chances to successfully hit a serve, and if they miss on their second chance, they are said to double-fault, and what Braden realized was that he always knew when a player was about to double-fault. A player would toss the ball up in the air and draw his racket back, and just as he was about to make contact, Braden would blurt out, "Oh, no, double fault," and sure enough, the ball would go wide or long or it would hit the net. It didn't seem to matter who was playing, man or woman, whether he was watching the match live or on television, or how well he knew the person serving. "I was calling double faults on girls from Russia I'd never seen before in my life," Braden says. Nor was Braden simply lucky. Lucky is when you call a coin toss correctly. But double-faulting is rare. In an entire match, a professional tennis player might hit hundreds of serves and double-fault no more than three or four times. One year, at the big professional tennis tournament at Indian Wells, near Braden's house in Southern California, he decided to keep track and found he correctly predicted sixteen out of seventeen double faults in the matches he watched. "For a while it got so bad that I got scared," Braden says. "It literally scared me. I was getting twenty out of twenty right, and we're talking about guys who almost never double-fault."

Braden is now in his seventies. When he was young, he was a world-class tennis player, and over the past fifty years, he has coached and counseled and known many of the greatest tennis players in the history of the game. He is a small and irrepressible man with the energy of someone half his age, and if you were to talk to people in the tennis world, they'd tell you that Vic Braden knows as much about the nuances and subtleties of the game as any man alive. It isn't surprising, then, that Vic Braden should be really good at reading a serve in the blink of an eye. It really isn't any different from the ability of an art expert to look at the Getty kouros and know, instantly, that it's a fake. Something in the way the tennis players hold themselves, or the way they toss the ball, or the fluidity of their motion triggers something in his unconscious. He instinctively picks up the "giss" of a double fault. He thin-slices some part of the service motion and — *blink!* — he just *knows.* But here's the catch: much to Braden's frustration, he simply cannot figure out *how* he knows.

"What did I see?" he says. "I would lie in bed, thinking, How did I do this? I don't know. It drove me crazy. It tortured me. I'd go back and I'd go over the serve in my mind and I'd try to figure it out. Did they stumble? Did they take another step? Did they add a bounce to the ball — something that changed their motor program?" The evidence he used to draw his conclusions seemed to be buried somewhere in his unconscious, and he could not dredge it up.

This is the second critical fact about the thoughts and decisions that bubble up from our unconscious. Snap judgments are, first of all, enormously quick: they rely on the thinnest slices of experience. But they are also unconscious. In the Iowa gambling experiment, the gamblers started avoiding the dangerous red decks long before they were actually aware that they were avoiding them. It took another seventy cards for the conscious brain to finally figure out what was going on. When Harrison and Hoving and the Greek experts first confronted the kouros, they experienced waves of repulsion and words popping into their heads, and Harrison blurted out, "I'm sorry to hear that." But at that moment of first doubt, they were a long way from being able to enumerate precisely why they felt the way they did. Hoving has talked to many art experts whom he calls fakebusters, and they all describe the act of getting at the truth of a work of art as an extraordinarily imprecise process. Hoving says they feel "a kind of mental rush, a flurry of visual facts flooding their minds when looking at a work of art. One fakebuster described the experience as if his eyes and senses were a flock of hummingbirds popping in and out of dozens of way stations. Within minutes, sometimes seconds, this fakebuster registered hosts of things that seemed to call out to him, 'Watch out!'"

Here is Hoving on the art historian Bernard Berenson. "[He] sometimes distressed his colleagues with his inability to articulate how he could see so clearly the tiny defects and inconsistencies in a particular work that branded it either an unintelligent reworking or a fake. In one court case, in fact, Berenson was able to say only that his stomach felt wrong. He had a curious ringing in his ears. He was struck by a momentary depression. Or he felt woozy and off balance. Hardly scientific descriptions of how he knew he was in the presence of something cooked up or faked. But that's as far as he was able to go."

Snap judgments and rapid cognition take place behind a locked door. Vic Braden tried to look inside that room. He stayed up at night, trying to figure out what it is in the delivery of a tennis serve that primes his judgment. But he couldn't.

I don't think we are very good at dealing with the fact of that locked door. It's one thing to acknowledge the enormous power of snap judgments and thin slices but quite another to place our trust in something so seemingly mysterious. "My father will sit down and give you theories to explain why he does this or that," the son of the billionaire investor George Soros has said. "But I remember seeing it as a kid and thinking, At least half of this is bull. I mean, you know the reason he changes his position on the market or whatever is because his back starts killing him. He literally goes into a spasm, and it's this early warning sign."

Clearly this is part of the reason why George Soros is so good at what he does: he is someone who is aware of the value of the products of his unconscious reasoning. But if you or I were to invest our money with Soros, we'd feel nervous if the only reason he could give for a decision was that his back hurt. A highly successful CEO like Jack Welch may entitle his memoir *Jack: Straight from the Gut*, but he then makes it clear that what set him apart wasn't just his gut but carefully worked-out theories of management, systems, and principles as well. Our world requires that decisions be sourced and footnoted, and if we say *how* we feel, we must also be prepared to elaborate on *why* we feel that way. This is why it was so hard for the Getty, at least in the beginning, to accept the opinion of people like Hoving and Harrison and Zeri: it was a lot easier to listen to the scientists and the lawyers, because the scientists and the lawyers could provide pages and pages of documentation supporting their conclusions. I think that approach is a mistake, and if we are to learn to improve the quality of the decisions we make, we need to accept the mysterious nature of our snap judgments. We need to respect the fact that it is possible to know without knowing why we know and accept that — sometimes — we're better off that way.

1. Primed for Action

Imagine that I'm a professor, and I've asked you to come and see me in my office. You walk down a long corridor, come through the doorway, and sit down at a table. In front of you is a sheet of paper with a list of five-word sets. I want you to make a grammatical four-word sentence as quickly as possible out of each set. It's called a scrambled-sentence test. Ready?

01   him was worried she always
02   from are Florida oranges temperature

03 ball the throw toss silently
04 shoes give replace old the
05 he observes occasionally people watches
06 be will sweat lonely they
07 sky the seamless gray is
08 should now withdraw forgetful we
09 us bingo sing play let
10 sunlight makes temperature wrinkle raisins

That seemed straightforward, right? Actually it wasn't. After you finished that test — believe it or not — you would have walked out of my office and back down the hall more slowly than you walked in. With that test, I affected the way you behaved. How? Well, look back at the list. Scattered throughout it are certain words, such as "worried," "Florida," "old," "lonely," "gray," "bingo," and "wrinkle." You thought that I was just making you take a language test. But, in fact, what I was also doing was making the big computer in your brain — your adaptive unconscious — think about the state of being old. It didn't inform the rest of your brain about its sudden obsession. But it took all this talk of old age so seriously that by the time you finished and walked down the corridor, you acted old. You walked slowly.

This test was devised by a very clever psychologist named John Bargh. It's an example of what is called a priming experiment, and Bargh and others have done numerous even more fascinating variations of it, all of which show just how much goes on behind that locked door of our unconscious. For example, on one occasion Bargh and two colleagues at New York University, Mark Chen and

Lara Burrows, staged an experiment in the hallway just down from Bargh's office. They used a group of undergraduates as subjects and gave everyone in the group one of two scrambled-sentence tests. The first was sprinkled with words like "aggressively," "bold," "rude," "bother," "disturb," "intrude," and "infringe." The second was sprinkled with words like "respect," "considerate," "appreciate," "patiently," "yield," "polite," and "courteous." In neither case were there so many similar words that the students picked up on what was going on. (Once you become conscious of being primed, of course, the priming doesn't work.) After doing the test — which takes only about five minutes — the students were instructed to walk down the hall and talk to the person running the experiment in order to get their next assignment.

Whenever a student arrived at the office, however, Bargh made sure that the experimenter was busy, locked in conversation with someone else — a confederate who was standing in the hallway, blocking the doorway to the experimenter's office. Bargh wanted to learn whether the people who were primed with the polite words would take longer to interrupt the conversation between the experimenter and the confederate than those primed with the rude words. He knew enough about the strange power of unconscious influence to feel that it would make a difference, but he thought the effect would be slight. Earlier, when Bargh had gone to the committee at NYU that approves human experiments, they had made him promise that he would cut off the conversation in the hall at ten minutes. "We looked at them when they said that and thought, You've got to be kidding," Bargh remembered. "The joke was that we would be measuring the difference in milliseconds. I mean, these are New Yorkers. They aren't going to just stand there. We thought maybe a few seconds, or a minute at most."

But Bargh and his colleagues were wrong. The people primed to be rude eventually interrupted — on average after about five minutes. But of the people primed to be polite, the overwhelming majority — 82 percent — *never interrupted at all*. If the experiment hadn't ended after ten minutes, who knows how long they would have stood in the hallway, a polite and patient smile on their faces?

"The experiment was right down the hall from my office," Bargh remembers. "I had to listen to the same conversation over and over again. Every hour, whenever there was a new subject. It was boring, *boring*. The people would come down the hallway, and they would see the confederate whom the experimenter was talking to through the doorway. And the confederate would be going on and on about how she didn't understand what she was supposed to do. She kept asking and asking, for ten minutes, 'Where do I mark this? I don't get it.'" Bargh winced at the memory and the strangeness of it all. "For a whole semester this was going on. And the people who had done the polite test *just stood there*."

Priming is not, it should be said, like brainwashing. I can't make you reveal deeply personal details about your childhood by priming you with words like "nap" and "bottle" and "teddy bear." Nor can I program you to rob a bank for me. On the other hand, the effects of priming aren't trivial. Two Dutch researchers did a study in which they had groups of students answer forty-two fairly demanding questions from the board game Trivial Pursuit. Half were asked to take five minutes beforehand to think about what it would mean to be a professor and write down everything that came to mind. Those students got 55.6 percent of the questions right. The other half of the students were asked to first sit and think about soccer hooligans. They ended up getting 42.6 percent of the Trivial Pursuit questions right. The "professor" group didn't know more than the "soccer hooligan" group. They weren't smarter or more focused or more serious. They were simply in a "smart" frame of mind, and, clearly, associating themselves with the idea of something smart, like a professor, made it a lot easier — in that stressful instant after a trivia question was asked — to blurt out the right answer. The difference between 55.6 and 42.6 percent, it should be pointed out, is enormous. That can be the difference between passing and failing.

The psychologists Claude Steele and Joshua Aronson created an even more extreme version of this test, using black college students and twenty questions taken from the Graduate Record Examination, the standardized test used for entry into graduate school. When the students were asked to identify their race on a pretest questionnaire, that simple act was sufficient to prime them with all the negative stereotypes associated with African Americans and academic achievement — and the number of items they got right was cut *in half*. As a society, we place enormous faith in tests because we think that they are a reliable indicator of the test taker's ability and knowledge.

But are they really? If a white student from a prestigious private high school gets a higher SAT score than a black student from an inner-city school, is it because she's truly a better student, or is it because to be white and to attend a prestigious high school is to be constantly primed with the idea of "smart"?

Even more impressive, however, is how mysterious these priming effects are. When you took that sentence-completion test, you didn't know that you were being primed to think "old." Why would you? The clues were pretty subtle. What is striking, though, is that even after people walked slowly out of the room and down the hall, they *still* weren't aware of how their behavior had been affected. Bargh once had people play board games in which the only way the participants could win was if they learned how to cooperate with one another. So he primed the players with thoughts of cooperativeness, and sure enough, they were far more cooperative, and the game went far more smoothly. "Afterward," Bargh says, "we ask them questions like How strongly did you cooperate? How much did you want to cooperate? And then we correlate that with their actual behavior — and the correlation is zero. This is a game that goes on for fifteen minutes, and at the end, people don't know what they have done. They just don't know it. Their explanations are just random, noise. That surprised me. I thought that people could at least have consulted their memories. But they couldn't."

Aronson and Steele found the same thing with the black students who did so poorly after they were reminded of their race. "I talked to the black students afterward, and I asked them, 'Did anything lower your performance?'" Aronson said. "I would ask, 'Did it bug you that I asked you to indicate your race?' Because it clearly had a huge effect on their performance. And they would always say no and something like 'You know, I just don't think I'm smart enough to be here.'"

The results from these experiments are, obviously, quite disturbing. They suggest that what we think of as free will is largely an illusion: much of the time, we are simply operating on automatic pilot, and the way we think and act — and *how well* we think and act on the spur of the moment — are a lot more susceptible to outside influences than we realize. But there is also, I think, a significant advantage to how secretly the unconscious does its work. In the example of the sentence-completion task I gave you with all the words about old age, how long did it take you to make sentences out of those words? My guess is that it took you no more than a few seconds per sentence. That's fast, and you were able to perform that experiment quickly because you were able to concentrate on the task and block out distractions. If you had been on the lookout for possible patterns in the lists of words, there is no way you would have completed the task that quickly. You would have been distracted. Yes, the references to old people changed the speed at which you walked out of the room, but was that bad? Your unconscious was simply telling your body: I've picked up some clues that we're in an environment that is really concerned about old age — and let's behave accordingly. Your unconscious, in this sense, was acting as a kind of mental valet. It was taking care of all the minor mental details in your life. It was keeping tabs on everything going on around you and making sure you were acting appropriately, while leaving you free to concentrate on the main problem at hand.

The team that created the Iowa gambling experiments was headed by the neurologist Antonio Damasio, and Damasio's group has done some fascinating research on just what happens when too much of our thinking takes place outside the locked door. Damasio studied patients with damage to a small but critical part of the brain called the ventromedial prefrontal cortex, which lies behind the nose. The ventromedial area plays a critical role in decision making. It works out contingencies and relationships and sorts through the mountain of information we get from the outside world, prioritizing it and putting flags on things that demand our immediate attention. People with damage to their ventromedial area are perfectly rational. They can be highly intelligent and functional, but they lack judgment. More precisely, they don't have that mental valet in their unconscious that frees them up to concentrate on what really matters. In his book *Descartes' Error*, Damasio describes trying to set up an appointment with a patient with this kind of brain damage:

> I suggested two alternative dates, both in the coming month and just a few days apart from each other. The patient pulled out his appointment book and began consulting the calendar. The behavior that ensued, which was witnessed by several investigators, was remarkable. For the better part of a half hour, the patient enumerated reasons for and against each of the two dates: previous engagements, proximity to other engagements, possible

meteorological conditions, virtually anything that one could think about concerning a simple date. [He was] walking us through a tiresome cost-benefit analysis, an endless outlining and fruitless comparison of options and possible consequences. It took enormous discipline to listen to all of this without pounding on the table and telling him to stop.

Damasio and his team also gave the gambler's test to their ventromedial patients. Most of the patients, just like the rest of us, eventually figured out that the red decks were a problem. But at no time did the ventromedial patients ever get a prickling of sweat on their palms; at no time did they get a hunch that the blue decks were preferable to the red cards, and at no time — not even after they had figured the game out — did the patients adjust their strategy to stay away from the problem cards. They knew intellectually what was right, but that knowledge wasn't enough to change the way they played the game. "It's like drug addiction," says Antoine Bechara, one of the researchers on the Iowa team. "Addicts can articulate very well the consequences of their behavior. But they fail to act accordingly. That's because of a brain problem. That's what we were putting our finger on. Damage in the ventromedial area causes a disconnect between what you know and what you do." What the patients lacked was the valet silently pushing them in the right direction, adding that little emotional extra — the prickling of the palms — to make sure they did the right thing. In high-stakes, fast-moving situations, we don't want to be as dispassionate and purely rational as the

Iowa ventromedial patients. We don't want to stand there endlessly talking through our options. Sometimes we're better off if the mind behind the locked door makes our decisions for us.

2. *The Storytelling Problem*

On a brisk spring evening not long ago, two dozen men and women gathered in the back room of a Manhattan bar to engage in a peculiar ritual known as speed-dating. They were all young professionals in their twenties, a smattering of Wall Street types and medical students and schoolteachers, as well as four women who came in a group from the nearby headquarters of Anne Klein Jewelry. The women were all in red or black sweaters, and jeans or dark-colored pants. The men, with one or two exceptions, were all wearing the Manhattan work uniform of a dark blue shirt and black slacks. At the beginning they mingled awkwardly, clutching their drinks, and then the coordinator of the evening, a tall, striking woman named Kailynn, called the group to order.

Each man would have, she said, six minutes of conversation with each woman. The women would sit for the duration of the evening against the wall on the long, low couches that ringed the room, and the men would rotate from woman to woman, moving to the next woman whenever Kailynn rang a bell, signaling that the six minutes were over. The daters were all given a badge, a number, and a short form to complete, with the instruction that if they liked someone after six minutes, they should check the box next to his or her number. If the person whose box they checked also checked their box, both daters would be notified of the other's e-mail address within twenty-four hours. There was a murmur of anticipation. Several people made a last-minute dash to the bathroom. Kailynn rang her bell.

The men and women took their places, and immediately a surge of conversation filled the room. The men's chairs were far enough away from the women's couches that the two parties had to lean forward, their elbows on their knees. One or two of the women were actually bouncing up and down on the sofa cushions. The man talking to the woman at table number three spilled his beer on her lap. At table one, a brunette named Melissa, desperate to get her date to talk, asked him in quick succession, "If you had three wishes, what would they be? Do you have siblings? Do you live alone?" At another table, a very young and blond man named David asked his date why she signed up for the evening. "I'm twenty-six," she replied. "A lot of my friends have boyfriends that they have known since high school, and they are engaged or already married, and I'm still single and I'm like — *ahhhh*."

Kailynn stood to the side, by the bar that ran across one wall of the room. "If you are enjoying the connection, time goes quickly. If you aren't, it's the longest six minutes of your life," she said as she watched the couples nervously chatter. "Sometimes strange things happen. I'll never forget, back in November, there was a guy from Queens who showed up with a dozen red roses, and he gave one to every girl he spoke to. He had a suit on." She gave a half smile. "He was ready to *go*."

Speed-dating has become enormously popular around the world over the last few years, and it's not hard to understand why. It's the distillation of dating to a simple snap judgment. Everyone who sat down at one of those tables was trying to answer a very simple question: Do I want to see this person again? And to answer that, we don't need an entire evening. We really need only a few minutes. Velma, for instance, one of the four Anne Klein women, said that she picked none of the men and that she made up her mind about each of them right away. "They lost me at hello," she said, rolling her eyes. Ron, who worked as a financial analyst at an investment bank, picked two of the women, one of whom he settled on after about a minute and a half of conversation and one of whom, Lillian at table two, he decided on the instant he sat down across from her. "Her tongue was pierced," he said, admiringly. "You come to a place like this and you expect a bunch of lawyers. But she was a whole different story." Lillian liked Ron, too. "You know why?" she asked. "He's from Louisiana. I loved the accent. And I dropped my pen, just to see what he would do, and he picked it up right away." As it turned out, lots of the women there liked Ron the instant they met him, and lots of the men liked Lillian the instant they met her. Both of them had a kind of contagious, winning spark. "You know, girls are really smart," Jon, a medical student in a blue suit, said at the end of the evening. "They know in the first minute, Do I like this guy, can I take him home to my parents, or is he just a wham-bam kind of jerk?" Jon is quite right, except it isn't just girls who are smart. When it comes to thin-slicing potential dates, pretty much everyone is smart.

But suppose I were to alter the rules of speed-dating just slightly. What if I tried to look behind the locked door and made everyone explain their choices? We know, of course, that that can't be done: the machinery of our unconscious thinking is forever hidden. But what if I threw caution to the winds and forced people to explain their first impressions and snap judgments *anyway*? That is what two professors from Columbia University, Sheena Iyengar and Raymond Fisman, have done, and they have discovered that if you make people explain themselves, something very strange and troubling happens. What once seemed like the most transparent and pure of thin-slicing exercises turns into something quite confusing.

Iyengar and Fisman make something of an odd couple: Iyengar is of Indian descent. Fisman is Jewish. Iyengar is a psychologist. Fisman is an economist. The only reason they got involved in speed-dating is that they once had an argument at a party about the relative merits of arranged marriages and love marriages. "We've supposedly spawned one long-term romance," Fisman told me. He is a slender man who looks like a teenager, and he has a wry sense of humor. "It makes me proud. Apparently all you need is three to get into Jewish heaven, so I'm well on my way." The two professors run their speed-dating nights at the back of the West End Bar on Broadway, across the street from the Columbia campus. They are identical to standard New York speed-dating evenings, with one exception. Their participants don't just date and then check the yes or no box. On four occasions — before the speed-dating starts, after the evening ends, a month later, and then six months after the speed-dating evening — they have to fill out a short questionnaire that asks them to rate what they are looking for in a potential partner on a scale of 1 to 10. The categories are attractiveness, shared interests, funny/sense of humor, sincerity, intelligence, and ambition. In addition, at the end of every "date," they rate the person they've just met, based on the same categories. By the end of one of their evenings, then, Fisman and Iyengar have an incredibly detailed picture of exactly what everyone says they were feeling during the dating process. And it's when you look at that picture that the strangeness starts.

For example, at the Columbia session, I paid particular attention to a young woman with pale skin and blond, curly hair and a tall, energetic man with green eyes and long brown hair. I don't know their names, but let's call them Mary and John. I watched them for the duration of their date, and it was immediately clear that Mary really liked John and John really liked Mary. John sat down at Mary's table. Their eyes locked. She looked down shyly. She seemed a little nervous. She leaned forward in her chair. It seemed, from the outside, like a perfectly straightforward case of instant attraction. But let's dig below the surface and ask a few simple questions. First of all, did Mary's assessment of John's personality match the personality that she said she wanted in a man before the evening started? In other words, how good is Mary at predicting what she likes in a man? Fisman and Iyengar can answer that question really easily, and what they find when they compare what speed-daters say they want with what they are actually attracted to in the moment is that those two things don't match. For example, if Mary said at the start of the evening that she wanted someone intelligent and sincere, that in no way means she'll be attracted only to intelligent and sincere men. It's just as likely that John, whom she likes more than anyone else, could turn out to be attractive and funny but not particularly sincere or smart at all. Second, if all the men Mary ends up liking during the speed-dating are more attractive and funny than they are smart and sincere, on the next day, when she's asked to describe her perfect man, Mary will say that she likes attractive and funny men. But that's just the next day. If you ask her again a month later, she'll be back to saying that she wants intelligent and sincere.

You can be forgiven if you found the previous paragraph confusing. It *is* confusing: Mary says that she wants a certain kind of person. But then she is given a roomful of choices and she meets someone whom she really likes, and in that instant she completely changes her mind about what kind of person she wants. But then a month passes, and she goes back to what she originally said she wanted. So what does Mary really want in a man?

"I don't know," Iyengar said when I asked her that question. "Is the real me the one that I described beforehand?"

She paused, and Fisman spoke up: "No, the real me is the me revealed by my actions. That's what an economist would say."

Iyengar looked puzzled. "I don't know that's what a psychologist would say."

They couldn't agree. But then, that's because there isn't a right answer. Mary has an idea about what she wants in a man, and that idea isn't wrong. It's just incomplete. The description that she starts with is her conscious ideal: what she believes she wants when she sits down and thinks about it. But what she cannot be as certain about are the criteria she uses to form her preferences in that first instant of meeting someone face-to-face. That information is behind the locked door.

Braden has had a similar experience in his work with professional athletes. Over the years, he has made a point of talking to as many of the world's top tennis players as possible, asking them questions about why and how they play the way they do, and invariably he comes away disappointed. "Out of all the research that we've done with top players, we haven't found a single player who is consistent in knowing and explaining exactly what he does," Braden says. "They give different answers at different times, or they have answers that simply are not meaningful." One of the things he does, for instance, is videotape top tennis players and then digitize their movements, breaking them down frame by frame on a computer so that he knows, say, precisely how many degrees Pete Sampras rotates his shoulder on a cross-court backhand.

One of Braden's digitized videotapes is of the tennis great Andre Agassi hitting a forehand. The image has been stripped down. Agassi has been reduced to a skeleton, so that as he moves to hit the ball, the movement of every joint in his body is clearly visible and measurable. The Agassi tape is a perfect illustration of our inability to describe how we behave in the moment. "Almost every pro in the world says that he uses his wrist to roll the racket over the ball when he hits a forehand," Braden says.

"Why? What are they seeing? Look" — and here Braden points to the screen — "see when he hits the ball? We can tell with digitized imaging whether a wrist turns an *eighth* of a degree. But players almost never move their wrist at all. Look how fixed it is. He doesn't move his wrist until long after the ball is hit. He thinks he's moving it at impact, but he's actually not moving it until long after impact. How can so many people be fooled? People are going to coaches and paying hundreds of dollars to be taught how to roll their wrist over the ball, and all that's happening is that the number of injuries to the arm is exploding."

Braden found the same problem with the baseball player Ted Williams. Williams was perhaps the greatest hitter of all time, a man revered for his knowledge and insight into the art of hitting. One thing he always said was that he could look the ball onto the bat, that he could track it right to the point where he made contact. But Braden knew from his work in tennis that that is impossible. In the final five feet of a tennis ball's flight toward a player, the ball is far too close and moving much too fast to be seen. The player, at that moment, is effectively blind. The same is true with baseball. No one can look a ball onto the bat. "I met with Ted Williams once," Braden says. "We both worked for Sears and were both appearing at the same event. I said, 'Gee, Ted. We just did a study that showed that human beings can't track the ball onto the bat. It's a three-millisecond event.' And he was honest. He said, 'Well, I guess it just *seemed* like I could do that.'"

Ted Williams could hit a baseball as well as anyone in history, and he could explain with utter confidence how to do it. But his explanation did not match his actions, just as

Mary's explanation for what she wanted in a man did not necessarily match who she was attracted to in the moment. We have, as human beings, a storytelling problem. We're a bit too quick to come up with explanations for things we don't really have an explanation for.

Many years ago, the psychologist Norman R. F. Maier hung two long ropes from the ceiling of a room that was filled with all kinds of different tools, objects, and furniture. The ropes were far enough apart that if you held the end of one rope, you couldn't get close enough to grab hold of the other rope. Everyone who came into the room was asked the same question: How many different ways can you come up with for tying the ends of those two ropes together? There are four possible solutions to this problem. One is to stretch one rope as far as possible toward the other, anchor it to an object, such as a chair, and then go and get the second rope. Another is to take a third length, such as an extension cord, and tie it to the end of one of the ropes so that it will be long enough to reach the other rope. A third strategy is to grab one rope in one hand and use an implement, such as a long pole, to pull the other rope toward you. What Maier found is that most people figured out those three solutions pretty easily. But the fourth solution — to swing one rope back and forth like a pendulum and then grab hold of the other rope — occurred to only a few people. The rest were stumped. Maier let them sit and stew for ten minutes and then, without saying anything, he walked across the room toward the window and casually brushed one of the ropes, setting it in motion back and forth. Sure enough, after he did that, most people suddenly said *aha!* and came up with the pendulum solution. But when Maier asked all those people to describe how they figured it out, only one of them gave the right reason. As Maier wrote: "They made such statements as: 'It just dawned on me'; 'It was the only thing left'; 'I just realized the cord would swing if I fastened a weight to it'; 'Perhaps a course in physics suggested it to me'; 'I tried to think of a way to get the cord over here, and the only way was to make it swing over.' A professor of Psychology reported as follows: 'Having exhausted everything else, the next thing was to swing it. I thought of the situation of swinging across a river. I had imagery of monkeys swinging from trees. This imagery appeared simultaneously with the solution. The idea appeared complete.'"

Were these people lying? Were they ashamed to admit that they could solve the problem only after getting a hint? Not at all. It's just that Maier's hint was so subtle that it was picked up on only on an unconscious level. It was processed behind the locked door, so, when pressed for an explanation, all Maier's subjects could do was make up what seemed to them the most plausible one.

This is the price we pay for the many benefits of the locked door. When we ask people to explain their thinking — particularly thinking that comes from the unconscious — we need to be careful in how we interpret their answers. When it comes to romance, of course, we understand that. We know we cannot rationally describe the kind of person we will fall in love with: that's why we go on dates — to test our theories about who attracts us. And everyone knows that it's better to have an expert show you — and not just tell you — how to play tennis or golf or a musical instrument. We learn by example and by direct experience because there are real limits to the adequacy of verbal instruction. But in other aspects of our lives, I'm not sure we always respect the mysteries of the locked door and the dangers of the storytelling problem. There are times when we demand an explanation when an explanation really isn't possible, and, as we'll explore in the upcoming chapters of this book, doing so can have serious consequences. "After the O.J. Simpson verdict, one of the jurors appeared on TV and said with absolute conviction, 'Race had absolutely *nothing* to do with my decision,'" psychologist Joshua Aronson says. "But how on earth could she know that? What my research with priming race and test performance, and Bargh's research with the interrupters, and Maier's experiment with the ropes show is that people are ignorant of the things that affect their actions, yet they rarely *feel* ignorant. We need to accept our ignorance and say 'I don't know' more often."

Of course, there is a second, equally valuable, lesson in the Maier experiment. His subjects were stumped. They were frustrated. They were sitting there for ten minutes, and no doubt many of them felt that they were failing an important test, that they had been exposed as stupid. But they weren't stupid. Why not? Because everyone in that room had not one mind but two, and all the while their conscious mind was blocked, their unconscious was scanning the room, sifting through possibilities, processing every conceivable clue. And the instant it found the answer, it guided them — silently and surely — to the solution.

THREE

The Warren Harding Error: Why We Fall For Tall, Dark, and Handsome Men

Early one morning in 1899, in the back garden of the Globe Hotel in Richwood, Ohio, two men met while having their shoes shined. One was a lawyer and lobbyist from the state capital of Columbus. His name was Harry Daugherty. He was a thick-set, red-faced man with straight black hair, and he was brilliant. He was the Machiavelli of Ohio politics, the classic behind-the-scenes fixer, a shrewd and insightful judge of character or, at least, political opportunity. The second man was a newspaper editor from the small town of Marion, Ohio, who was at that moment a week away from winning election to the Ohio state senate. His name was Warren Harding. Daugherty looked over at Harding and was instantly overwhelmed by what he saw. As the journalist Mark Sullivan wrote, of that moment in the garden:

> Harding was worth looking at. He was at the time about 35 years old. His head, features, shoulders and torso had

a size that attracted attention; their proportions to each other made an effect which in any male at any place would justify more than the term handsome — in later years, when he came to be known beyond his local world, the word "Roman" was occasionally used in descriptions of him. As he stepped down from the stand, his legs bore out the striking and agreeable proportions of his body; and his lightness on his feet, his erectness, his easy bearing, added to the impression of physical grace and virility. His suppleness, combined with his bigness of frame, and his large, wide-set rather glowing eyes, heavy black hair, and markedly bronze complexion gave him some of the handsomeness of an Indian. His courtesy as he surrendered his seat to the other customer suggested genuine friendliness toward all mankind. His voice was noticeably resonant, masculine, warm. His pleasure in the attentions of the bootblack's whisk reflected a consciousness about clothes unusual in a small-town man. His manner as he bestowed a tip suggested generous good-nature, a wish to give pleasure, based on physical well-being and sincere kindliness of heart.

In that instant, as Daugherty sized up Harding, an idea came to him that would alter American history: Wouldn't that man make a great President?

Warren Harding was not a particularly intelligent man. He liked to play poker and golf and to drink and, most of all, to chase women; in fact, his sexual appetites were the stuff of legend. As he rose from one political office to another, he never once distinguished himself. He was vague and ambivalent on matters of policy. His speeches were once described as "an army of pompous phrases moving over the landscape in search of an idea." After being elected to the U.S. Senate in 1914, he was absent for the debates on women's suffrage and Prohibition — two of the biggest political issues of his time. He advanced steadily from local Ohio politics only because he was pushed by his wife, Florence, and stage-managed by the scheming Harry Daugherty and because, as he grew older, he grew more and more irresistibly distinguished-looking. Once, at a banquet, a supporter cried out, "Why, the son of a bitch *looks* like a senator," and so he did. By early middle age, Harding's biographer Francis Russell writes, his "lusty black eyebrows contrasted with his steel-gray hair to give the effect of force, his massive shoulders and bronzed complexion gave the effect of health." Harding, according to Russell, could have put on a toga and stepped onstage in a production of *Julius Caesar.* Daugherty arranged for Harding to address the 1916 Republican presidential convention because he knew that people only had to see Harding and hear that magnificent rumbling voice to be convinced of his worthiness for higher office. In 1920, Daugherty convinced Harding, against Harding's better judgment, to run for the White House. Daugherty wasn't being facetious. He was serious.

"Daugherty, ever since the two had met, had carried in the back of his mind the idea that Harding would make a 'great President,'" Sullivan writes. "Sometimes, unconsciously, Daugherty expressed it, with more fidelity to exactness, 'a great-*looking* President.'" Harding entered the Republican convention that summer sixth among a field of six. Daugherty was unconcerned. The convention was deadlocked between the two leading candidates, so,

Daugherty predicted, the delegates would be forced to look for an alternative. To whom else would they turn, in that desperate moment, if not to the man who radiated common sense and dignity and all that was presidential? In the early morning hours, as they gathered in the smoke-filled back rooms of the Blackstone Hotel in Chicago, the Republican Party bosses threw up their hands and asked, wasn't there a candidate they could all agree on? And one name came immediately to mind: Harding! Didn't he *look* just like a presidential candidate? So Senator Harding became candidate Harding, and later that fall, after a campaign conducted from his front porch in Marion, Ohio, candidate Harding became President Harding. Harding served two years before dying unexpectedly of a stroke. He was, most historians agree, one of the worst presidents in American history.

1. The Dark Side of Thin-Slicing

So far in *Blink*, I have talked about how extraordinarily powerful thin-slicing can be, and what makes thin-slicing possible is our ability to very quickly get below the surface of a situation. Thomas Hoving and Evelyn Harrison and the art experts were instantly able to see behind the forger's artifice. Susan and Bill seemed, at first, to be the embodiment of a happy, loving couple. But when we listened closely to their interaction and measured the ratio of positive to negative emotions, we got a different story. Nalini Ambady's research showed how much we can learn about a surgeon's likelihood of being sued if we get beyond the diplomas on the wall and the white coat and focus on his or her tone of voice. But what happens if that rapid chain of thinking gets interrupted somehow? What if we reach a snap judgment without *ever* getting below the surface?

In the previous chapter, I wrote about the experiments conducted by John Bargh in which he showed that we have such powerful associations with certain words (for example, "Florida," "gray," "wrinkles," and "bingo") that just being exposed to them can cause a change in our behavior. I think that there are facts about people's appearance — their size or shape or color or sex — that can trigger a very similar set of powerful associations. Many people who looked at Warren Harding saw how extraordinarily handsome and distinguished-looking he was and jumped to the immediate — and entirely unwarranted — conclusion that he was a man of courage and intelligence and integrity. They didn't dig below the surface. The way he looked carried so many powerful connotations that it stopped the normal process of thinking dead in its tracks.

The Warren Harding error is the dark side of rapid cognition. It is at the root of a good deal of prejudice and discrimination. It's why picking the right candidate for a job is so difficult and why, on more occasions than we may care to admit, utter mediocrities sometimes end up in positions of enormous responsibility. Part of what it means to take thin-slicing and first impressions seriously is accepting the fact that sometimes we can know more about someone or something in the blink of an eye than we can after months of study. But we also have to acknowledge and understand those circumstances when rapid cognition leads us astray.

2. Blink in Black and White

Over the past few years, a number of psychologists have begun to look more closely at the role these kinds of unconscious — or, as they like to call them, implicit — associations play in our beliefs and behavior, and much of their work has focused on a very fascinating tool called the Implicit Association Test (IAT). The IAT was devised by Anthony G. Greenwald, Mahzarin Banaji, and Brian Nosek, and it is based on a seemingly obvious — but nonetheless quite profound — observation. We make connections much more quickly between pairs of ideas that are already related in our minds than we do between pairs of ideas that are unfamiliar to us. What does that mean? Let me give you an example. Below is a list of words. Take a pencil or pen and assign each name to the category to which it belongs by putting a check mark either to the left or to the right of the word. You can also do it by tapping your finger in the appropriate column. Do it as quickly as you can. Don't skip over words. And don't worry if you make any mistakes.

Male	Female
...................John...................
...................Bob...................
...................Amy...................
...................Holly...................
...................Joan...................
...................Derek...................
...................Peggy...................

..................Jason........................
..................Lisa.........................
..................Matt.........................
..................Sarah........................

That was easy, right? And the reason that was easy is that when we read or hear the name "John" or "Bob" or "Holly," we don't even have to think about whether it's a masculine or a feminine name. We all have a strong prior association between a first name like John and the male gender, or a name like Lisa and things female.

That was a warm-up. Now let's complete an actual IAT. It works like the warm-up, except that now I'm going to mix two entirely separate categories together. Once again, put a check mark to either the right or the left of each word, in the category to which it belongs.

Male	Female
or	or
Career	Family

...............Lisa............................
...............Matt............................
...............Laundry.........................
...............Entrepreneur....................
...............John............................
...............Merchant........................
...............Bob.............................
...............Capitalist......................
...............Holly...........................
...............Joan............................

...............Home.....................

...............Corporation.............

...............Siblings..................

...............Peggy....................

...............Jason.....................

...............Kitchen..................

...............Housework.............

...............Parents..................

...............Sarah.....................

...............Derek....................

My guess is that most of you found that a little harder, but that you were still pretty fast at putting the words into the right categories. Now try this:

Male or Family	Female or Career

...............Babies......................

...............Sarah......................

...............Derek......................

...............Merchant..................

...............Employment................

...............John.......................

...............Bob........................

...............Holly......................

...............Domestic..................

...............Entrepreneur..............

...............Office......................

...............Joan.......................

................Peggy..............................
................Cousins.........................
................Grandparents...................
................Jason............................
................Home............................
................Lisa.............................
................Corporation....................
................Matt............................

Did you notice the difference? This test was quite a bit harder than the one before it, wasn't it? If you are like most people, it took you a little longer to put the word "Entrepreneur" into the "Career" category when "Career" was paired with "Female" than when "Career" was paired with "Male." That's because most of us have much stronger mental associations between maleness and career-oriented concepts than we do between femaleness and ideas related to careers. "Male" and "Capitalist" go together in our minds a lot like "John" and "Male" did. But when the category is "Male or Family," we have to stop and think — even if it's only for a few hundred milliseconds — before we decide what to do with a word like "Merchant."

When psychologists administer the IAT, they usually don't use paper and pencil tests like the ones I've just given you. Most of the time, they do it on a computer. The words are flashed on the screen one at a time, and if a given word belongs in the left-hand column, you hit the letter *e*, and if the word belongs in the right-hand column, you hit the letter *i*. The advantage of doing the IAT on a computer is that the responses are measurable down to the millisecond, and those measurements are used in assigning the test taker's score. So, for example, if it took you a little bit longer to complete part two of the Work/Family IAT than it did part one, we would say that you have a moderate association between men and the workforce. If it took you a lot longer to complete part two, we'd say that when it comes to the workforce, you have a strong automatic male association.

One of the reasons that the IAT has become so popular in recent years as a research tool is that the effects it is measuring are not subtle; as those of you who felt yourself slowing down on the second half of the Work/Family IAT above can attest, the IAT is the kind of tool that hits you over the head with its conclusions. "When there's a strong prior association, people answer in between four hundred and six hundred milliseconds," says Greenwald. "When there isn't, they might take two hundred to three hundred milliseconds longer than that — which in the realm of these kinds of effects is huge. One of my cognitive psychologist colleagues described this as an effect you can measure with a sundial."

If you'd like to try a computerized IAT, you can go to www.implicit.harvard.edu. There you'll find several tests, including the most famous of all the IATs, the Race IAT. I've taken the Race IAT on many occasions, and the result always leaves me feeling a bit creepy. At the beginning of the test, you are asked what your attitudes toward blacks and whites are. I answered, as I am sure most of you would, that I think of the races as equal. Then comes the test. You're encouraged to complete it quickly. First comes the warm-up. A series of pictures of faces flash on the screen.

When you see a black face, you press *e* and put it in the left-hand category. When you see a white face, you press *i* and put it in the right-hand category. It's *blink, blink, blink:* I didn't have to think at all. Then comes part one.

European American   African American
or   or
Bad   Good

......................Hurt.......................
.............................Evil.........................
....................Glorious....................

....

....
....................Wonderful....................

And so on. Immediately, something strange happened to me. The task of putting the words and faces in the right categories suddenly became more difficult. I found myself slowing down. I had to think. Sometimes I assigned something to one category when I really meant to assign it to the other category. I was trying as hard as I could, and in the back of my mind was a growing sense of mortification. Why was I having such trouble when I had to put a word like "Glorious" or "Wonderful" into the "Good" category when "Good" was paired with "African American" or when I had to put the word "Evil" into the "Bad" category when "Bad" was paired with "European American"? Then came part two. This time the categories were reversed.

European American   African American
            or   or
         Good   Bad

........................Hurt........................
........................Evil.........................
.....................Glorious.....................

....

....
....................Wonderful....................

And so on. Now my mortification grew still further. Now I was having no trouble at all.

Evil? *African American or Bad.*

Hurt? *African American or Bad.*

Wonderful? *European American or Good.*

I took the test a second time, and then a third time, and then a fourth time, hoping that the awful feeling of bias would go away. It made no difference. It turns out that more than 80 percent of all those who have ever taken the test end up having pro-white associations, meaning that it takes them measurably longer to complete answers when they are required to put good words into the "Black" category than when they are required to link bad things with black people. I didn't do quite so badly. On the Race IAT, I was rated as having a "moderate automatic preference for whites." But then again, I'm half black. (My mother is Jamaican.)

So what does this mean? Does this mean I'm a racist, a self-hating black person? Not exactly. What it means is that our attitudes toward things like race or gender operate on two levels. First of all, we have our conscious attitudes. This is what we choose to believe. These are our stated values, which we use to direct our behavior deliberately. The apartheid policies of South Africa or the laws in the American South that made it difficult for African Americans to vote are manifestations of conscious discrimination, and when we talk about racism or the fight for civil rights, this is the kind of discrimination that we usually refer to. But the IAT measures something else. It measures our second level of attitude, our racial attitude on an *unconscious* level — the immediate, automatic associations that tumble out before we've even had time to think. We don't deliberately choose our unconscious attitudes. And as I wrote about in the first chapter, we may not even be aware of them. The giant computer that is our unconscious silently crunches all the data it can from the experiences we've had, the people we've met, the lessons we've learned, the books we've read, the movies we've seen, and so on, and it forms an opinion. That's what is coming out in the IAT.

The disturbing thing about the test is that it shows that our unconscious attitudes may be utterly incompatible with our stated conscious values. As it turns out, for example, of the fifty thousand African Americans who have taken the Race IAT so far, about half of them, like me, have stronger associations with whites than with blacks. How could we not? We live in North America, where we are surrounded every day by cultural messages linking white with good. "You don't choose to make positive associations with the dominant group," says Mahzarin Banaji, who teaches psychology at Harvard University and is one of the leaders in IAT research. "But you are required to. All around you, that group is being paired with good things. You open the newspaper and you turn on the television, and you can't escape it."

The IAT is more than just an abstract measure of attitudes. It's also a powerful predictor of how we act in certain kinds of spontaneous situations. If you have a strongly pro-white pattern of associations, for example, there is evidence that that will affect the way you behave in the presence of a black person. It's not going to affect what you'll choose to say or feel or do. In all likelihood, you won't be aware that you're behaving any differently than you would around a white person. But chances are you'll lean forward a little less, turn away slightly from him or her, close your body a bit, be a bit less expressive, maintain less eye contact, stand a little farther away, smile a lot less, hesitate and stumble over your words a bit more, laugh at jokes a bit less. Does that matter? Of course it does. Suppose the conversation is a job interview. And suppose the applicant is a black man. He's going to pick up on that uncertainty and distance, and that may well make him a little less certain of himself, a little less confident, and a little less friendly. And what will you think then? You may well get a gut feeling that the applicant doesn't really have what it takes, or maybe that he is a bit standoffish, or maybe that he doesn't really want the job. What this unconscious first impression will do, in other words, is throw the interview hopelessly off course.

Or what if the person you are interviewing is tall? I'm sure that on a conscious level we don't think that we treat tall people any differently from how we treat short people. But there's plenty of evidence to suggest that height — particularly in men — does trigger a certain set of very positive unconscious associations. I polled about half of the companies on the Fortune 500 list — the list of the largest corporations in the United States — asking each company questions about its CEO. Overwhelmingly, the heads of big companies are, as I'm sure comes as no surprise to anyone, white men, which undoubtedly reflects some kind of implicit bias. But they are also almost all tall: in my sample, I found that on average, male CEOs were just a shade under six feet tall. Given that the average American male is five foot nine, that means that CEOs as a group have about three inches on the rest of their sex. But this statistic actually understates the matter. In the U.S. population, about 14.5 percent of all men are six feet or taller. Among CEOs of Fortune 500 companies, that number is 58 percent. Even more striking, in the general American population, 3.9 percent of adult men are six foot two or taller. Among my CEO sample, almost a third were six foot two or taller.

The lack of women or minorities among the top executive ranks at least has a plausible explanation. For years, for a number of reasons having to do with discrimination and cultural patterns, there simply weren't a lot of women and minorities entering the management ranks of American corporations. So, today, when boards of directors look for people with the necessary experience to be candidates for top positions, they can argue somewhat plausibly that there aren't a lot of women and minorities in the executive pipeline. But this is not true of short people. It is possible to staff a large company entirely with white males, but it is not possible to staff a large company without short people. There simply aren't enough tall people to go around. Yet few of those short people ever make it into the executive suite. Of the tens of millions of American men below five foot six, a grand total of ten in my sample have reached the level of CEO, which says that being short is probably as much of a handicap to corporate success as being a woman or an African American. (The grand exception to all of these trends is American Express CEO Kenneth Chenault, who is both on the short side—five foot nine—and black. He must be a remarkable man to have overcome *two* Warren Harding errors.)

Is this a deliberate prejudice? Of course not. No one ever says dismissively of a potential CEO candidate that he's too short. This is quite clearly the kind of unconscious bias that the IAT picks up on. Most of us, in ways that we are not entirely aware of, automatically associate leadership ability with imposing physical stature. We have a sense of what a leader is supposed to look like, and that stereotype is so powerful that when someone fits it, we simply become blind to other considerations. And this isn't confined to the executive suite. Not long ago, researchers who analyzed the data from four large research studies that had followed thousands of people from birth to adulthood calculated that when corrected for such variables as age and gender and weight, an inch of height is worth $789 a year in salary. That means that a person who is six feet tall but otherwise identical to someone who is five foot five will make on average $5,525 more per year. As Timothy Judge, one of the authors of the height-salary study, points out: "If you take this over the course of a 30-year career and compound it, we're talking about a tall person enjoying literally hundreds of thousands of dollars of earnings advantage." Have you ever wondered why so many mediocre people find their way into positions of authority in companies and organizations? It's because when it comes to even the most important positions, our selection decisions are a good deal less rational than we think. We see a tall person and we swoon.

3. Taking Care of the Customer

The sales director of the Flemington Nissan dealership in the central New Jersey town of Flemington is a man named Bob Golomb. Golomb is in his fifties, with short, thinning black hair and wire-rimmed glasses. He wears dark, conservative suits, so that he looks like a bank manager or a stockbroker. Since starting in the car business more than a decade ago, Golomb has sold, on average, about twenty cars a month, which is more than double what the average car salesman sells. On his desk Golomb has a row of five gold stars, given to him by his dealership in honor of his performance. In the world of car salesmen, Golomb is a virtuoso.

Being a successful salesman like Golomb is a task that places extraordinary demands on the ability to thin-slice. Someone you've never met walks into your dealership, perhaps about to make what may be one of the most expensive purchases of his or her life. Some people are insecure. Some are nervous. Some know exactly what they want. Some have no idea. Some know a great deal about cars and will be offended by a salesman who adopts a patronizing tone. Some are desperate for someone to take them by the hand and make sense of what seems to them like an overwhelming process. A salesman, if he or she is to be successful, has to gather all of that information—figuring out, say, the dynamic that exists between a husband and a wife, or a father and a daughter — process it, and adjust his or her own behavior accordingly, and do all of that within the first few moments of the encounter.

Bob Golomb is clearly the kind of person who seems to do that kind of thin-slicing effortlessly. He's the Evelyn Harrison of car selling. He has a quiet, watchful intelligence and a courtly charm. He is thoughtful and attentive. He's a wonderful listener. He has, he says, three simple rules that guide his every action: "Take care of the customer. Take care of the customer. Take care of the customer." If you buy a car from Bob Golomb, he will be on the phone to you the next day, making sure everything is all right. If you come to the dealership but don't end up buying anything, he'll call you the next day, thanking you for stopping by. "You always put on your best face, even if you are having a bad day. You leave that behind," he says. "Even if things are horrendous at home, you give the customer your best."

When I met Golomb, he took out a thick three-ring binder filled with the mountain of letters he had received over the years from satisfied customers. "Each one of these has a story to tell," he said. He seemed to remember every one. As he flipped through the book, he pointed randomly at a short typewritten letter. "Saturday afternoon, late November 1992. A couple. They came in with this glazed look on their faces. I said, 'Folks, have you been shopping for cars all day?' They said yes. No one had taken them seriously. I ended up selling them a car, and we had to get it from, I want to say, Rhode Island. We sent a driver four hundred miles. They were so happy." He pointed at another letter. "This gentleman here. We've delivered six cars to him already since 1993, and every time we deliver another car, he writes another letter. There's a lot like that. Here's a guy who lives way down by Keyport, New Jersey, forty miles away. He brought me up a platter of scallops."

There is another even more important reason for Golomb's success, however. He follows, he says, another very simple rule. He may make a million snap judgments about a customer's needs and state of mind, but he tries never to judge anyone on the basis of his or her appearance. He assumes that everyone who walks in the door has the exact same chance of buying a car.

"You cannot prejudge people in this business," he said over and over when we met, and each time he used that phrase, his face took on a look of utter conviction. "Prejudging is the kiss of death. You have to give everyone your best shot. A green salesperson looks at a customer and says, 'This person looks like he can't afford a car,' which is the worst thing you can do, because sometimes the most unlikely person is flush," Golomb says. "I have a farmer I deal with, who I've sold all kinds of cars over the years. We seal our deal with a handshake, and he hands me a hundred-dollar bill and says, 'Bring it out to my farm.' We don't even have to write the order up. Now, if you saw this man, with his coveralls and his cow dung, you'd figure he was not a worthy customer. But in fact, as we say in the trade, he's all cashed up. Or sometimes people see a teenager and they blow him off. Well, then later that night, the teenager comes back with Mom and Dad, and they pick up a car, and it's the other salesperson that writes them up."

What Golomb is saying is that most salespeople are prone to a classic Warren Harding error. They see someone, and somehow they let the first impression they have about that person's appearance drown out every other piece of information they manage to gather in that first instant. Golomb, by contrast, tries to be more selective. He has his antennae out to pick up on whether someone is confident or insecure, knowledgeable or naïve, trusting or suspicious — but from that thin-slicing flurry he tries to edit out those impressions based solely on physical appearance. The secret of Golomb's success is that he has decided to fight the Warren Harding error.

4. Spotting the Sucker

Why does Bob Golomb's strategy work so well? Because Warren Harding errors, it turns out, play an enormous, largely unacknowledged role in the car-selling business. Consider, for example, a remarkable social experiment conducted in the 1990s by a law professor in Chicago named Ian Ayres. Ayres put together a team of thirty-eight people — eighteen white men, seven white women, eight black women, and five black men. Ayres took great pains to make them appear as similar as possible. All were in their mid-twenties. All were of average attractiveness. All were instructed to dress in conservative casual wear: the women in blouses, straight skirts, and flat shoes; the men in polo shirts or button-downs, slacks, and loafers. All were given the same cover story. They were instructed to go to a total of 242 car dealerships in the Chicago area and present themselves as college-educated young professionals (sample job: systems analyst at a bank) living in the tony Chicago neighborhood of Streeterville. Their instructions for what to do were even more specific. They should walk in. They should wait to be approached by a salesperson. "I'm interested in buying this car," they were supposed to say, pointing to the lowest-priced car in the showroom. Then, after they heard the salesman's initial offer, they were instructed to bargain back and forth until the salesman either accepted an offer or refused to bargain any further — a process that in almost all cases took about forty minutes. What Ayres was trying to do was zero in on a very specific question: All other things being absolutely equal, how does skin color or gender affect the price that a salesman in a car dealership offers?

The results were stunning. The white men received initial offers from the salesmen that were $725 above the dealer's invoice (that is, what the dealer paid for the car from the manufacturer). White women got initial offers of $935 above invoice. Black women were quoted a price, on average, of $1,195 above invoice. And black men? Their initial offer was $1,687 above invoice. Even after forty minutes of bargaining, the black men could get the price, on average, down to only $1,551 above invoice. After lengthy negotiations, Ayres's black men still ended up with a price that was nearly $800 higher than Ayres's white men were offered without having to say a word.

What should we make of this? Are the car salesmen of Chicago incredible sexists and bigots? That's certainly the most extreme explanation for what happened. In the car-selling business, if you can convince someone to pay the sticker price (the price on the window of the car in the showroom), and if you can talk them into the full pre-mium package, with the leather seats and the sound system and the aluminum wheels, you can make as much in com-mission off that one gullible customer as you might from half a dozen or so customers who are prepared to drive a hard bargain. If you are a salesman, in other words, there is a tremendous temptation to try to spot the sucker. Car salesmen even have a particular word to describe the cus-tomers who pay the sticker price. They're called a lay-down.

One interpretation of Ayres's study is that these car sales-men simply made a blanket decision that women and blacks are lay-downs. They saw someone who wasn't a white male and thought to themselves, "Aha! This person is so stupid and naïve that I can make a lot of money off them."

This explanation, however, doesn't make much sense. Ayres's black and female car buyers, after all, gave one re-ally obvious sign after another that they weren't stupid and naïve. They were college-educated professionals. They had high-profile jobs. They lived in a wealthy neighbor-hood. They were dressed for success. They were savvy enough to bargain for forty minutes. Does anything about these facts suggest a sucker? If Ayres's study is evidence of conscious discrimination, then the car salesmen of Chicago are either the most outrageous of bigots (which seems unlikely) or so dense that they were oblivious to every one of those clues (equally unlikely). I think, in-stead, that there is something more subtle going on here. What if, for whatever reason — experience, car-selling lore, what they've heard from other salesmen — they have a strong automatic association between lay-downs and women and minorities? What if they link those two con-cepts in their mind unconsciously, the same way that mil-lions of Americans link the words "Evil" and "Criminal" with "African American" on the Race IAT, so that when women and black people walk through the door, they in-stinctively think "sucker"?

These salesmen may well have a strong conscious commitment to racial and gender equality, and they would probably insist, up and down, that they were quoting prices based on the most sophisticated reading of their customers' character. But the decisions they made on the spur of the moment as each customer walked through the door was of another sort. This was an unconscious reaction. They were silently picking up on the most immediate and obvious fact about Ayres's car buyers — their sex and their color — and sticking with that judgment even in the face of all manner of new and contradictory evidence. They were behaving just like the voters did in the 1920 presidential election when they took one look at Warren Harding, jumped to a conclusion, and stopped thinking. In the case of the voters, their error gave them one of the worst U.S. Presidents ever. In the case of the car salesmen, their decision to quote an outrageously high price to women and blacks alienated people who might otherwise have bought a car.

Golomb tries to treat every customer exactly the same because he's aware of just how dangerous snap judgments are when it comes to race and sex and appearance. Sometimes the unprepossessing farmer with his filthy coveralls is actually an enormously rich man with a four-thousand-acre spread, and sometimes the teenager is coming back later with Mom and Dad. Sometimes the young black man has an MBA from Harvard. Sometimes the petite blonde makes the car decisions for her whole family. Sometimes the man with the silver hair and broad shoulders and lantern jaw is a lightweight. So Golomb doesn't try to spot the lay-down. He quotes everyone the same price, sacrificing high profit margins on an individual car for the benefits of volume, and word of his fairness has spread to the point where he gets up to a third of his business from the referrals of satisfied customers. "Can I simply look at someone and say, 'This person is going to buy a car'?" asks Golomb. "You'd have to be pretty darn good to do that, and there's no way I could. Sometimes I get completely taken aback. Sometimes I'll have a guy come in waving a checkbook, saying, 'I'm here to buy a car today. If the numbers are right, I'll buy a car today.' And you know what? Nine times out of ten, he never buys."

5. Think About Dr. King

What should we do about Warren Harding errors? The kinds of biases we're talking about here aren't so obvious that it's easy to identify a solution. If there's a law on the books that says that black people can't drink at the same water fountains as white people, the obvious solution is to change the law. But unconscious discrimination is a little bit trickier. The voters in 1920 didn't think they were being suckered by Warren Harding's good looks any more than Ayres's Chicago car dealers realized how egregiously they were cheating women and minorities or boards of directors realize how absurdly biased they are in favor of the tall. If something is happening outside of awareness, how on earth do you fix it?

The answer is that we are not helpless in the face of our first impressions. They may bubble up from the unconscious — from behind a locked door inside of our brain — but just because something is outside of awareness doesn't mean it's outside of control. It is true, for instance, that you can take the Race IAT or the Career IAT as many times as you want and try as hard as you can to respond faster to the more problematic categories, and it won't make a whit of difference. But, believe it or not, if, before you take the IAT, I were to ask you to look over a series of pictures or articles about people like Martin Luther King or Nelson Mandela or Colin Powell, your reaction time would change. Suddenly it won't seem so hard to associate positive things with black people. "I had a student who used to take the IAT every day," Banaji says. "It was the first thing he did, and his idea was just to let the data gather as he went. Then this one day, he got a positive association with blacks. And he said, 'That's odd. I've never gotten that before,' because we've all tried to change our IAT score and we couldn't. But he's a track-and-field guy, and what he realized is that he'd spent the morning watching the Olympics."

Our first impressions are generated by our experiences and our environment, which means that we can change our first impressions — we can alter the way we thin-slice — by changing the experiences that comprise those impressions. If you are a white person who would like to treat black people as equals in every way — who would like to have a set of associations with blacks that are as positive as those that you have with whites — it requires more than a simple commitment to equality. It requires that you change your life so that you are exposed to minorities on a regular basis and become comfortable with them and familiar with the best of their culture, so that when you want to meet, hire, date, or talk with a member of a minority, you aren't betrayed by your hesitation and discomfort. Taking rapid cognition seriously — acknowledging the incredible power, for good and ill, that first impressions play in our lives — requires that we take active steps to manage and control those impressions. In the next section of this book, I'm going to tell three stories about people who confronted the consequences of first impressions and snap judgments. Some were successful. Some were not. But all, I think, provide us with critical lessons of how we can better understand and come to terms with the extraordinary power of thin-slicing.

FOUR

Paul Van Riper's Big Victory: Creating Structure for Spontaneity

Paul Van Riper is tall and lean with a gleaming bald dome and wire-rimmed glasses. He walks with his shoulders square and has a gruff, commanding voice. His friends call him Rip. Once when he and his twin brother were twelve, they were sitting in a car with their father as he read a newspaper story about the Korean War. "Well, boys," he said, "the war's about to be over. Truman's sending in the marines." That's when Van Riper decided that when he grew up, he would join the Marine Corps. In his first tour in Vietnam, he was almost cut in half by gunfire while taking out a North Vietnamese machine gun in a rice paddy outside Saigon. In 1968, he returned to Vietnam, and this time he was the commander of Mike Company (Third Battalion, Seventh Marines, First Marine Division) in the rice-paddy-and-hill country of South Vietnam between two treacherous regions the marines called Dodge City and the Arizona Territory. There his task was to stop the North Vietnamese from firing rockets into Danang. Before he got there, the rocket attacks in his patrol area were happening once or even twice a week. In the three months he was in the bush, there was only one.

"I remember when I first met him like it was yesterday," says Richard Gregory, who was Van Riper's gunnery sergeant in Mike Company. "It was between Hill Fifty-five and Hill Ten, just southeast of Danang. We shook hands. He had that crisp voice, low to middle tones. Very direct. Concise. Confident, without a lot of icing on the cake. That's how he was, and he maintained that every day of the war. He had an office in our combat area — a hooch — but I never saw him in there. He was always out in the field or out near his bunker, figuring out what to do next. If he had an idea and he had a scrap of paper in his pocket, he would write that idea on the scrap, and then, when we had a meeting, he would pull out seven or eight little pieces of paper. Once he and I were in the jungle a few yards away from a river, and he wanted to reconnoiter over certain areas, but he couldn't get the view he wanted. The bush was in the way. Damned if he didn't take off his shoes, dive into the river, swim out to the middle, and tread water so he could see downstream."

In the first week of November of 1968, Mike Company was engaged in heavy fighting with a much larger North Vietnamese regiment. "At one point we called in a medevac to take out some wounded. The helicopter was landing, and the North Vietnamese army was shooting rockets and killing everybody in the command post," remembers John Mason, who was one of the company's platoon commanders. "We suddenly had twelve dead marines. It was bad. We got out of there three or four days later, and we took a number of casualties, maybe forty-five total. But we reached our objective. We got back to Hill Fifty-five, and the very next day, we were working on squad tactics and inspection and, believe it or not, physical training. It had never dawned on me as a young lieutenant that we would do PT in the bush. But we did. It did not dawn on me that we would practice platoon and squad tactics or bayonet training in the bush, but we did. And we did it on a routine basis. After a battle, there would be a brief respite, then we would be back to training. That's how Rip ran his company."

Van Riper was strict. He was fair. He was a student of war, with clear ideas about how his men ought to conduct themselves in combat. "He was a gunslinger," another of his soldiers from Mike Company remembers, "somebody who doesn't sit behind a desk but leads the troops from the front. He was always very aggressive but in such a way that you didn't mind doing what he was asking you to do. I remember one time I was out with a squad on a night ambush. I got a call from the skipper [what marines call the company commander] on the radio. He told me that there were one hundred twenty-one little people, meaning Vietnamese, heading toward my position, and my job was to resist them. I said, 'Skipper, I have nine men.' He said he would bring out a reactionary force *if I needed one*. That's the way he was. The enemy was out there and there may have been nine of us and one hundred twenty-one of them, but there was no doubt in his mind that we had to engage them. Wherever the skipper operated, the enemy was put off by his tactics. He was not 'live and let live.'"

In the spring of 2000, Van Riper was approached by a group of senior Pentagon officials. He was retired at that point, after a long and distinguished career. The Pentagon was in the earliest stages of planning for a war game that they were calling Millennium Challenge '02. It was the largest and most expensive war game thus far in history. By the time the exercise was finally staged — in July and early August of 2002, two and a half years later — it would end up costing a quarter of a billion dollars, which is more than some countries spend on their entire defense budget. According to the Millennium Challenge scenario, a rogue military commander had broken away from his government somewhere in the Persian Gulf and was threatening to engulf the entire region in war. He had a considerable power base from strong religious and ethnic loyalties, and he was harboring and sponsoring four different terrorist organizations. He was virulently anti-American. In Millennium Challenge — in what would turn out to be an inspired (or, depending on your perspective, disastrous) piece of casting — Paul Van Riper was asked to play the rogue commander.

1. One Morning in the Gulf

The group that runs war games for the U.S. military is called the Joint Forces Command, or, as it is better known, JFCOM. JFCOM occupies two rather nondescript low-slung concrete buildings at the end of a curving driveway in Suffolk, Virginia, a few hours' drive south and east of Washington, D.C. Just before the entrance to the parking lot, hidden from the street, is a small guard hut. A chain-link fence rings the perimeter. There is a Wal-Mart across the street. Inside, JFCOM looks like a very ordinary office building, with conference rooms and rows of cubicles and long, brightly lit carpetless corridors. The business of JFCOM, however, is anything but ordinary. JFCOM is where the Pentagon tests new ideas about military organization and experiments with new military strategies.

Planning for the war game began in earnest in the summer of 2000. JFCOM brought together hundreds of military analysts and specialists and software experts. In war game parlance, the United States and its allies are always known as Blue Team, and the enemy is always known as Red Team, and JFCOM generated comprehensive portfolios for each team, covering everything they would be expected to know about their own forces and their adversary's forces. For several weeks leading up to the game, the Red and Blue forces took part in a series of "spiral" exercises that set the stage for the showdown. The rogue commander was getting more and more belligerent, the United States more and more concerned.

In late July, both sides came to Suffolk and set up shop in the huge, windowless rooms known as test bays on the first floor of the main JFCOM building. Marine Corps, air force, army, and navy units at various military bases around the country stood by to enact the commands of Red and Blue Team brass. Sometimes when Blue Team fired a missile or launched a plane, a missile actually fired or a plane actually took off, and whenever it didn't, one of forty-two separate computer models simulated each of those actions so precisely that the people in the war room often couldn't tell it wasn't real. The game lasted for two and a half weeks. For future analysis, a team of JFCOM specialists monitored and recorded every conversation, and a computer kept track of every bullet fired and missile launched and tank deployed. This was more than an experiment. As became clear less than a year later — when the United States invaded a Middle Eastern state with a rogue commander who had a strong ethnic power base and was thought to be harboring terrorists — this was a full dress rehearsal for war.

The stated purpose of Millennium Challenge was for the Pentagon to test a set of new and quite radical ideas about how to go to battle. In Operation Desert Storm in 1991, the United States had routed the forces of Saddam Hussein in Kuwait. But that was an utterly conventional kind of war: two heavily armed and organized forces meeting and fighting in an open battlefield. In the wake of Desert Storm, the Pentagon became convinced that that kind of warfare would soon be an anachronism: no one would be foolish enough to challenge the United States head-to-head in pure military combat. Conflict in the future would be diffuse. It would take place in cities as often as on battlefields, be fueled by ideas as much as by weapons, and engage cultures and economies as much as armies. As one JFCOM analyst puts it: "The next war is not just going to be military on military. The deciding factor is not going to be how many tanks you kill, how many ships you sink, and how many planes you shoot down. The decisive factor is how you take apart your adversary's system.

Instead of going after war-fighting capability, we have to go after war-making capability. The military is connected to the economic system, which is connected to their cultural system, to their personal relationships. We have to understand the links between all those systems."

With Millennium Challenge, then, Blue Team was given greater intellectual resources than perhaps any army in history. JFCOM devised something called the Operational Net Assessment, which was a formal decision-making tool that broke the enemy down into a series of systems — military, economic, social, political — and created a matrix showing how all those systems were interrelated and which of the links among the systems were the most vulnerable. Blue Team's commanders were also given a tool called Effects-Based Operations, which directed them to think beyond the conventional military method of targeting and destroying an adversary's military assets. They were given a comprehensive, real-time map of the combat situation called the Common Relevant Operational Picture (CROP). They were given a tool for joint interactive planning. They were given an unprecedented amount of information and intelligence from every corner of the U.S. government and a methodology that was logical and systematic and rational and rigorous. They had every toy in the Pentagon's arsenal.

"We looked at the full array of what we could do to affect our adversary's environment — political, military, economic, societal, cultural, institutional. All those things we looked at very comprehensively," the commander of JFCOM, General William F. Kernan, told reporters in a

Pentagon press briefing after the war game was over.
"There are things that the agencies have right now that can
interrupt people's capabilities. There are things that you
can do to disrupt their ability to communicate, to provide
power to their people, to influence their national will ...
to take out power grids." Two centuries ago, Napoleon
wrote that "a general never knows anything with certainty, never sees his enemy clearly, and never knows posi-
tively where he is." War was shrouded in fog. The point
of Millennium Challenge was to show that, with the full
benefit of high-powered satellites and sensors and super-
computers, that fog could be lifted.

This is why, in many ways, the choice of Paul Van
Riper to head the opposing Red Team was so inspired, because if Van Riper stood for anything, it was the antithesis
of that position. Van Riper didn't believe you could lift the
fog of war. His library on the second floor of his house in
Virginia is lined with rows upon rows of works on com-
plexity theory and military strategy. From his own experiences in Vietnam and his reading of the German military
theorist Carl von Clausewitz, Van Riper became convinced
that war was inherently unpredictable and messy and non-
linear. In the 1980s, Van Riper would often take part in
training exercises, and, according to military doctrine, he
would be required to perform versions of the kind of ana-
lytical, systematic decision making that JFCOM was testing in Millennium Challenge. He hated it. It took far too
long. "I remember once," he says, "we were in the middle
of the exercise. The division commander said, 'Stop. Let's
see where the enemy is.' We'd been at it for eight or nine

hours, and they were already behind us. The thing we were planning for had changed." It wasn't that Van Riper hated all rational analysis. It's that he thought it was inappropriate in the midst of battle, where the uncertainties of war and the pressures of time made it impossible to compare options carefully and calmly.

In the early 1990s, when Van Riper was head of the Marine Corps University at Quantico, Virginia, he became friendly with a man named Gary Klein. Klein ran a consulting firm in Ohio and wrote a book called *Sources of Power,* which is one of the classic works on decision making. Klein studied nurses, intensive care units, firefighters, and other people who make decisions under pressure, and one of his conclusions is that when experts make decisions, they don't logically and systematically compare all available options. That is the way people are taught to make decisions, but in real life it is much too slow. Klein's nurses and firefighters would size up a situation almost immediately and *act,* drawing on experience and intuition and a kind of rough mental simulation. To Van Riper, that seemed to describe much more accurately how people make decisions on the battlefield.

Once, out of curiosity, Van Riper and Klein and a group of about a dozen Marine Corp generals flew to the Mercantile Exchange in New York to visit the trading floor. Van Riper thought to himself, I've never seen this sort of pandemonium except in a military command post in war — we can learn something from this. After the bell rang at the end of the day, the generals went onto the floor and played trading games. Then they took a group of traders from Wall Street across New York Harbor to the military base on Governor's Island and played war games on computers. The traders did brilliantly. The war games required them to make decisive, rapid-fire decisions under conditions of high pressure and with limited information, which is, of course, what they did all day at work. Van Riper then took the traders down to Quantico, put them in tanks, and took them on a live fire exercise. To Van Riper, it seemed clearer and clearer that these "overweight, unkempt, long-haired" guys and the Marine Corps brass were fundamentally engaged in the same business — the only difference being that one group bet on money and the other bet on lives. "I remember the first time the traders met the generals," Gary Klein says. "It was at the cocktail party, and I saw something that really startled me. You had all these marines, these two- and three-star generals, and you know what a Marine Corps general is like. Some of them had never been to New York. Then there were all these traders, these brash, young New Yorkers in their twenties and thirties, and I looked at the room and there were groups of two and three, and there was not a single group that did not include members of both sides. They weren't just being polite. They were animatedly talking to each other. They were comparing notes and connecting. I said to myself, These guys are soul mates. They were treating each other with total respect."

Millennium Challenge, in other words, was not just a battle between two armies. It was a battle between two perfectly opposed military philosophies. Blue Team had their databases and matrixes and methodologies for systematically understanding the intentions and capabilities of the enemy. Red Team was commanded by a man who looked at a long-haired, unkempt, seat-of-the pants commodities trader yelling and pushing and making a thousand instant decisions an hour and saw in him a soul mate.

On the opening day of the war game, Blue Team poured tens of thousands of troops into the Persian Gulf. They parked an aircraft carrier battle group just offshore of Red Team's home country. There, with the full weight of its military power in evidence, Blue Team issued an eight-point ultimatum to Van Riper, the eighth point being the demand to surrender. They acted with utter confidence, because their Operational Net Assessment matrixes told them where Red Team's vulnerabilities were, what Red Team's next move was likely to be, and what Red Team's range of options was. But Paul Van Riper did not behave as the computers predicted.

Blue Team knocked out his microwave towers and cut his fiber-optics lines on the assumption that Red Team would now have to use satellite communications and cell phones and they could monitor his communications.

"They said that Red Team would be surprised by that," Van Riper remembers. "Surprised? Any moderately informed person would know enough not to count on those technologies. That's a Blue Team mind-set. Who would use cell phones and satellites after what happened to Osama bin Laden in Afghanistan? We communicated with couriers on motorcycles, and messages hidden inside prayers. They said, 'How did you get your airplanes off the airfield without the normal chatter between pilots and the tower?' I said, 'Does anyone remember World War Two? We'll use lighting systems.'"

Suddenly the enemy that Blue Team thought could be read like an open book was a bit more mysterious. What was Red Team doing? Van Riper was supposed to be cowed and overwhelmed in the face of a larger foe. But he was too much of a gunslinger for that. On the second day of the war, he put a fleet of small boats in the Persian Gulf to track the ships of the invading Blue Team navy. Then, without warning, he bombarded them in an hour-long assault with a fusillade of cruise missiles. When Red Team's surprise attack was over, sixteen American ships lay at the bottom of the Persian Gulf. Had Millennium Challenge been a real war instead of just an exercise, twenty thousand American servicemen and women would have been killed before their own army had even fired a shot.

"As the Red force commander, I'm sitting there and I realize that Blue Team had said that they were going to adopt a strategy of preemption," Van Riper says. "So I struck first. We'd done all the calculations on how many cruise missiles their ships could handle, so we simply launched more than that, from many different directions, from offshore and onshore, from air, from sea. We probably got half of their ships. We picked the ones we wanted. The aircraft carrier. The biggest cruisers. There were six amphibious ships. We knocked out five of them."

In the weeks and months that followed, there were numerous explanations from the analysts at JFCOM about exactly what happened that day in July. Some would say that it was an artifact of the particular way war games are run.

Others would say that in real life, the ships would never have been as vulnerable as they were in the game. But none of the explanations change the fact that Blue Team suffered a catastrophic failure. The rogue commander did what rogue commanders do. He fought back, yet somehow this fact caught Blue Team by surprise. In a way, it was a lot like the kind of failure suffered by the Getty when it came to evaluating the kouros: they had conducted a thoroughly rational and rigorous analysis that covered every conceivable contingency, yet that analysis somehow missed a truth that should have been picked up instinctively. In that moment in the Gulf, Red Team's powers of rapid cognition were intact — and Blue Team's were not. How did that happen?

2. The Structure of Spontaneity

One Saturday evening not long ago, an improvisation comedy group called Mother took the stage in a small theater in the basement of a supermarket on Manhattan's West Side. It was a snowy evening just after Thanksgiving, but the room was full. There are eight people in Mother, three women and five men, all in their twenties and thirties. The stage was bare except for a half dozen white folding chairs. Mother was going to perform what is known in the improv world as a Harold. They would get up onstage, without any idea whatsoever of what character they would be playing or what plot they would be acting out, take a random suggestion from the audience, and then, without so much as a moment's consultation, make up a thirty-minute play from scratch.

One of the group members called out to the audience for a suggestion. "Robots," someone yelled back. In improv, the suggestion is rarely taken literally, and in this case, Jessica, the actress who began the action, said later that the thing that came to mind when she heard the word "robots" was emotional detachment and the way technology affects relationships. So, right then and there, she walked onstage, pretending to read a bill from the cable television company. There was one other person onstage with her, a man seated in a chair with his back to her. They began to talk. Did he know what character he was playing at that moment? Not at all; nor did she or anyone in the audience. But somehow it emerged that she was the wife, and the man was her husband, and she had found charges on the cable bill for porn movies and was distraught. He, in turn, responded by blaming their teenaged son, and after a spirited back-and-forth, two more actors rushed onstage, playing two different characters in the same narrative. One was a psychiatrist helping the family with their crisis. In another scene, an actor angrily slumped in a chair. "I'm doing time for a crime I didn't commit," the actor said. He was the couple's son. At no time as the narrative unfolded did anyone stumble or freeze or look lost. The action proceeded as smoothly as if the actors had rehearsed for days. Sometimes what was said and done didn't quite work. But often it was profoundly hilarious, and the audience howled with delight. And at every point it was riveting: here was a group of eight people up on a stage without a net, creating a play before our eyes.

Improvisation comedy is a wonderful example of the kind of thinking that *Blink* is about. It involves people making very sophisticated decisions on the spur of the moment, without the benefit of any kind of script or plot. That's what makes it so compelling and — to be frank — terrifying. If I were to ask you to perform in a play that I'd written, before a live audience with a month of rehearsal, I suspect that most of you would say no. What if you got stage fright? What if you forgot your lines? What if the audience booed? But at least a conventional play has structure. Every word and movement has been scripted. Every performer gets to rehearse. There's a director in charge, telling everyone what to do. Now suppose that I were to ask you to perform again before a live audience — only this time without a script, without any clue as to what part you were playing or what you were supposed to say, and with the added requirement that you were expected to be funny. I'm quite sure you'd rather walk on hot coals. What is terrifying about improv is the fact that it appears utterly random and chaotic. It seems as though you have to get up onstage and make everything up, right there on the spot.

But the truth is that improv isn't random and chaotic at all. If you were to sit down with the cast of Mother, for instance, and talk to them at length, you'd quickly find out that they aren't all the sort of zany, impulsive, free-spirited comedians that you might imagine them to be. Some are quite serious, even nerdy. Every week they get together for a lengthy rehearsal. After each show they gather backstage and critique each other's performance soberly. Why do they practice so much? Because improv is an art form governed by a series of rules, and they want to make sure that when they're up onstage, everyone abides by those rules. "We think of what we're doing as a lot like basketball," one of the Mother players said, and that's an apt analogy. Basketball is an intricate, high-speed game filled with split-second, spontaneous decisions. But that spontaneity is possible only when everyone first engages in hours of highly repetitive and structured practice — perfecting their shooting, dribbling, and passing and running plays over and over again — and agrees to play a carefully defined role on the court. This is the critical lesson of improv, too, and it is also a key to understanding the puzzle of Millennium Challenge: *spontaneity isn't random.* Paul Van Riper's Red Team did not come out on top in that moment in the Gulf because they were smarter or luckier at that moment than their counterparts over at Blue Team. How good people's decisions are under the fast-moving, high-stress conditions of rapid cognition is a function of training and rules and rehearsal.

One of the most important of the rules that make improv possible, for example, is the idea of agreement, the notion that a very simple way to create a story — or humor — is to have characters accept everything that happens to them. As Keith Johnstone, one of the founders of improv theater, writes: "If you'll stop reading for a moment and think of something you wouldn't want to happen to you, or to someone you love, then you'll have thought of something worth staging or filming. We don't want to walk into a restaurant and be hit in the face by a custard pie, and we don't want to suddenly glimpse Granny's wheelchair racing towards the edge of a cliff, but we'll pay money to attend enactments of such events. In life, most of us are highly skilled at suppressing action. All the improvisation teacher has to do is to reverse this skill and he creates very 'gifted' improvisers. Bad improvisers block action, often with a high degree of skill. Good improvisers develop action."

Here, for instance, is an improvised exchange between two actors in a class that Johnstone was teaching:

A: I'm having trouble with my leg.
B: I'm afraid I'll have to amputate.
A: You can't do that, Doctor.
B: Why not?
A: Because I'm rather attached to it.
B: (Losing heart) Come on, man.
A: I've got this growth on my arm too, Doctor.

The two actors involved in this scene quickly became very frustrated. They couldn't keep the scene going. Actor A had made a joke — and a rather clever one ("I'm rather attached to it") — but the scene itself wasn't funny. So Johnstone stopped them and pointed out the problem. Actor A had violated the rule of agreement. His partner had made a suggestion, and he had turned it down. He had said, "You can't do that, Doctor."

So the two started again, only this time with a renewed commitment to agreeing:

A: Augh!
B: Whatever is it, man?
A: It's my leg, Doctor.
B: This looks nasty. I shall have to amputate.
A: It's the one you amputated last time, Doctor.
B: You mean you've got a pain in your wooden leg?

A: Yes, Doctor.

B: You know what this means?

A: Not woodworm, Doctor!

B: Yes. We'll have to remove it before it spreads to the rest of you.

(A's chair collapses.)

B: My God! It's spreading to the furniture!

Here are the same two people, with the same level of skill, playing exactly the same roles, and beginning almost exactly the same way. However, in the first case, the scene comes to a premature end, and in the second case, the scene is full of possibility. By following a simple rule, A and B became *funny*. "Good improvisers seem telepathic; everything looks pre-arranged," Johnstone writes. "This is because they accept all offers made — which is something no 'normal' person would do."

Here's one more example, from a workshop conducted by Del Close, another of the fathers of improv. One actor is playing a police officer, the other a robber he's chasing.

Cop: (Panting) Hey — I'm 50 years old and a little overweight. Can we stop and rest for a minute?

Robber: (Panting) You're not gonna grab me if we rest?

Cop: Promise. Just for a few seconds — on the count of three. One, Two, Three.

Do you have to be particularly quick-witted or clever or light on your feet to play that scene? Not really. It's a perfectly straightforward conversation. The humor arises entirely out of how steadfastly the participants adhere to the rule that no suggestion can be denied. If you can create the right framework, all of a sudden, engaging in the kind of fluid, effortless, spur-of-the-moment dialogue that makes for good improv theater becomes a lot easier. This is what Paul Van Riper understood in Millennium Challenge. He didn't just put his team up onstage and hope and pray that funny dialogue popped into their heads. He created the conditions for successful spontaneity.

3. The Perils of Introspection

On Paul Van Riper's first tour in Southeast Asia, when he was out in the bush, serving as an advisor to the South Vietnamese, he would often hear gunfire in the distance. He was then a young lieutenant new to combat, and his first thought was always to get on the radio and ask the troops in the field what was happening. After several weeks of this, however, he realized that the people he was calling on the radio had no more idea than he did about what the gunfire meant. It was just gunfire. It was the beginning of something — but what that something was was not yet clear. So Van Riper stopped asking. On his second tour of Vietnam, whenever he heard gunfire, he would wait. "I would look at my watch," Van Riper says, "and the reason I looked was that I wasn't going to do a thing for five minutes. If they needed help, they were going to holler. And after five minutes, if things had settled down, I still wouldn't do anything. You've got to let people work out the situation and work out what's happening. The danger in calling is that they'll tell you anything to get you off their backs, and if you act on that and take it at face value, you could make a mistake. Plus you are diverting them. Now they are looking upward instead of downward. You're preventing them from resolving the situation."

Van Riper carried this lesson with him when he took over the helm of Red Team. "The first thing I told our staff is that we would be in command and out of control," Van Riper says, echoing the words of the management guru Kevin Kelly. "By that, I mean that the overall guidance and the intent were provided by me and the senior leadership, but the forces in the field wouldn't depend on intricate orders coming from the top. They were to use their own initiative and be innovative as they went forward. Almost every day, the commander of the Red air forces came up with different ideas of how he was going to pull this together, using these general techniques of trying to overwhelm Blue Team from different directions. But he never got specific guidance from me of how to do it. Just the intent."

Once the fighting started, Van Riper didn't want introspection. He didn't want long meetings. He didn't want explanations. "I told our staff that we would use none of the terminology that Blue Team was using. I never wanted to hear that word 'effects,' except in a normal conversation. I didn't want to hear about Operational Net Assessment. We would not get caught up in any of these mechanistic processes. We would use the wisdom, the experience, and the good judgment of the people we had."

This kind of management system clearly has its risks. It meant Van Riper didn't always have a clear idea of what his troops were up to. It meant he had to place a lot of trust in his subordinates. It was, by his own admission, a "messy" way to make decisions. But it had one overwhelming advantage: allowing people to operate without having to explain themselves constantly turns out to be like the rule of agreement in improv. It enables rapid cognition.

Let me give you a very simple example of this. Picture, in your mind, the face of the waiter or waitress who served you the last time you ate at a restaurant, or the person who sat next to you on the bus today. Any stranger whom you've seen recently will do. Now, if I were to ask you to pick that person out of a police lineup, could you do it? I suspect you could. Recognizing someone's face is a classic example of unconscious cognition. We don't have to think about it. Faces just pop into our minds. But suppose I were to ask you to take a pen and paper and write down in as much detail as you can what your person looks like. Describe her face. What color was her hair? What was she wearing? Was she wearing any jewelry? Believe it or not, you will now do a lot worse at picking that face out of a lineup. This is because the act of describing a face has the effect of impairing your otherwise effortless ability to subsequently recognize that face.

The psychologist Jonathan W. Schooler, who pioneered research on this effect, calls it verbal overshadowing. Your brain has a part (the left hemisphere) that thinks in words, and a part (the right hemisphere) that thinks in pictures, and what happened when you described the face in words was that your actual visual memory was displaced. Your thinking was bumped from the right to the left hemisphere. When you were faced with the lineup the second time around, what you were drawing on was your memory of what you *said* the waitress looked like, not your memory of what you *saw* she looked like. And that's a problem because when it comes to faces, we are an awful lot better at visual recognition than we are at verbal description. If I were to show you a picture of Marilyn Monroe or Albert Einstein, you'd recognize both faces in a fraction of a second. My guess is that right now you can "see" them both almost perfectly in your imagination. But how accurately can you describe them? If you wrote a paragraph on Marilyn Monroe's face, without telling me whom you were writing about, could I guess who it was? We all have an instinctive memory for faces. But by forcing you to verbalize that memory — to explain yourself — I separate you from those instincts.

Recognizing faces sounds like a very specific process, but Schooler has shown that the implications of verbal overshadowing carry over to the way we solve much broader problems. Consider the following puzzle:

> A man and his son are in a serious car accident. The father is killed, and the son is rushed to the emergency room. Upon arrival, the attending doctor looks at the child and gasps, "This child is my son!" Who is the doctor?

This is an insight puzzle. It's not like a math or a logic problem that can be worked out systematically with pencil and paper. The only way you can get the answer is if it comes to you suddenly in the blink of an eye. You need to make a leap beyond the automatic assumption that doctors are always men. They aren't always, of course. The doctor is the boy's mother! Here's another insight puzzle:

A giant inverted steel pyramid is perfectly balanced on its point. Any movement of the pyramid will cause it to topple over. Underneath the pyramid is a $100 bill. How do you remove the bill without disturbing the pyramid?

Think about this problem for a few moments. Then, after a minute or so, write down, in as much detail as you can, everything you can remember about how you were trying to solve the problem — your strategy, your approach, or any solutions you've thought of. When Schooler did this experiment with a whole sheet of insight puzzles, he found that people who were asked to explain themselves ended up solving *30 percent* fewer problems than those who weren't. In short, when you write down your thoughts, your chances of having the flash of insight you need in order to come up with a solution are significantly impaired — just as describing the face of your waitress made you unable to pick her out of a police lineup. (The solution to the pyramid problem, by the way, is to destroy the bill in some way — tear it or burn it.)

With a logic problem, asking people to explain themselves doesn't impair their ability to come up with the answers. In some cases, in fact, it may help. But problems that require a flash of insight operate by different rules. "It's the same kind of paralysis through analysis you find in sports contexts," Schooler says. "When you start becoming reflective about the process, it undermines your ability. You lose the flow. There are certain kinds of fluid, intuitive, nonverbal kinds of experience that are vulnerable to this process." As human beings, we are capable of extraordinary leaps of insight and instinct. We can hold a face in memory, and we can solve a puzzle in a flash. But what Schooler is saying is that all these abilities are incredibly fragile. Insight is not a lightbulb that goes off inside our heads. It is a flickering candle that can easily be snuffed out.

Gary Klein, the decision-making expert, once did an interview with a fire department commander in Cleveland as part of a project to get professionals to talk about times when they had to make tough, split-second decisions. The story the fireman told was about a seemingly routine call he had taken years before, when he was a lieutenant. The fire was in the back of a one-story house in a residential neighborhood, in the kitchen. The lieutenant and his men broke down the front door, laid down their hose, and then, as firemen say, "charged the line," dousing the flames in the kitchen with water. Something should have happened at that point: the fire should have abated. But it didn't. So the men sprayed again. Still, it didn't seem to make much difference. The firemen retreated back through the archway into the living room, and there, suddenly, the lieutenant thought to himself, There's something wrong. He turned to his men. "Let's get out, *now!*" he said, and moments after they did, the floor on which they had been standing collapsed. The fire, it turned out, had been in the basement.

"He didn't know why he had ordered everyone out," Klein remembers. "He believed it was ESP. He was serious. He thought he had ESP, and he felt that because of that ESP, he'd been protected throughout his career."

Klein is a decision researcher with a Ph.D., a deeply intelligent and thoughtful man, and he wasn't about to accept that as an answer. Instead, for the next two hours, again and again he led the firefighter back over the events of that day in an attempt to document precisely what the lieutenant did and didn't know. "The first thing was that the fire didn't behave the way it was supposed to," Klein says. Kitchen fires should respond to water. This one didn't. "Then they moved back into the living room," Klein went on. "He told me that he always keeps his earflaps up because he wants to get a sense of how hot the fire is, and he was surprised at how hot this one was. A kitchen fire shouldn't have been that hot. I asked him, 'What else?' Often a sign of expertise is noticing what doesn't happen, and the other thing that surprised him was that the fire wasn't noisy. It was quiet, and that didn't make sense given how much heat there was."

In retrospect all those anomalies make perfect sense. The fire didn't respond to being sprayed in the kitchen because it wasn't centered in the kitchen. It was quiet because it was muffled by the floor. The living room was hot because the fire was underneath the living room, and heat rises. At the time, though, the lieutenant made none of those connections consciously. All of his thinking was going on behind the locked door of his unconscious. This is a beautiful example of thin-slicing in action. The fireman's internal computer effortlessly and instantly found a pattern in the chaos. But surely the most striking fact about that day is how close it all came to disaster. Had the lieutenant stopped and discussed the situation with his men, had he said to them, let's talk this over and try to figure out what's going on, had he done, in other words, what we often think leaders are supposed to do to solve difficult problems, he might have destroyed his ability to jump to the insight that saved their lives.

In Millennium Challenge, this is exactly the mistake that Blue Team made. They had a system in place that forced their commanders to stop and talk things over and figure out what was going on. That would have been fine if the problem in front of them demanded logic. But instead, Van Riper presented them with something different. Blue Team thought they could listen to Van Riper's communications. But he started sending messages by couriers on motorcycles. They thought he couldn't launch his planes. But he borrowed a forgotten technique from World War II and used lighting systems. They thought he couldn't track their ships. But he flooded the Gulf with little PT boats. And then, on the spur of the moment, Van Riper's field commanders attacked, and all of a sudden what Blue Team thought was a routine "kitchen fire" was something they could not factor into their equations at all. They needed to solve an insight problem, but their powers of insight had been extinguished.

"What I heard is that Blue Team had all these long discussions," Van Riper says. "They were trying to decide what the political situation was like. They had charts with up arrows and down arrows. I remember thinking, Wait a minute. You were doing that while you were *fighting?* They had all these acronyms. The elements of national power were diplomatic, informational, military, and economic. That gives you DIME. They would always talk about the Blue DIME. Then there were the political, military, economic, social, infrastructure, and information instruments, PMESI. So they'd have these terrible conversations where it would be our DIME versus their PMESI. I wanted to gag. What are you talking about? You know, you get caught up in forms, in matrixes, in computer programs, and it just draws you in. They were so focused on the mechanics and the process that they never looked at the problem holistically. In the act of tearing something apart, you lose its meaning."

"The Operational Net Assessment was a tool that was supposed to allow us to see all, know all," Major General Dean Cash, one of the senior JFCOM officials involved in the war game, admitted afterward. "Well, obviously it failed."

4. A Crisis in the ER

On West Harrison Street in Chicago, two miles west of the city's downtown, there is an ornate, block-long building designed and built in the early part of the last century. For the better part of one hundred years, this was the home of Cook County Hospital. It was here that the world's first blood bank opened, where cobalt-beam therapy was pioneered, where surgeons once reattached four severed fingers, and where the trauma center was so famous — and so busy treating the gunshot wounds and injuries of the surrounding gangs — that it inspired the television series *ER*. In the late 1990s, however, Cook County Hospital started a project that may one day earn the hospital as much acclaim as any of those earlier accomplishments. Cook County changed the way its physicians diagnose patients coming to the ER complaining of chest pain, and how and why they did that offers another way of understanding Paul Van Riper's unexpected triumph in Millennium Challenge.

Cook County's big experiment began in 1996, a year after a remarkable man named Brendan Reilly came to Chicago to become chairman of the hospital's Department of Medicine. The institution that Reilly inherited was a mess. As the city's principal public hospital, Cook County was the place of last resort for the hundreds of thousands of Chicagoans without health insurance. Resources were stretched to the limit. The hospital's cavernous wards were built for another century. There were no private rooms, and patients were separated by flimsy plywood dividers. There was no cafeteria or private telephone — just a payphone for everyone at the end of the hall. In one possibly apocryphal story, doctors once trained a homeless man to do routine lab tests because there was no one else available.

"In the old days," says one physician at the hospital, "if you wanted to examine a patient in the middle of the night, there was only one light switch, so if you turned on the light, the whole ward lit up. It wasn't until the mid-seventies that they got individual bed lights. Because it wasn't air-conditioned, they had these big fans, and you can imagine the racket they made. There would be all kinds of police around because Cook County was where they brought patients from the jails, so you'd see prisoners shackled to the beds. The patients would bring in TVs and radios, and they would be blaring, and people would sit out in the hallways like they were sitting on a porch on a summer evening. There was only one bathroom for these hallways filled with patients, so people would be walking up and down, dragging their IVs. Then there were the nurses' bells that you buzzed to get a nurse. But of course there weren't enough nurses, so the bells would constantly be going, ringing and ringing. Try listening to someone's heart or lungs in that setting. It was a crazy place."

Reilly had begun his medical career at the medical center at Dartmouth College, a beautiful, prosperous state-of-the-art hospital nestled in the breezy, rolling hills of New Hampshire. West Harrison Street was another world. "The first summer I was here was the summer of ninety-five, when Chicago had a heat wave that killed hundreds of people, and of course the hospital wasn't air-conditioned," Reilly remembers. "The heat index inside the hospital was a hundred and twenty. We had patients — sick patients — trying to live in that environment. One of the first things I did was grab one of the administrators and just walk her down the hall and have her stand in the middle of one of the wards. She lasted about eight seconds."

The list of problems Reilly faced was endless. But the Emergency Department (the ED) seemed to cry out for special attention. Because so few Cook County patients had health insurance, most of them entered the hospital through the Emergency Department, and the smart patients would come first thing in the morning and pack a lunch and a dinner. There were long lines down the hall.

The rooms were jammed. A staggering 250,000 patients came through the ED every year.

"A lot of times," says Reilly, "I'd have trouble even walking through the ED. It was one gurney on top of another. There was constant pressure about how to take care of these folks. The sick ones had to be admitted to the hospital, and that's when it got interesting. It's a system with constrained resources. How do you figure out who needs what? How do you figure out how to direct resources to those who need them the most?" A lot of those people were suffering from asthma, because Chicago has one of the worst asthma problems in the United States. So Reilly worked with his staff to develop specific protocols for efficiently treating asthma patients, and another set of programs for treating the homeless.

But from the beginning, the question of how to deal with heart attacks was front and center. A significant number of those people filing into the ED — on average, about thirty a day — were worried that they were having a heart attack. And those thirty used more than their share of beds and nurses and doctors and stayed around a lot longer than other patients. Chest-pain patients were resource-intensive. The treatment protocol was long and elaborate and — worst of all — maddeningly inconclusive.

A patient comes in clutching his chest. A nurse takes his blood pressure. A doctor puts a stethoscope on his chest and listens for the distinctive crinkling sound that will tell her whether the patient has fluid in his lungs — a sure sign that his heart is having trouble keeping up its pumping responsibilities. She asks him a series of questions: How long have you been experiencing chest pain? Where does it hurt?

Are you in particular pain when you exercise? Have you had heart trouble before? What's your cholesterol level? Do you use drugs? Do you have diabetes (which has a powerful association with heart disease)? Then a technician comes in, pushing a small device the size of a desktop computer printer on a trolley. She places small plastic stickers with hooks on them at precise locations on the patient's arms and chest. An electrode is clipped to each sticker, which "reads" the electrical activity of his heart and prints out the pattern on a sheet of pink graph paper. This is the electrocardiogram. In theory, a healthy patient's heart will produce a distinctive — and consistent — pattern on the page that looks like the profile of a mountain range. And if the patient is having heart trouble, the pattern will be distorted. Lines that usually go up may now be moving down. Lines that once were curved may now be flat or elongated or spiked, and if the patient is in the throes of a heart attack, the ECG readout is supposed to form two very particular and recognizable patterns. The key words, though, are "supposed to." The ECG is far from perfect. Sometimes someone with an ECG that looks perfectly normal can be in serious trouble, and sometimes someone with an ECG that looks terrifying can be perfectly healthy. There are ways to tell with absolute certainty whether someone is having a heart attack, but those involve tests of particular enzymes that can take hours for results. And the doctor confronted in the emergency room with a patient in agony and another hundred patients in a line down the corridor doesn't have hours. So when it comes to chest pain, doctors gather as much information as they can, and then they make an estimate.

The problem with that estimate, though, is that it isn't very accurate. One of the things Reilly did early in his campaign at Cook, for instance, was to put together twenty perfectly typical case histories of people with chest pain and give the histories to a group of doctors — cardiologists, internists, emergency room docs, and medical residents — people, in other words, who had lots of experience making estimates about chest pain. The point was to see how much agreement there was about who among the twenty cases was actually having a heart attack. What Reilly found was that there really wasn't any agreement at all. The answers were all over the map. The same patient might be sent home by one doctor and checked into intensive care by another. "We asked the doctors to estimate on a scale of zero to one hundred the probability that each patient was having an acute myocardial infarction [heart attack] and the odds that each patient would have a major life-threatening complication in the next three days," Reilly says. "In each case, the answers we got pretty much ranged from zero to one hundred. It was extraordinary."

The doctors thought they were making reasoned judgments. But in reality they were making something that looked a lot more like a guess, and guessing, of course, leads to mistakes. Somewhere between 2 and 8 percent of the time in American hospitals, a patient having a genuine heart attack gets sent home — because the doctor doing the examination thinks for some reason that the patient is healthy. More commonly, though, doctors correct for their uncertainty by erring heavily on the side of caution. As long as there is a chance that someone might be having a heart attack, why take even the smallest risk by ignoring her problem?

"Say you've got a patient who presents to ER complaining of severe chest pain," Reilly says. "He's old and he smokes and he has high blood pressure. There are lots of things to make you think, Gee, it's his heart. But then, after evaluating the patient, you find out his ECG is normal. What do you do? Well, you probably say to yourself, This is an old guy with a lot of risk factors who's having chest pain. I'm not going to trust the ECG." In recent years, the problem has gotten worse because the medical community has done such a good job of educating people about heart attacks that patients come running to the hospital at the first sign of chest pain. At the same time, the threat of malpractice has made doctors less and less willing to take a chance on a patient, with the result that these days only about 10 percent of those admitted to a hospital on suspicion of having a heart attack actually have a heart attack.

This, then, was Reilly's problem. He wasn't back at Dartmouth or over in one of the plush private hospitals on Chicago's north side, where money wasn't an issue. He was at Cook County. He was running the Department of Medicine on a shoestring. Yet every year, the hospital found itself spending more and more time and money on people who were not actually having a heart attack. A single bed in Cook County's coronary care unit, for instance, cost roughly $2,000 a night — and a typical chest pain patient might stay for three days — yet the typical chest pain patient might have nothing, at that moment, wrong with him. Is this, the doctors at Cook County asked themselves, any way to run a hospital?

"The whole sequence began in 1996," Reilly says. "We just didn't have the number of beds we needed to deal with patients with chest pain. We were constantly fighting about which patient needs what." Cook County at that time had eight beds in its coronary care unit, and another twelve beds in what's called intermediate coronary care, which is a ward that's a little less intensive and cheaper to run (about $1,000 a night instead of $2,000) and staffed by nurses instead of cardiologists. But that wasn't enough beds. So they opened another section, called the observation unit, where they could put a patient for half a day or so under the most basic care. "We created a third, lower-level option and said, 'Let's watch this. Let's see if it helps.' But pretty soon what happened is that we started fighting about who gets into the observation unit," Reilly went on. "I'd be getting phone calls all through the night. It was obvious that there was no standardized, rational way of making this decision."

Reilly is a tall man with a runner's slender build. He was raised in New York City, the product of a classical Jesuit education: Regis for high school, where he had four years of Latin and Greek, and Fordham University for college, where he read everything from the ancients to Wittgenstein and Heidegger and thought about an academic career in philosophy before settling on medicine. Once, as an assistant professor at Dartmouth, Reilly grew frustrated with the lack of any sort of systematic textbook on the everyday problems that doctors encounter in the outpatient setting — things like dizziness, headaches, and abdominal pain. So he sat down and, in his free evenings and weekends, wrote an eight-hundred-page textbook on the subject, painstakingly reviewing the available evidence for the most common problems a general practitioner might encounter. "He's always exploring different topics, whether it's philosophy or Scottish poetry or the history of medicine," says his friend and colleague Arthur Evans, who worked with Reilly on the chest pain project. "He's usually reading five books at once, and when he took a sabbatical leave when he was at Dartmouth, he spent the time writing a novel."

No doubt Reilly could have stayed on the East Coast, writing one paper after another in air-conditioned comfort on this or that particular problem. But he was drawn to Cook County. The thing about a hospital that serves only the poorest and the neediest is that it attracts the kinds of nurses and doctors who want to serve the poorest and neediest — and Reilly was one of those. The other thing about Cook County was that because of its relative poverty, it was a place where it was possible to try something radical — and what better place to go for someone interested in change?

Reilly's first act was to turn to the work of a cardiologist named Lee Goldman. In the 1970s, Goldman got involved with a group of mathematicians who were very interested in developing statistical rules for telling apart things like subatomic particles. Goldman wasn't much interested in physics, but it struck him that some of the same mathematical principles the group was using might be helpful in deciding whether someone was suffering a heart attack. So he fed hundreds of cases into a computer, looking at what kinds of things actually predicted a heart attack, and came up with an algorithm — an equation — that he believed would take much of the guesswork out of treating chest pain. Doctors, he concluded, ought to combine the evidence of the ECG with three of what he called urgent risk factors: (1) Is the pain felt by the patient unstable angina? (2) Is there fluid in the patient's lungs? and (3) Is the patient's systolic blood pressure below 100?

For each combination of risk factors, Goldman drew up a decision tree that recommended a treatment option. For example, a patient with a normal ECG who was positive on all three urgent risk factors would go to the intermediate unit; a patient whose ECG showed acute ischemia (that is, the heart muscle wasn't getting enough blood) but who had either one or no risk factors would be considered low-risk and go to the short-stay unit; someone with an ECG positive for ischemia and two or three risk factors would be sent directly to the cardiac care unit — and so on.

Goldman worked on his decision tree for years, steadily refining and perfecting it. But at the end of his scientific articles, there was always a plaintive sentence about how much more hands-on, real-world research needed to be done before the decision tree could be used in clinical practice. As the years passed, however, no one volunteered to do that research — not even at Harvard Medical School, where Goldman began his work, or at the equally prestigious University of California at San Francisco, where he completed it. For all the rigor of his calculations, it seemed that no one wanted to believe what he was saying, that an equation could perform better than a trained physician.

Ironically, a big chunk of the funding for Goldman's initial research had come not from the medical community itself but from the navy. Here was a man trying to come up with a way to save lives and improve the quality of care in every hospital in the country and save billions of dollars in health care costs, and the only group that got excited was the Pentagon. Why? For the most arcane of reasons: If you are in a submarine at the bottom of the ocean, quietly snooping in enemy waters, and one of your sailors starts suffering from chest pain, you really want to know whether you need to surface (and give away your position) in order to rush him to a hospital or whether you can stay underwater and just send him to his bunk with a couple of Rolaids.

But Reilly shared none of the medical community's qualms about Goldman's findings. He was in a crisis. He took Goldman's algorithm, presented it to the doctors in the Cook County ED and the doctors in the Department of Medicine, and announced that he was holding a bake-off. For the first few months, the staff would use their own judgment in evaluating chest pain, the way they always had. Then they would use Goldman's algorithm, and the diagnosis and outcome of every patient treated under the two systems would be compared. For two years, data were collected, and in the end, the result wasn't even close. Goldman's rule won hands down in two directions: it was a whopping *70 percent* better than the old method at recognizing the patients who weren't actually having a heart attack. At the same time, it was safer. The whole point of chest pain prediction is to make sure that patients who end up having major complications are assigned right away to the coronary and intermediate units. Left to their own devices, the doctors guessed right on the most serious patients somewhere between 75 and 89 percent of the time. The algorithm guessed right more than 95 percent of the time. For Reilly, that was all the evidence he needed. He went to the ED and changed the rules. In 2001, Cook County Hospital became one of the first medical institutions in the country to devote itself full-time to the Goldman algorithm for chest pain, and if you walk into the Cook County ER, you'll see a copy of the heart attack decision tree posted on the wall.

5. When Less Is More

Why is the Cook County experiment so important? Because we take it, as a given, that the more information decision makers have, the better off they are. If the specialist we are seeing says she needs to do more tests or examine us in more detail, few of us think that's a bad idea. In Millennium Challenge, Blue Team took it for granted that because they had more information at their fingertips than Red Team did, they had a considerable advantage. This was the second pillar of Blue Team's aura of invincibility. They were more logical and systematic than Van Riper, and they knew more. But what does the Goldman algorithm say? Quite the opposite: that all that extra information isn't actually an advantage at all; that, in fact, you need to know very little to find the underlying signature of a complex phenomenon. All you need is the evidence of the

ECG, blood pressure, fluid in the lungs, and unstable angina.

That's a radical statement. Take, for instance, the hypothetical case of a man who comes into the ER complaining of intermittent left-side chest pain that occasionally comes when he walks up the stairs and that lasts from five minutes to three hours. His chest exam, heart exam, and ECG are normal, and his systolic blood pressure is 165, meaning it doesn't qualify as an urgent factor. But he's in his sixties. He's a hard-charging executive. He's under constant pressure. He smokes. He doesn't exercise. He's had high blood pressure for years. He's overweight. He had heart surgery two years ago. He's sweating. It certainly seems like he ought to be admitted to the coronary care unit right away. But the algorithm says he shouldn't be. All those extra factors certainly matter in the long term. The patient's condition and diet and lifestyle put him at serious risk of developing heart disease over the next few years. It may even be that those factors play a very subtle and complex role in increasing the odds of something happening to him in the next seventy-two hours. What Goldman's algorithm indicates, though, is that the role of those other factors is so small in determining what is happening to the man right now that an accurate diagnosis can be made without them. In fact — and this is a key point in explaining the breakdown of Blue Team that day in the Gulf — that extra information is more than useless. It's harmful. It confuses the issues. What screws up doctors when they are trying to predict heart attacks is that they take *too much* information into account.

The problem of too much information also comes up in studies of why doctors sometimes make the mistake of missing a heart attack entirely — of failing to recognize when someone is on the brink of or in the midst of a major cardiac complication. Physicians, it turns out, are more likely to make this kind of mistake with women and minorities. Why is that? Gender and race are not irrelevant considerations when it comes to heart problems; blacks have a different overall risk profile than whites, and women tend to have heart attacks much later in life than men. The problem arises when the additional information of gender and race is factored into a decision about an individual patient. It serves only to overwhelm the physician still further. Doctors would do better in these cases if they knew *less* about their patients — if, that is, they had no idea whether the people they were diagnosing were white or black, male or female.

It is no surprise that it has been so hard for Goldman to get his ideas accepted. It doesn't seem to make sense that we can do better by ignoring what seems like perfectly valid information. "This is what opens the decision rule to criticism," Reilly says. "This is precisely what docs don't trust. They say, 'This process must be more complicated than just looking at an ECG and asking these few questions. Why doesn't this include whether the patient has diabetes? How old he is? Whether he's had a heart attack before?' These are obvious questions. They look at it and say, 'This is nonsense, this is not how you make decisions.'" Arthur Evans says that there is a kind of automatic tendency among physicians to believe that a life-or-death decision has to be a difficult decision. "Doctors think it's mundane to follow guidelines," he says. "It's much more gratifying to come up with a decision on your own. Anyone can follow an algorithm. There is a tendency to say, 'Well, certainly I can do better. It can't be this simple and efficient; otherwise, why are they paying me so much money?'" The algorithm doesn't *feel* right.

Many years ago a researcher named Stuart Oskamp conducted a famous study in which he gathered together a group of psychologists and asked each of them to consider the case of a twenty-nine-year-old war veteran named Joseph Kidd. In the first stage of the experiment, he gave them just basic information about Kidd. Then he gave them one and a half single-spaced pages about his childhood. In the third stage, he gave each person two more pages of background on Kidd's high school and college years. Finally, he gave them a detailed account of Kidd's time in the army and his later activities. After each stage, the psychologists were asked to answer a twenty-five-item multiple-choice test about Kidd. Oskamp found that as he gave the psychologists more and more information about Kidd, their confidence in the accuracy of their diagnoses increased dramatically. But were they really getting more accurate? As it turns out, they weren't. With each new round of data, they would go back over the test and change their answers to eight or nine or ten of the questions, but their overall accuracy remained pretty constant at about 30 percent.

"As they received more information," Oskamp concluded, "their certainty about their own decisions became entirely out of proportion to the actual correctness of those decisions." This is the same thing that happens with doctors in the ER. They gather and consider far more information than is truly necessary because it makes them feel more confident — and with someone's life in the balance, they need to feel more confident. The irony, though, is that that very desire for confidence is precisely what ends up undermining the accuracy of their decision. They feed the extra information into the already overcrowded equation they are building in their heads, and they get even more muddled.

What Reilly and his team at Cook County were trying to do, in short, was provide some structure for the spontaneity of the ER. The algorithm is a rule that protects the doctors from being swamped with too much information — the same way that the rule of agreement protects improv actors when they get up onstage. The algorithm frees doctors to attend to all of the other decisions that need to be made in the heat of the moment: If the patient isn't having a heart attack, what *is* wrong with him? Do I need to spend more time with this patient or turn my attention to someone with a more serious problem? How should I talk to and relate to him? What does this person need from me to get better?

"One of the things Brendan tries to convey to the house staff is to be meticulous in talking to patients and listening to them and giving a very careful and thorough physical examination — skills that have been neglected by many training programs," Evans says. "He feels strongly that those activities have intrinsic value in terms of connecting you to another person. He thinks it's impossible to care for someone unless you know about their circumstances — their home, their neighborhood, their life. He thinks that there are a lot of social and psychological aspects to medicine that physicians don't pay enough attention to." Reilly believes that a doctor has to understand the patient as a *person*, and if you believe in the importance of empathy and respect in the doctor-patient relationship, you have to create a place for that. To do so, you have to relieve the pressure of decision making in other areas.

There are, I think, two important lessons here. The first is that truly successful decision making relies on a balance between deliberate and instinctive thinking. Bob Golomb is a great car salesman because he is very good, in the moment, at intuiting the intentions and needs and emotions of his customers. But he is also a great salesman because he understands when to put the brakes on that process: when to consciously resist a particular kind of snap judgment. Cook County's doctors, similarly, function as well as they do in the day-to-day rush of the ER because Lee Goldman sat down at his computer and over the course of many months painstakingly evaluated every possible piece of information that he could. Deliberate thinking is a wonderful tool when we have the luxury of time, the help of a computer, and a clearly defined task, and the fruits of that type of analysis can set the stage for rapid cognition.

The second lesson is that in good decision making, frugality matters. John Gottman took a complex problem and reduced it to its simplest elements: even the most complicated of relationships and problems, he showed, have an identifiable underlying pattern. Lee Goldman's research proves that in picking up these sorts of patterns, less is more. Overloading the decision makers with information, he proves, makes picking up that signature harder, not easier. To be a successful decision maker, we have to edit.

When we thin-slice, when we recognize patterns and make snap judgments, we do this process of editing unconsciously. When Thomas Hoving first saw the kouros, the thing his eyes were drawn to was how fresh it looked. Federico Zeri focused instinctively on the fingernails. In both cases, Hoving and Zeri brushed aside a thousand other considerations about the way the sculpture looked and zeroed in on a specific feature that told them everything they needed to know. I think we get in trouble when this process of editing is disrupted — when we can't edit, or we don't know what to edit, or our environment doesn't let us edit.

Remember Sheena Iyengar, who did the research on speed-dating? She once conducted another experiment in which she set up a tasting booth with a variety of exotic gourmet jams at the upscale grocery store Draeger's in Menlo Park, California. Sometimes the booth had six different jams, and sometimes Iyengar had twenty-four different jams on display. She wanted to see whether the number of jam choices made any difference in the number of jams sold. Conventional economic wisdom, of course, says that the more choices consumers have, the more likely they are to buy, because it is easier for consumers to find the jam that perfectly fits their needs. But Iyengar found the opposite to be true. Thirty percent of those who stopped by the six-choice booth ended up buying some jam, while only *3 percent* of those who stopped by the bigger booth bought anything. Why is that? Because buying jam is a snap decision. You say to yourself, instinctively, I want that one. And if you are given too many choices, if you are forced to consider much more than your unconscious is comfortable with, you get paralyzed. Snap judgments can be made in a snap because they are frugal, and if we want to protect our snap judgments, we have to take steps to protect that frugality.

This is precisely what Van Riper understood with Red Team. He and his staff did their analysis. But they did it first, before the battle started. Once hostilities began, Van Riper was careful not to overload his team with irrelevant information. Meetings were brief. Communication between headquarters and the commanders in the field was limited. He wanted to create an environment where rapid cognition was possible. Blue Team, meanwhile, was gorging on information. They had a database, they boasted, with forty thousand separate entries in it. In front of them was the CROP — a huge screen showing the field of combat in real time. Experts from every conceivable corner of the U.S. government were at their service. They were seamlessly connected to the commanders of the four military services in a state-of-the-art interface. They were the beneficiaries of a rigorous ongoing series of analyses about what their opponent's next moves might be.

But once the shooting started, all of that information became a burden. "I can understand how all the concepts that Blue was using translate into planning for an engagement," Van Riper says. "But does it make a difference in the moment? I don't believe it does. When we talk about analytic versus intuitive decision making, neither is good or bad. What is bad is if you use either of them in an inappropriate circumstance. Suppose you had a rifle company pinned down by machine-gun fire. And the company commander calls his troops together and says, 'We have to go through the command staff with the decision-making process.' That's crazy. He should make a decision on the spot, execute it, and move on. If we had had Blue's processes, everything we did would have taken twice as long, maybe four times as long. The attack might have happened six or eight days later. The process draws you in. You disaggregate everything and tear it apart, but you are never able to synthesize the whole. It's like the weather. A commander does not need to know the barometric pressure or the winds or even the temperature. He needs to know the forecast. If you get too caught up in the production of information, you drown in the data."

Paul Van Riper's twin brother, James, also joined the Marine Corps, rising to the rank of colonel before his retirement, and, like most of the people who know Paul Van Riper well, he wasn't at all surprised at the way Millennium Challenge turned out. "Some of these new thinkers say if we have better intelligence, if we can see everything, we can't lose," Colonel Van Riper said. "What my brother always says is, 'Hey, say you are looking at a chess board. Is there anything you can't see? No. But are you guaranteed to win? Not at all, because you can't see what the other guy is thinking.' More and more commanders want to know everything, and they get imprisoned by that idea. They get locked in. But you can never know everything." Did it really matter that Blue Team was many times the size of Red Team? "It's like *Gulliver's Travels*," Colonel Van Riper says. "The big giant is tied down by those little rules and regulations and procedures. And the little guy? He just runs around and does what he wants."

6. Millennium Challenge, Part Two

For a day and a half after Red Team's surprise attack on Blue Team in the Persian Gulf, an uncomfortable silence fell over the JFCOM facility. Then the JFCOM staff stepped in. They turned back the clock. Blue Team's sixteen lost ships, which were lying at the bottom of the Persian Gulf, were refloated. In the first wave of his attack, Van Riper had fired twelve theater ballistic missiles at various ports in the Gulf region where Blue Team troops were landing. Now, JFCOM told him, all twelve of those missiles had been shot down, miraculously and mysteriously, with a new kind of missile defense. Van Riper had assassinated the leaders of the pro-U.S. countries in the region. Now, he was told, those assassinations had no effect.

"The day after the attack, I walked into the command room and saw the gentleman who was my number two giving my team a completely different set of instructions," Van Riper said. "It was things like — shut off the radar so Blue force are not interfered with. Move ground forces so marines can land without any interference. I asked, 'Can I shoot down one V-twenty-two?' and he said, 'No, you can't shoot down any V-twenty-two's.' I said, 'What the hell's going on in here?' He said, 'Sir, I've been given guidance by the program director to give completely different directions.' The second round was all scripted, and if they didn't get what they liked, they would just run it again."

Millennium Challenge, the sequel, was won by Blue Team in a rout. There were no surprises the second time around, no insight puzzles, no opportunities for the complexities and confusion of the real world to intrude on the Pentagon's experiment. And when the sequel was over, the analysts at JFCOM and the Pentagon were jubilant. The fog of war had been lifted. The military had been transformed, and with that, the Pentagon confidently turned its attention to the real Persian Gulf. A rogue dictator was threatening the stability of the region. He was virulently anti-American. He had a considerable power base from strong religious and ethnic loyalties and was thought to be harboring terrorist organizations. He needed to be replaced and his country restored to stability, and if they did it right — if they had CROP and PMESI and DIME — how hard could that be?

FIVE

Kenna's Dilemma:
The Right — and
Wrong — Way to Ask
People What They Want

The rock musician known as Kenna grew up in Virginia Beach, the child of Ethiopian immigrants. His father got his degree from Cambridge University and was an economics professor. As a family, they watched Peter Jennings and CNN, and if music was played, it was Kenny Rogers. "My father loves Kenny Rogers because he had a message to tell in that song 'The Gambler,'" Kenna explains. "Everything was about learning lessons and money and how the world worked. My parents wanted me to do better than they did." Occasionally, Kenna's uncle would visit and expose Kenna to different things, such as disco or dancing or Michael Jackson. And Kenna would look at him and say, "I don't understand." Kenna's main interest was skateboarding. He built a ramp in the backyard, and he would play with a boy from across the street. Then one day his neighbor showed him his bedroom, and on the walls were pictures of bands Kenna had never heard of. The boy gave Kenna a tape of U2's *The Joshua Tree*. "I destroyed that tape, I played it so much," Kenna says. "I just didn't know. It never dawned on me that music was like this. I think I was eleven or twelve, and that was that. Music opened the door."

Kenna is very tall and strikingly handsome, with a shaved head and a goatee. He looks like a rock star, but he has none of a rock star's swagger and braggadocio and staginess. There is something gentle about him. He is polite and thoughtful and unexpectedly modest, and he talks with the quiet earnestness of a graduate student. When Kenna got one of his first big breaks and opened at a rock concert for the well-respected band No Doubt, he either forgot to tell the audience his name (which is how his manager tells it) or decided against identifying himself (which is how he tells it.) "Who *are* you?" the fans were yelling by the end. Kenna is the sort of person who is constantly at odds with your expectations, and that is both one of the things that make him so interesting and one of the things that have made his career so problematic.

By his midteens Kenna had taught himself to play piano. He wanted to learn how to sing, so he listened to Stevie Wonder and Marvin Gaye. He entered a talent show. There was a piano at the audition but not at the show, so he got up onstage and sang a Brian McKnight song a cappella. He started writing music. He scraped together some money to rent a studio. He recorded a demo. His songs were different — not weird, exactly, but different. They were hard to classify. Sometimes people want to put Kenna in the rhythm-and-blues category, which irritates him because he thinks people do that just because he's black. If you look at some of the Internet servers that store songs, you can sometimes find his music in the alternative section and sometimes in the electronica section and sometimes in the unclassified section. One enterprising rock critic has tried to solve the problem simply by calling his music a cross between the British new wave music of the 1980s and hip-hop.

How to classify Kenna is a difficult question, but, at least in the beginning, it wasn't one that he thought about a great deal. Through a friend from high school, he was lucky enough to get to know some people in the music business. "In my life, everything seems to fall in place," Kenna says. His songs landed in the hands of a so-called A and R man — a talent scout for a record company — and through that contact, his demo CD landed in the hands of Craig Kallman, the co-president of Atlantic Records. That was a lucky break. Kallman is a self-described music junkie with a personal collection of two hundred thousand records and CDs. In the course of a week, he might be given between one hundred and two hundred songs by new artists, and every weekend he sits at home, listening to them one after another. The overwhelming majority of those, he realizes in an instant, aren't going to work: in five to ten seconds, he'll have popped them out of his CD player. But every weekend, there are at least a handful that catch his ear, and once in a blue moon, there is a singer or a song that makes him jump out of his seat. That's what Kenna was. "I was blown away," Kallman remembers. "I thought, I've got to meet this guy. I brought him immediately to New York. He sang for me, literally, like this" — and here Kallman gestures with his hand to indicate a space of no more than two feet — "face-to-face."

Later, Kenna happened to be in a recording studio with one of his friends, who is a producer. There was a man there named Danny Wimmer who worked with Fred Durst, the lead singer of a band called Limpbizkit, which was then one of the most popular rock groups in the country. Danny listened to Kenna's music. He was entranced. He called Durst and played him one of Kenna's songs, "Freetime," over the phone. Durst said, "Sign him!" Then Paul McGuinness, the manager of U2, the world's biggest rock band, heard Kenna's record and flew him to Ireland for a meeting. Next Kenna made a music video for next to nothing for one of his songs and took it to MTV2, the MTV channel for more serious music lovers. Record companies spend hundreds of thousands of dollars on promotion, trying to get their videos on MTV, and if they can get them broadcast one hundred or two hundred times, they consider themselves very lucky. Kenna walked his video over to MTV himself, and MTV ended up playing it 475 times over the next few months. Kenna then made a complete album. He gave it to Kallman again, and Kallman gave the album to all of his executives at Atlantic. "Everyone wanted it," Kallman remembers. "That's amazingly unusual." Soon after Kenna's success opening for No Doubt, his manager got a call from the Roxy, a nightclub in Los Angeles that is prominent in the city's rock music scene. Did Kenna want to play the following night? Yes, he said, and then posted a message on his Website, announcing his appearance. That was at four-thirty the day before the show. "By the next afternoon, we got a call from the Roxy. They were turning people away. I figured we'd have at most a hundred people," Kenna says.

"It was jam-packed, and the people up front were singing along to all the lyrics. It tripped me out."

In other words, people who truly know music (the kind of people who run record labels, go to clubs, and know the business well) love Kenna. They hear one of his songs, and, in the blink of an eye, they think, *Wow!* More precisely, they hear Kenna and their instinct is that he is the kind of artist whom other people — the mass audience of music buyers — are going to like. But this is where Kenna runs into a problem, because whenever attempts have been made to verify this instinct that other people are going to like him, other people haven't liked him.

When Kenna's album was making the rounds in New York, being considered by music industry executives, on three separate occasions it was given to an outside market-research firm. This is common practice in the industry. In order to be successful, an artist has to get played on the radio. And radio stations will play only a small number of songs that have been proven by market research to appeal — immediately and overwhelmingly — to their audience. So, before they commit millions of dollars to signing an artist, record companies will spend a few thousand dollars to test his or her music first, using the same techniques as the radio stations.

There are firms, for example, that post new songs on the Web and then collect and analyze the ratings of anyone who visits the Website and listens to the music. Other companies play songs over the phone or send sample CDs to a stable of raters. Hundreds of music listeners end up voting on particular songs, and over the years the rating systems have become extraordinarily sophisticated. Pick the Hits, for instance, a rating service outside Washington, D.C., has a base of two hundred thousand people who from time to time rate music, and they have learned that if a song aimed, say, at Top 40 radio (listeners 18 to 24) averages above 3.0 on a score of 1 to 4 (where 1 is "I dislike the song"), there's roughly an 85 percent chance that it will be a hit.

These are the kinds of services that Kenna's record was given to — and the results were dismal. Music Research, a California-based firm, sent Kenna's CD to twelve hundred people preselected by age, gender, and ethnicity. They then called them up three days later and interviewed as many as they could about what they thought of Kenna's music on a scale of 0 to 4. The response was, as the conclusion to the twenty-five-page "Kenna" report stated politely, "subdued." One of his most promising songs, "Freetime," came in at 1.3 among listeners to rock stations, and .8 among listeners to R&B stations. Pick the Hits rated every song on the album, with two scoring average ratings and eight scoring below average. The conclusion was even more blunt this time: "Kenna, as an artist, and his songs lack a core audience and have limited potential to gain significant radio airplay."

Kenna once ran into Paul McGuinness, the manager of U2, backstage at a concert. "This man right here," McGuinness said, pointing at Kenna, "he's going to change the world." That was his instinctive feeling, and the manager of a band like U2 is a man who knows music. But the people whose world Kenna was supposed to be changing, it seemed, couldn't disagree more, and when the results of all of the consumer research came in, Kenna's once promising career suddenly stalled. To get on the radio, there had to be hard evidence that the public liked him — and the evidence just wasn't there.

1. A Second Look at First Impressions

In *Behind the Oval Office,* his memoir of his years as a political pollster, Dick Morris writes about going to Arkansas in 1977 to meet with the state's thirty-one-year-old attorney general, an ambitious young man by the name of Bill Clinton:

> I explained that I got this idea from the polling my friend Dick Dresner had done for the movie industry. Before a new James Bond movie or a sequel to a film like *Jaws* came out, a film company would hire Dresner to summarize the plot and then ask people whether they wanted to see the movie. Dresner would read respondents proposed PR blurbs and slogans about the movie to find out which ones worked the best. Sometimes he even read them different endings or described different places where the same scenes were shot to see which they preferred.
>
> "And you just apply these techniques to politics?" Clinton asked.
>
> I explained how it could be done. "Why not do the same thing with political ads? Or speeches? Or arguments about the issues? And after each statement, ask them again whom they're going to vote for. Then you can see which arguments move how many voters and which voters they move."

We talked for almost four hours and ate lunch at his desk. I showed the attorney general sample polls I'd done.

He was fascinated by the process. Here was a tool he could use, a process that could reduce the mysterious ways of politics to scientific testing and evaluation.

Morris would go on to become a key advisor to Clinton when Clinton became President, and many people came to view his obsession with polling as deeply problematic — as a corruption of the obligation of elected officials to provide leadership and act upon principle. In truth, that's a little harsh. Morris was simply bringing to the world of politics the very same notions that guide the business world. Everyone wants to capture the mysterious and powerful reactions we have to the world around us. The people who make movies or detergent or cars or music all want to know what we think of their products. That's why it wasn't enough for the people in the music business who loved Kenna to act on their gut feelings. Gut feelings about what the public wants are too mysterious and too iffy. Kenna was sent to the market researchers because it seems as though the most accurate way to find out how consumers feel about something is to ask them directly.

But is that really true? If we had asked the students in John Bargh's experiment why they were standing in the hall so patiently after they had been primed to be polite, they wouldn't have been able to tell us. If we had asked the Iowa gamblers why they were favoring cards from the blue decks, they wouldn't have been able to say — at least not until they had drawn eighty cards. Sam Gosling and

John Gottman found that we can learn a lot more about what people think by observing their body language or facial expressions or looking at their bookshelves and the pictures on their walls than by asking them directly. And Vic Braden discovered that while people are very willing and very good at volunteering information explaining their actions, those explanations, particularly when it comes to the kinds of spontaneous opinions and decisions that arise out of the unconscious, aren't necessarily correct. In fact, it sometimes seems as if they are just plucked out of thin air. So, when marketers ask consumers to give them their reactions to something — to explain whether they liked a song that was just played or a movie they just saw or a politician they just heard — how much trust should be placed in their answers? Finding out what people think of a rock song sounds as if it should be easy. But the truth is that it isn't, and the people who run focus groups and opinion polls haven't always been sensitive to this fact. Getting to the bottom of the question of how good Kenna really is requires a more searching exploration of the intricacies of our snap judgments.

2. Pepsi's Challenge

In the early 1980s, the Coca-Cola Company was profoundly nervous about its future. Once, Coke had been far and away the dominant soft drink in the world. But Pepsi had been steadily chipping away at Coke's lead. In 1972, 18 percent of soft drink users said they drank Coke exclusively, compared with 4 percent who called themselves exclusive Pepsi drinkers. By the early 1980s, Coke had dropped to 12 percent and Pepsi had risen to 11 percent — and this despite the fact that Coke was much more widely available than Pepsi and spending at least $100 million more on advertising per year.

In the midst of this upheaval, Pepsi began running television commercials around the country, pitting Coke head-to-head with Pepsi in what they called the Pepsi Challenge. Dedicated Coke drinkers were asked to take a sip from two glasses, one marked Q and one marked M. Which did they prefer? Invariably, they would say M, and, lo and behold, M would be revealed as Pepsi. Coke's initial reaction to the Pepsi Challenge was to dispute its findings. But when they privately conducted blind head-to-head taste tests of their own, they found the same thing: when asked to choose between Coke and Pepsi, the majority of tasters — 57 percent — preferred Pepsi. A 57 to 43 percent edge is a lot, particularly in a world where millions of dollars hang on a tenth of a percentage point, and it is not hard to imagine how devastating this news was to Coca-Cola management. The Coca-Cola mystique had always been based on its famous secret formula, unchanged since the earliest days of the company. But here was seemingly incontrovertible evidence that time had passed Coke by.

Coca-Cola executives next did a flurry of additional market research projects. The news seemed to get worse. "Maybe the principal characteristics that made Coke distinctive, like its bite, consumers now describe as harsh," the company's head of American operations, Brian Dyson, said at the time. "And when you mention words like 'rounded' and 'smooth,' they say Pepsi. Maybe the way we assuage our thirst has changed." The head of Coke's consumer marketing research department in those years was a man named Roy Stout, and Stout became one of the leading advocates in the company for taking the results of the Pepsi Challenge seriously. "If we have twice as many vending machines, have more shelf space, spend more on advertising, and are competitively priced, why are we losing [market] share?" he asked Coke's top management. "You look at the Pepsi Challenge, and you have to begin asking about taste."

This was the genesis of what came to be known as New Coke. Coke's scientists went back and tinkered with the fabled secret formula to make it a little lighter and sweeter — more like Pepsi. Immediately Coke's market researchers noticed an improvement. In blind tastes of some of the early prototypes, Coke pulled even with Pepsi. They tinkered some more. In September of 1984, they went back out and tested what would end up as the final version of New Coke. They rounded up not just thousands but hundreds of thousands of consumers all across North America, and in head-to-head blind taste tests, New Coke beat Pepsi by 6 to 8 percentage points. Coca-Cola executives were elated. The new drink was given the green light. In the press conference announcing the launch of New Coke, the company's CEO, Roberto C. Goizueta, called the new product "the surest move the company's ever made," and there seemed little reason to doubt what he said. Consumers, in the simplest and most direct manner imaginable, had been asked for their reaction, and they had said they didn't much like the old Coke but they very much liked the new Coke. How could New Coke fail?

But it did. It was a disaster. Coke drinkers rose up in outrage against New Coke. There were protests around the country. Coke was plunged into crisis, and just a few months later, the company was forced to bring back the original formula as Classic Coke — at which point, sales of New Coke virtually disappeared. The predicted success of New Coke never materialized. But there was an even bigger surprise. The seemingly inexorable rise of Pepsi — which had also been so clearly signaled by market research — never materialized either. For the last twenty years, Coke has gone head-to-head with Pepsi with a product that taste tests say is inferior, and Coke is still the number one soft drink in the world. The story of New Coke, in other words, is a really good illustration of how complicated it is to find out what people really think.

3. The Blind Leading the Blind

The difficulty with interpreting the Pepsi Challenge findings begins with the fact that they were based on what the industry calls a sip test or a CLT (central location test). Tasters don't drink the entire can. They take a sip from a cup of each of the brands being tested and then make their choice. Now suppose I were to ask you to test a soft drink a little differently. What if you were to take a case of the drink home and tell me what you think after a few weeks? Would that change your opinion? It turns out it would.

Carol Dollard, who worked for Pepsi for many years in new-product development, says, "I've seen many times when the CLT will give you one result and the home-use test will give you the exact opposite. For example, in a CLT, consumers might taste three or four different products in a row, taking a sip or a couple sips of each. A sip is very different from sitting and drinking a whole beverage on your own. Sometimes a sip tastes good and a whole bottle doesn't. That's why home-use tests give you the best information. The user isn't in an artificial setting. They are at home, sitting in front of the TV, and the way they feel in that situation is the most reflective of how they will behave when the product hits the market."

Dollard says, for instance, that one of the biases in a sip test is toward sweetness: "If you only test in a sip test, consumers will like the sweeter product. But when they have to drink a whole bottle or can, that sweetness can get really overpowering or cloying." Pepsi is sweeter than Coke, so right away it had a big advantage in a sip test. Pepsi is also characterized by a citrusy flavor burst, unlike the more raisiny-vanilla taste of Coke. But that burst tends to dissipate over the course of an entire can, and that is another reason Coke suffered by comparison. Pepsi, in short, is a drink built to shine in a sip test. Does this mean that the Pepsi Challenge was a fraud? Not at all. It just means that we have two different reactions to colas. We have one reaction after taking a sip, and we have another reaction after drinking a whole can. In order to make sense of people's cola judgments, we need to first decide which of those two reactions most interests us.

Then there's the issue of what is called sensation transference. This is a concept coined by one of the great figures
in twentieth-century marketing, a man named Louis Cheskin, who was born in Ukraine at the turn of the century
and immigrated to the United States as a child. Cheskin was
convinced that when people give an assessment of something they might buy in a supermarket or a department
store, without realizing it, they transfer sensations or impressions that they have about the packaging of the product
to the product itself. To put it another way, Cheskin believed that most of us don't make a distinction — on an unconscious level — between the package and the product.
The product is the package and the product combined.

One of the projects Cheskin worked on was margarine. In the late 1940s, margarine was not very popular.
Consumers had no interest in either eating it or buying it.
But Cheskin was curious. Why didn't people like margarine? Was their problem with margarine intrinsic to the
food itself? Or was it a problem with the associations
people had with margarine? He decided to find out. In that
era, margarine was white. Cheskin colored it yellow so that
it would look like butter. Then he staged a series of luncheons with homemakers. Because he wanted to catch
people unawares, he didn't call the luncheons margarine-
testing luncheons. He merely invited a group of women to
an event. "My bet is that all the women wore little white
gloves," says Davis Masten, who today is one of the princi-
pals in the consulting firm Cheskin founded. "[Cheskin]
brought in speakers and served food, and there were little
pats of butter for some and little pats of margarine for
others. The margarine was yellow. In the context of it, they

didn't let people know there was a difference. Afterwards, everyone was asked to rate the speakers and the food, and it ended up that people thought the 'butter' was just fine. Market research had said there was no future for margarine. Louis said, 'Let's go at this more indirectly.'

Now the question of how to increase sales of margarine was much clearer. Cheskin told his client to call their product Imperial Margarine, so they could put an impressive-looking crown on the package. As he had learned at the luncheon, the color was critical: he told them the margarine had to be yellow. Then he told them to wrap it in foil, because in those days foil was associated with high quality. And sure enough, if they gave someone two identical pieces of bread — one buttered with white margarine and the other buttered with foil-wrapped yellow Imperial Margarine — the second piece of bread won hands-down in taste tests every time. "You never ask anyone, 'Do you want foil or not?' because the answer is always going to be 'I don't know' or 'Why would I?' says Masten. "You just ask them which tastes better, and by that indirect method you get a picture of what their true motivations are."

The Cheskin company demonstrated a particularly elegant example of sensation transference a few years ago, when they studied two competing brands of inexpensive brandy, Christian Brothers and E & J (the latter of which, to give some idea of the market segment to which the two belong, is known to its clientele as Easy Jesus). Their client, Christian Brothers, wanted to know why, after years of being the dominant brand in the category, it was losing market share to E & J. Their brandy wasn't more expensive. It wasn't harder to find in the store. And they weren't being out-advertised (since there is very little advertising at this end of the brandy segment). So, why were they losing ground?

Cheskin set up a blind taste test with two hundred brandy drinkers. The two brandies came out roughly the same. Cheskin then decided to go a few steps further. "We went out and did another test with two hundred different people," explains Darrel Rhea, another principal in the firm. "This time we told people which glass was Christian Brothers and which glass was E & J. Now you are having sensation transference from the name, and this time Christian Brothers' numbers are up." Clearly people had more positive associations with the name Christian Brothers than with E & J. That only deepened the mystery, because if Christian Brothers had a stronger brand, why where they losing market share? "So, now we do another two hundred people. This time the actual bottles of each brand are in the background. We don't ask about the packages, but they are there. And what happens? Now we get a statistical preference for E & J. So we've been able to isolate what Christian Brothers' problem is. The problem is not the product and it's not the branding. *It's the package.*" Rhea pulled out a picture of the two brandy bottles as they appeared in those days. Christian Brothers looked like a bottle of wine: it had a long, slender spout and a simple off-white label. E & J, by contrast, had a far more ornate bottle: more squat, like a decanter, with smoked glass, foil wrapping around the spout, and a dark, richly textured label. To prove their point, Rhea and his colleagues did one more test. They served two hundred people Christian

Brothers Brandy out of an E & J bottle, and E & J Brandy out of a Christian Brothers bottle. Which brandy won? Christian Brothers, hands-down, by the biggest margin of all. Now they had the right taste, the right brand, *and* the right bottle. The company redesigned their bottle to be a lot more like E & J's, and, sure enough, their problem was solved.

Cheskin's offices are just outside San Francisco, and after we talked, Masten and Rhea took me to a Nob Hill Farms supermarket down the street, one of those shiny, cavernous food emporia that populate the American suburbs. "We've done work in just about every aisle," Masten said as we walked in. In front of us was the beverage section. Rhea leaned over and picked up a can of 7-Up. "We tested Seven-Up. We had several versions, and what we found is that if you add fifteen percent more yellow to the green on the package — if you take this green and add more yellow — what people report is that the taste experience has a lot more lime or lemon flavor. And people were upset. 'You are changing my Seven-Up! Don't do a 'New Coke' on me.' It's exactly the same product, but a different set of sensations have been transferred from the bottle, which in this case isn't necessarily a good thing."

From the cold beverage section, we wandered to the canned-goods aisle. Masten picked up a can of Chef Boyardee Ravioli and pointed at the picture of the chef on the label of the can. "His name is Hector. We know a lot about people like this, like Orville Redenbacher or Betty Crocker or the woman on the Sun-Maid Raisins package. The general rule is, the closer consumers get to the food itself, the more consumers are going to be conservative. What that means for Hector is that in this case he needs to look pretty literal. You want to have the face as a recognizable human being that you can relate to. Typically, close-ups of the face work better than full-body shots. We tested Hector in a number of different ways. Can you make the ravioli taste better by changing him? Mostly you can blow it, like by making him a cartoon figure. We looked at him in the context of photography down to cartoon character kinds of things. The more you go to cartoon characters, the more of an abstraction Hector becomes, the less and less effective you are in perceptions of the taste and quality of the ravioli."

Masten picked up a can of Hormel canned meat. "We did this, too. We tested the Hormel logo." He pointed at the tiny sprig of parsley between the *r* and the *m*. "That little bit of parsley helps bring freshness to canned food."

Rhea held out a bottle of Classico tomato sauce and talked about the meanings attached to various kinds of containers. "When Del Monte took the peaches out of the tin and put them in a glass container, people said, 'Ahh, this is something like my grandmother used to make.' People say peaches taste better when they come in a glass jar. It's just like ice cream in a cylindrical container as opposed to a rectangular package. People expect it's going to taste better and they are willing to pay five, ten cents more — just on the strength of that package."

What Masten and Rhea do is tell companies how to manipulate our first impressions, and it's hard not to feel a certain uneasiness about their efforts. If you double the size of the chips in chocolate chip ice cream and say on the package, "New! Bigger Chocolate Chips!" and charge five to ten cents more, that seems honest and fair. But if you put your ice cream in a round as opposed to a rectangular container and charge five to ten cents more, that seems like you're pulling the wool over people's eyes. If you think about it, though, there really isn't any practical difference between those two things. We are willing to pay more for ice cream when it tastes better, and putting ice cream in a round container convinces us it tastes better just as surely as making the chips bigger in chocolate chip ice cream does. Sure, we're conscious of one improvement and not conscious of the other, but why should that distinction matter? Why should an ice cream company be able to profit only from improvements that we are conscious of? You might say, "Well, they're going behind our back." But who is going behind our back? The ice cream company? Or our own unconscious?

Neither Masten nor Rhea believes that clever packaging allows a company to put out a bad-tasting product. The taste of the product itself matters a great deal. Their point is simply that when we put something in our mouth and in that blink of an eye decide whether it tastes good or not, we are reacting not only to the evidence from our taste buds and salivary glands but also to the evidence of our eyes and memories and imaginations, and it is foolish of a company to service one dimension and ignore the other.

In that context, then, Coca-Cola's error with New Coke becomes all the more egregious. It wasn't just that they placed too much emphasis on sip tests. It was that the entire principle of a blind taste test was ridiculous. They shouldn't have cared so much that they were losing blind taste tests with old Coke, and we shouldn't at all be surprised that Pepsi's dominance in blind taste tests never translated to much in the real world. Why not? *Because in the real world, no one ever drinks Coca-Cola blind.* We transfer to our sensation of the Coca-Cola taste all of the unconscious associations we have of the brand, the image, the can, and even the unmistakable red of the logo. "The mistake Coca-Cola made," Rhea says, "was in attributing their loss in share to Pepsi entirely to the product. But what counts for an awful lot in colas is the brand imagery, and they lost sight of that. All their decisions were made on changing the product itself, while Pepsi was focusing on youth and making Michael Jackson their spokesman and doing a lot of good branding things. Sure, people like a sweeter product in a sip test, but people don't make their product decisions on sip tests. Coke's problem is that the guys in white lab coats took over."

Did the guys in the white lab coats take over in Kenna's case as well? The market testers assumed that they could simply play one of his songs or part of one of his songs for someone over the telephone or on the Internet and the response of listeners would serve as a reliable guide to what music buyers would feel about the song. Their thinking was that music lovers can thin-slice a new song in a matter of seconds, and there is nothing wrong with that idea in principle. But thin-slicing has to be done in context. It is possible to quickly diagnose the health of a marriage. But you can't just watch a couple playing Ping-

Pong. You have to observe them while they are discussing something of relevance to their relationship. It's possible to thin-slice a surgeon's risk of being sued for malpractice on the basis of a small snippet of conversation. But it has to be a conversation with a patient. All of the people who warmed to Kenna had that kind of context. The people at the Roxy and the No Doubt concert saw him in the flesh. Craig Kallman had Kenna sing for him, right there in his office. Fred Durst heard Kenna through the prism of one of his trusted colleagues' excitement. The viewers of MTV who requested Kenna over and over had seen his video. Judging Kenna without that additional information is like making people choose between Pepsi and Coke in a blind taste test.

4. "The Chair of Death"

The Aeron chair was the brainchild of two well-known industrial designers, Don Chadwick and Bill Stumpf. The two had been hired by furniture maker Herman Miller, with whom they had worked before, most notably on chairs called the Ergon and the Equa. Yet they weren't entirely satisfied with their earlier efforts. Both had sold well, but the two men thought that the Ergon was clumsy — an immature effort. The Equa was better, but it had since been copied by so many other firms that it no longer seemed special. "The chairs we had done previously all looked alike," Stumpf says. "The Aeron was a deliberate attempt to come up with something that looked different."

Stumpf and Chadwick's first idea was to try to make the most ergonomically correct chair imaginable. They had done that to some extent with the Equa. But with the Aeron they went even further. An enormous amount of work, for instance, went into the mechanism connecting the back of the chair to what chair designers call the seat pan. In a typical chair, there is a simple hinge connecting the two so you can lean back in the chair. But the problem with the hinge is that the chair pivots in a different way from how our hips pivot, so tilting pulls the shirt out of our pants and puts undue stress on our back. On the Aeron, the seat pan and back of the chair moved independently through a complex mechanism. And there was much more. The design team at Herman Miller wanted fully adjustable arms, and that was easier if the arms of the chair were attached to the back of the Aeron, not underneath the seat pan, as is ordinarily the case. They wanted to maximize support for the shoulders, so the back of the chair was wider at the top than at the bottom. This was exactly the opposite of most chairs, which are wide at the bottom and tapered at the top. Finally, they wanted the chair to be comfortable for people who were stuck at their desks for long periods of time. "I looked at straw hats and other things, like wicker furniture," Stumpf says. "I've always hated foam chairs covered in fabric, because they seemed hot and sticky. The skin is an organ, it breathes. This idea of getting something breathable like the straw hat was intriguing to me." What they settled on was a specially engineered thin elastic mesh stretched tight over the plastic frame. If you looked closely through the mesh, you could see the levers and mechanisms and hard plastic appendages in plain sight below the seat pan.

In Herman Miller's years of working with consumers on seating, they had found that when it came to choosing office chairs, most people automatically gravitated toward the chair with the most presumed status — something senatorial or thronelike, with thick cushions and a high, imposing back. What was the Aeron? It was the exact opposite: a slender, transparent concoction of black plastic and odd protuberances and mesh that looked like the exoskeleton of a giant prehistoric insect. "Comfort in America is very much conditioned by La-Z-Boy recliners," says Stumpf. "In Germany, they joke about Americans wanting too much padding in their car seats. We have this fixation on softness. I always think of that glove that Disney put on Mickey Mouse's hand. If we saw his real claw, no one would have liked him. What we were doing was running counter to that idea of softness."

In May of 1992, Herman Miller started doing what they call use testing. They took prototypes of the Aeron to local companies in western Michigan and had people sit in them for at least half a day. In the beginning, the response was not positive. Herman Miller asked people to rate the chair's comfort on a scale of 1 to 10 — where 10 is perfect, and at least 7.5 is where you'd really love to be before you actually go to market — and the early prototypes of the Aeron came in at around 4.75. As a gag, one of the Herman Miller staffers put a picture of the chair on the mock-up cover of a supermarket tabloid, with the headline CHAIR OF DEATH: EVERYONE WHO SITS IN IT DIES and made it the cover of one of the early Aeron research reports. People would look at the wiry frame and wonder if it would hold them, and then look at the mesh and wonder if it could ever be comfortable. "It's very hard to get some-body to sit on something that doesn't look right," says Rob Harvey, who was Herman Miller's senior vice presi-dent of research and design at the time. "If you build a chair that has a wiry frame, people's perception is that it isn't going to hold them. They get very tentative about sit-ting in it. Seating is a very intimate kind of thing. The body comes intimately into contact with a chair, so there are a lot of visual cues like perceived temperature and hardness that drive people's perceptions." But as Herman Miller tinkered with the design, coming up with new and better prototypes, and got people to overcome their qualms, the scores began to inch up. By the time Herman Miller was ready to go to market, the comfort scores were, in fact, above 8. That was the good news.

The bad news? Just about everyone thought the chair was a monstrosity. "From the beginning, the aesthetic scores lagged way behind the comfort scores," said Bill Dowell, who was research lead on the Aeron. "This was an anomaly. We've tested thousands and thousands of people sitting in chairs, and one of the strongest correla-tions we've always found is between comfort and aesthet-ics. But here it didn't happen. The comfort scores got above eight, which is phenomenal. But the aesthetic scores started out between two and three and never got above six in any of our prototypes. We were quite perplexed and not unworried. We'd had the Equa chair. That chair was con-troversial, too. But it was always seen as beautiful."

In late 1993, as they prepared to launch the chair, Herman Miller put together a series of focus groups around the country. They wanted to get some ideas about pricing and marketing and make sure there was general support for the concept. They started with panels of architects and designers, and they were generally receptive. "They understood how radical the chair was," Dowell said. "Even if they didn't see it as a thing of beauty, they understood that it had to look the way it did." Then they presented the chair to groups of facility managers and ergonomic experts — the kinds of people who would ultimately be responsible for making the chair a commercial success.

This time the reception was downright chilly. "They didn't understand the aesthetic at all," says Dowell. Herman Miller was told to cover the Aeron with a solid fabric and that it would be impossible to sell it to corporate clients. One facility manager likened the chair to lawn furniture or old-fashioned car-seat covers. Another said it looked as though it came from the set of RoboCop, and another said that it looked as if it had been made entirely from recycled materials. "I remember one professor at Stanford who confirmed the concept and its function but said he wanted to be invited back when we got to an 'aesthetically refined prototype,'" Dowell remembers. "We were behind the glass saying, 'There isn't going to be an aesthetically refined prototype!'"

Put yourself, for a moment, in Herman Miller's shoes. You have committed yourself to a brand-new product. You have spent an enormous amount of money retooling your furniture factory, and still more making sure that, say, the mesh on the Aeron doesn't pinch the behinds of people who sit in it. But now you find out that people don't like the mesh. In fact, they think the whole chair is ugly, and if there is one thing you know from years and years in the business, it is that people don't buy chairs they think are ugly. So what do you do? You could scrap the chair entirely. You could go back and cover it in a nice familiar layer of foam. Or you could trust your instincts and dive ahead.

Herman Miller took the third course. They went ahead, and what happened? In the beginning, not much. The Aeron, after all, was ugly. Before long, however, the chair started to attract the attention of some of the very cutting-edge elements of the design community. It won a design of the decade award from the Industrial Designers Society of America. In California and New York, in the advertising world and in Silicon Valley, it became a kind of cult object that matched the stripped-down aesthetic of the new economy. It began to appear in films and television commercials, and from there its profile built and grew and blossomed. By the end of the 1990s, sales were growing 50 to 70 percent annually, and the people at Herman Miller suddenly realized that what they had on their hands was the best-selling chair in the history of the company. Before long, there was no office chair as widely imitated as the Aeron. Everyone wanted to make a chair that looked like the exoskeleton of a giant prehistoric insect. And what are the aesthetic scores today? The Aeron is now an 8. What once was ugly has become beautiful.

In the case of a blind sip test, first impressions don't work because colas aren't supposed to be sipped blind. The blind sip test is the wrong context for thin-slicing

Coke. With the Aeron, the effort to collect consumers' first impressions failed for a slightly different reason: the people reporting their first impressions misinterpreted their own feelings. They said they hated it. But what they really meant was that the chair was so new and unusual that they weren't used to it. This isn't true of everything we call ugly. The Edsel, the Ford Motor Company's famous flop from the 1950s, failed because people thought it looked funny. But two or three years later, every other car maker didn't suddenly start making cars that looked like the Edsel, the way everyone started copying the Aeron. The Edsel started out ugly, and it's still ugly. By the same token, there are movies that people hate when they see them for the first time, and they still hate them two or three years later. A bad movie is always a bad movie. The problem is that buried among the things that we hate is a class of products that are in that category only because they are weird. They make us nervous. They are sufficiently different that it takes us some time to understand that we actually like them.

"When you are in the product development world, you become immersed in your own stuff, and it's hard to keep in mind the fact that the customers you go out and see spend very little time with your product," says Dowell. "They know the experience of it then and there. But they don't have any history with it, and it's hard for them to imagine a future with it, especially if it's something very different. That was the thing with the Aeron chair. Office chairs in people's minds had a certain aesthetic. They were cushioned and upholstered. The Aeron chair of course isn't. It looked different. There was nothing familiar about it. Maybe the word 'ugly' was just a proxy for 'different.'"

The problem with market research is that often it is simply too blunt an instrument to pick up this distinction between the bad and the merely different. In the late 1960s, the screenwriter Norman Lear produced a television sitcom pilot for a show called *All in the Family*. It was a radical departure from the kind of fare then on television: it was edgy and political, and it tackled social issues that the television of the day avoided. Lear took it to ABC. They had it market-tested before four hundred carefully selected viewers at a theater in Hollywood. Viewers filled out questionnaires and turned a dial marked "very dull," "dull," "fair," "good," and "very good" as they watched the show, with their responses then translated into a score between 1 and 100. For a drama, a good score was one in the high 60s. For a comedy, the mid-70s. *All in the Family* scored in the low 40s. ABC said no. Lear took the show to CBS. They ran it through their own market research protocol, called the Program Analyzer, which required audiences to push red and green buttons, recording their impressions of the shows they were watching. The results were unimpressive. The recommendation of the research department was that Archie Bunker be rewritten as a soft-spoken and nurturing father. CBS didn't even bother promoting *All in the Family* before its first season. What was the point? The only reason it made it to the air at all was that the president of the company, Robert Wood, and the head of programming, Fred Silverman, happened to like it, and the network was so dominant at that point that it felt that it could afford to take a risk on the show.

That same year, CBS was also considering a new comedy show starring Mary Tyler Moore. It, too, was a departure for television. The main character, Mary Richards, was a young, single woman who was interested not in starting a family — as practically every previous television heroine had been — but in advancing her career. CBS ran the first show through the Program Analyzer. The results were devastating. Mary was a "loser." Her neighbor Rhoda Morgenstern was "too abrasive," and another of the major female characters on the show, Phyllis Lindstrom, was seen as "not believable." The only reason *The Mary Tyler Moore Show* survived was that by the time CBS tested it, it was already scheduled for broadcast. "Had *The MTM* been a mere pilot, such overwhelmingly negative comments would have buried it," Sally Bedell [Smith] writes in her biography of Silverman, *Up the Tube*.

All in the Family and *The Mary Tyler Moore Show*, in other words, were the television equivalents of the Aeron chair. Viewers said they hated them. But, as quickly became clear when these sitcoms became two of the most successful programs in television history, viewers didn't actually hate them. They were just shocked by them. And all of the ballyhooed techniques used by the armies of market researchers at CBS utterly failed to distinguish between these two very different emotions.

Market research isn't always wrong, of course. If *All in the Family* had been more traditional — and if the Aeron had been just a minor variation on the chair that came before it — the act of measuring consumer reactions would not have been nearly as difficult. But testing products or ideas that are truly revolutionary is another matter, and the most successful companies are those that understand that in those cases, the first impressions of their consumers need interpretation. We like market research because it provides certainty — a score, a prediction; if someone asks us why we made the decision we did, we can point to a number. But the truth is that for the most important decisions, there can be no certainty. Kenna did badly when he was subjected to market research. But so what? His music was new and different, and it is the new and different that is always most vulnerable to market research.

5. The Gift of Expertise

One bright summer day, I had lunch with two women who run a company in New Jersey called Sensory Spectrum. Their names are Gail Vance Civille and Judy Heylmun, and they taste food for a living. If Frito-Lay, for example, has a new kind of tortilla chip, they need to know where their chip prototype fits into the tortilla chip pantheon: How much of a departure is it from their other Doritos varieties? How does it compare to Cape Cod Tortilla Chips? Do they need to add, say, a bit more salt? Civille and Heylmun are the people they send their chips to.

Having lunch with professional food tasters, of course, is a tricky proposition. After much thought I decided on a restaurant called Le Madri, in downtown Manhattan, which is the kind of place where it takes five minutes to recite the list of daily specials. When I arrived,

Heylmun and Civille were seated, two stylish professional women in business suits. They had already spoken to the waiter. Civille told me the specials from memory. A great deal of thought obviously went into the lunch choices. Heylmun settled on pasta preceded by roasted-pumpkin chowder with a sprinkling of celery and onion, finished with crème fraîche and bacon-braised cranberry beans garnished with diced pumpkin, fried sage, and toasted pumpkin seeds. Civille had a salad, followed by risotto with Prince Edward Island mussels and Manila clams, finished with squid ink. (At Le Madri, rare is the dish that is not "finished" in some way or adorned with some kind of "reduction.") After we ordered, the waiter brought Heylmun a spoon for her soup. Civille held up her hand for another. "We share everything," she informed him.

"You should see us when we go out with a group of Sensory people," Heylmun said. "We take our bread plates and pass them around. What you get back is half your meal and a little bit of everyone else's."

The soup came. The two of them dug in. "Oh, it's fabulous," Civille said and cast her eyes heavenward. She handed me her spoon. "Taste it." Heylmun and Civille both ate with small, quick bites, and as they ate they talked, interrupting each other like old friends, jumping from topic to topic. They were very funny and talked very quickly. But the talking never overwhelmed the eating. The opposite was true: they seemed to talk only to heighten their anticipation of the next bite, and when the next bite came, their faces took on a look of utter absorption. Heylmun and Civille don't just taste food. They think about food. They dream about food. Having lunch with them is like going cello shopping with Yo-Yo Ma, or dropping in on Giorgio Armani one morning as he is deciding what to wear. "My husband says that living with me is like a taste-a-minute tour," Civille said. "It drives everyone in my family crazy. Stop talking about it! You know that scene in the deli from the movie *When Harry Met Sally?* That's what I feel about food when it's really good."

The waiter came offering dessert: crème brûlée, mango and chocolate sorbet, or strawberry saffron and sweet-corn vanilla gelato. Heylmun had the vanilla gelato and the mango sorbet but not before she thought hard about the crème brûlée. "Crème brûlée is the test of any restaurant," she said. "It comes down to the quality of the vanilla. I don't like my crème brûlée adulterated, because then you can't taste through to the quality of the ingredients." An espresso came for Civille. As she took her first sip, an almost imperceptible wince crossed her face. "It's good, not great," she said. "It's missing the whole winey texture. It's a little too woody."

Heylmun then started talking about "rework," which is the practice in some food factories of recycling leftover or rejected ingredients from one product batch into another product batch. "Give me some cookies and crackers," she said, "and I can tell you not only what factory they came from but what rework they were using." Civille jumped in. Just the previous night, she said, she had eaten two cookies — and here she named two prominent brands. "I could *taste* the rework," she said and made another face. "We've spent years and years developing these skills," she went on. "Twenty years. It's like medical training. You do your internship, and then you become a resident. And you do it and do it until you can look at something and say in a very objective way how sweet it is, how bitter it is, how caramelized it is, how much citrus character there is — and in terms of the citrus, this much lemon, this much lime, this much grapefruit, this much orange."

Heylmun and Civille, in other words, are experts. Would they get fooled by the Pepsi Challenge? Of course not. Nor would they be led astray by the packaging for Christian Brothers, or be as easily confused by the difference between something they truly don't like and something they simply find unusual. The gift of their expertise is that it allows them to have a much better understanding of what goes on behind the locked door of their unconscious. This is the last and most important lesson of the Kenna story, because it explains why it was such a mistake to favor the results of Kenna's market research so heavily over the enthusiastic reactions of the industry insiders, the crowd at the Roxy, and the viewers of MTV2. The first impressions of experts are *different*. By that I don't mean that experts like different things than the rest of us — although that is undeniable. When we become expert in something, our tastes grow more esoteric and complex. What I mean is that it is really only experts who are able to reliably account for their reactions.

Jonathan Schooler — whom I introduced in the previous chapter — once did an experiment with Timothy Wilson that beautifully illustrates this difference. It involved strawberry jam. *Consumer Reports* put together a panel of food experts and had them rank forty-four different brands of strawberry jam from top to bottom according to very specific measures of texture and taste. Wilson and Schooler took the first-, eleventh-, twenty-fourth-, thirty-second-, and forty-fourth-ranking jams — Knott's Berry Farm, Alpha Beta, Featherweight, Acme, and Sorrell Ridge — and gave them to a group of college students. Their question was, how close would the students' rankings come to the experts? The answer is, pretty close. The students put Knott's Berry Farm second and Alpha Beta first (reversing the order of the first two jams). The experts and the students both agreed that Featherweight was number three. And, like the experts, the students thought that Acme and Sorrell Ridge were markedly inferior to the others, although the experts thought Sorrell Ridge was worse than Acme, while the students had the order the other way around. Scientists use something called a correlation to measure how closely one factor predicts another, and overall, the students' ratings correlated with the experts' ratings by .55, which is quite a high correlation. What this says, in other words, is that our jam reactions are quite good: even those of us who aren't jam experts know good jam when we taste it.

But what would happen if I were to give you a questionnaire and ask you to enumerate your reasons for preferring one jam to another? Disaster. Wilson and Schooler had another group of students provide a written explanation for their rankings, and they put Knott's Berry Farm — the best jam of all, according to the experts — second to last, and Sorrell Ridge, the experts' worst jam, third. The overall correlation was now down to .11, which for all intents and purposes means that the students' evaluations had almost nothing at all to do with the experts' evaluations. This is reminiscent of Schooler's experiments that I described in the Van Riper story, in which introspection destroyed people's ability to solve insight problems. By making people think about jam, Wilson and Schooler turned them into jam idiots.

In the earlier discussion, however, I was referring to things that impair our ability to solve problems. Now I'm talking about the loss of a much more fundamental ability, namely the ability to know our own mind. Furthermore, in this case we have a much more specific explanation for why introspections mess up our reactions. It's that we simply don't have any way of explaining our feelings about jam. We know unconsciously what good jam is: it's Knott's Berry Farm. But suddenly we're asked to stipulate, according to a list of terms, why we think that, and the terms are meaningless to us. Texture, for instance. What does that mean? We may never have thought about the texture of any jam before, and we certainly don't understand what texture means, and texture may be something that we actually, on a deep level, don't particularly care much about. But now the idea of texture has been planted in our mind, and we think about it and decide that, well, the texture does seem a little strange, and in fact maybe we don't like this jam after all. As Wilson puts it, what happens is that we come up with a plausible-sounding reason for why we might like or dislike something, and then we adjust our true preference to be in line with that plausible-sounding reason.

Jam experts, though, don't have the same problem when it comes to explaining their feelings about jam. Expert food tasters are taught a very specific vocabulary, which allows them to describe precisely their reactions to specific foods. Mayonnaise, for example, is supposed to be evaluated along six dimensions of appearance (color, color intensity, chroma, shine, lumpiness, and bubbles), ten dimensions of texture (adhesiveness to lips, firmness, denseness, and so on), and fourteen dimensions of flavor, split among three subgroups — aromatics (eggy, mustardy, and so forth); basic tastes (salty, sour, and sweet); and chemical-feeling factors (burn, pungent, astringent). Each of those factors, in turn, is evaluated on a 15-point scale. So, for example, if we wanted to describe the oral texture of something, one of the attributes we would look at is slipperiness. And on the 15-point slipperiness scale, where 0 is not slippery at all and 15 is very slippery, Gerber's Beef and Beef Gravy baby food is a 2, Whitney's vanilla yogurt is a 7.5, and Miracle Whip is a 13. If you taste something that's not quite as slippery as Miracle Whip but more slippery than Whitney's vanilla yogurt, then, you might give it a 10. Or take crispiness. Quaker's low-fat Chewy Chocolate Chunk Granola Bars are a 2, Keebler Club Partners Crackers are a 5, and Kellogg's Corn Flakes are a 14. Every product in the supermarket can be analyzed along these lines, and after a taster has worked with these scales for years, they become embedded in the taster's unconscious. "We just did Oreos," said Heylmun, "and we broke them into ninety attributes of appearance, flavor, and texture." She paused, and I could tell that she was re-creating in her mind what an Oreo feels like. "It turns out there are eleven attributes that are probably critical."

Our unconscious reactions come out of a locked room, and we can't look inside that room. But with experience we become expert at using our behavior and our training to interpret — and decode — what lies behind our snap judgments and first impressions. It's a lot like what people do when they are in psychoanalysis: they spend years analyzing their unconscious with the help of a trained therapist until they begin to get a sense of how their mind works. Heylmun and Civille have done the same thing — only they haven't psychoanalyzed their feelings; they've psychoanalyzed their feelings for mayonnaise and Oreo cookies.

All experts do this, either formally or informally. Gottman wasn't happy with his instinctive reactions to couples. So he videotaped thousands of men and women, broke down every second of the tapes, and ran the data through a computer — and now he can sit down next to a couple in a restaurant and confidently thin-slice their marriage. Vic Braden, the tennis coach, was frustrated by the fact that he knew when someone was about to double-fault but didn't know how he knew. He is now teamed up with some experts in biomechanics who are going to film and digitally analyze professional tennis players in the act of serving so that they can figure out precisely what it is in the players' delivery that Braden is unconsciously picking up on. And why was Thomas Hoving so sure, in those first two seconds, that the Getty's kouros was a fake? Because, over the course of his life, he'd experienced countless ancient sculptures and learned to understand and interpret that first impression that crossed his mind. "In my second year working at the Met [Metropolitan Museum of Art in New York], I had the good luck of having this European curator come over and go through virtually everything with me," he says. "We spent evening after evening taking things out of cases and putting them on the table. We were down in the storerooms. There were thousands of things. I mean, we were there every night until ten o'clock, and it wasn't just a routine glance. It was really poring and poring and poring over things." What he was building, in those nights in the storerooms, was a kind of database in his unconscious. He was learning how to match the feeling he had about an object with what was formally understood about its style and background and value. Whenever we have something that we are good at — something we care about — that experience and passion fundamentally change the nature of our first impressions.

This does not mean that when we are outside our areas of passion and experience, our reactions are invariably wrong. It just means that they are shallow. They are hard to explain and easily disrupted. They aren't grounded in real understanding. Do you think, for example, that you can accurately describe the difference between Coke and Pepsi? It's actually surprisingly difficult. Food tasters like Civille and Heylmun use what they call a DOD (degree-of-difference) scale to compare products in the same category. It goes from 0 to 10, where 10 is for two things that are totally different and 1 or 2 might describe just the production-range differences between two batches of the same product. Wise's and Lay's salt and vinegar potato chips, for instance, have a DOD of 8. ("Ohmigod, they are so different," says Heylmun. "Wise is dark, and Lay's is uniform and light.") Things with a DOD of 5 or 6 are much closer but still possible to tell apart. Coke and Pepsi, though, are only a 4, and in some cases the difference may be even less, particularly if the colas have aged a bit and the level of carbonation has decreased and the vanilla has become a little more pronounced and pruney.

This means that if we are asked to give our thoughts on Coke and Pepsi, most of our answers aren't going to be very useful. We can say whether we like it. We can make some vague and general comments about the level of carbonation or flavor or sweetness and sourness. But with a DOD of 4, only someone schooled in colas is going to be able to pick up on the subtle nuances that distinguish each soft drink.

I imagine that some of you, particularly those who are diehard cola drinkers, are bristling at this point. I'm being a bit insulting. You think you really do know your way around Pepsi and Coke. Okay, let's concede that you can reliably tell Coke from Pepsi, even when the DOD hovers around 4. In fact, I urge you to test yourself. Have a friend pour Pepsi into one glass and Coke into another and try to tell them apart. Let's say you succeed. Congratulations. Now let's try the test again, in a slightly different form. This time have your tester give you *three* glasses, two of which are filled with one of the Colas and the third with the other. In the beverage business, this is called a triangle test. This time around, I don't want you to identify which is Coke and which is Pepsi. All I want you to say is which of the three drinks is not like the other two. Believe it or not, you will find this task incredibly hard. If a thousand people were to try this test, just over one-third would guess right — which is not much better than chance; we might as well just guess.

When I first heard about the triangle test, I decided to try it on a group of my friends. *None of them got it right.* These were all well-educated, thoughtful people, most of whom were regular cola drinkers, and they simply couldn't believe what had happened. They jumped up and down. They accused me of tricking them. They argued that there must have been something funny about the local Pepsi and Coke bottlers. They said that I had manipulated the order of the three glasses to make it more difficult for them. None of them wanted to admit to the truth: their knowledge of colas was incredibly shallow. With two colas, all we have to do is compare two first impressions. But with three glasses, we have to be able to describe and hold the taste of the first and then the second cola in our memory and somehow, however briefly, convert a fleeting sensory sensation into something permanent — and to do that requires knowledge and understanding of the vocabulary of taste. Heylmun and Civille can pass the triangle test with flying colors, because their knowledge gives their first impressions resiliency. My friends were not so fortunate. They may drink a lot of cola, but they don't ever really *think* about colas. They aren't cola experts, and to force them to be — to ask too much of them — is to render their reactions useless.

Isn't this what happened to Kenna?

6. "It Sucks What the Record Companies Are Doing to You"

After years of starts and stops, Kenna was finally signed by Columbia Records. He released an album called *New Sacred Cow*. Then he went on his first tour, playing in fourteen cities throughout the American West and Midwest. It was a modest beginning: he opened for another band and played for thirty-five minutes. Many people in the audience didn't even realize that he was on the bill. But once they heard him play, they were enthusiastic. He also made a video of one of his songs, which was nominated for an award on VH-1. College radio stations began playing *New Sacred Cow,* and it started to climb the college charts. He then got a few appearances on television talk shows. But the big prize still eluded him. His album didn't take off because he couldn't get his first single played on Top 40 radio.

It was the same old story. The equivalent of Gail Vance Civille and Judy Heylmun had loved Kenna. Craig Kallman heard his demo tape and got on the phone and said, "I want to see him *now*." Fred Durst heard one of his songs over the telephone and decided that this was *it*. Paul McGuinness flew him to Ireland. The people who had a way to structure their first impressions, the vocabulary to capture them, and the experience to understand them, loved Kenna, and in a perfect world, that would have counted for more than the questionable findings of market research. But the world of radio is not as savvy as the world of food or the furniture makers at Herman Miller.

They prefer a system that cannot measure what it promises to measure.

"I guess they've gone to their focus groups, and the focus groups have said, 'No, it's not a hit.' They don't want to put money into something that doesn't test well," Kenna says. "But that's not the way this music works. This music takes faith. And faith isn't what the music business is about anymore. It's absolutely frustrating, and it's overwhelming as well. I can't sleep. My mind is running. But if nothing else, I get to play, and the response from the kids is so massive and beautiful that it makes me get up the next day and fight again. The kids come up to me after the show and say, 'It sucks what the record companies are doing to you. But we're here for you, and we're telling everybody.'"

SIX

Seven Seconds in the Bronx: The Delicate Art of Mind Reading

The 1100 block of Wheeler Avenue in the Soundview neighborhood of the South Bronx is a narrow street of modest two-story houses and apartments. At one end is the bustle of Westchester Avenue, the neighborhood's main commercial strip, and from there, the block runs about two hundred yards, flanked by trees and twin rows of parked cars. The buildings were built in the early part of the last century. Many have an ornate façade of red brick, with four- or five-step stoops leading to the front door. It is a poor and working-class neighborhood, and in the late 1990s, the drug trade in the area, particularly on Westchester Avenue and one street over on Elder Avenue, was brisk. Soundview is just the kind of place where you would go if you were an immigrant in New York City who was looking to live somewhere cheap and close to a subway, which is why Amadou Diallo made his way to Wheeler Avenue.

Diallo was from Guinea. In 1999, he was twenty-two and working as a peddler in lower Manhattan, selling videotapes and socks and gloves from the sidewalk along Fourteenth Street. He was short and unassuming, about five foot six and 150 pounds, and he lived at 1157 Wheeler, on the second floor of one of the street's narrow apartment houses. On the night of February 3, 1999, Diallo returned home to his apartment just before midnight, talked to his roommates, and then went downstairs and stood at the top of the steps to his building, taking in the night. A few minutes later, a group of plainclothes police officers turned slowly onto Wheeler Avenue in an unmarked Ford Taurus. There were four of them — all white, all wearing jeans and sweatshirts and baseball caps and bulletproof vests, and all carrying police-issue 9-millimeter semiautomatic handguns. They were part of what is called the Street Crime Unit, a special division of the New York Police Department, dedicated to patrolling crime "hot spots" in the city's poorest neighborhoods. Driving the Taurus was Ken Boss. He was twenty-seven. Next to him was Sean Carroll, thirty-five, and in the backseat were Edward McMellon, twenty-six, and Richard Murphy, twenty-six.

It was Carroll who spotted Diallo first. "Hold up, hold up," he said to the others in the car. "What's that guy doing there?" Carroll claimed later that he had had two thoughts. One was that Diallo might be the lookout for a "push-in" robber — that is, a burglar who pretends to be a visitor and pushes his way into people's apartments. The other was that Diallo fitted the description of a serial rapist who had been active in the neighborhood about a year earlier. "He was just standing there," Carroll recalled.

"He was just standing on the stoop, looking up and down the block, peeking his head out and then putting his head back against the wall. Within seconds, he does the same thing, looks down, looks right. And it appeared that he stepped backwards into the vestibule as we were approaching, like he didn't want to be seen. And then we passed by, and I am looking at him, and I'm trying to figure out what's going on. What's this guy up to?"

Boss stopped the car and backed up until the Taurus was right in front of 1157 Wheeler. Diallo was still there, which Carroll would later say "amazed" him. "I'm like, all right, definitely something is going on here." Carroll and McMellon got out of the car. "Police," McMellon called out, holding up his badge. "Can we have a word?" Diallo didn't answer. Later, it emerged that Diallo had a stutter, so he may well have tried to say something but simply couldn't. What's more, his English wasn't perfect, and it was rumored as well that someone he knew had recently been robbed by a group of armed men, so he must have been terrified: here he was, outside in a bad neighborhood after midnight with two very large men in baseball caps, their chests inflated by their bulletproof vests, striding toward him. Diallo paused and then ran into the vestibule. Carroll and McMellon gave chase. Diallo reached the inside door and grabbed the doorknob with his left hand while, as the officers would later testify, turning his body sideways and "digging" into his pocket with his other hand. "Show me your hands!" Carroll called out. McMellon was yelling, too: "Get your hands out of your pockets. Don't make me fucking kill you!" But Diallo was growing more and more agitated, and Carroll was starting to get nervous, too, because it seemed to him that the reason Diallo was turning his body sideways was that he wanted to hide whatever he was doing with his right hand.

"We were probably at the top steps of the vestibule, trying to get to him before he got through that door," Carroll remembered. "The individual turned, looked at us. His hand was on — still on the doorknob. And he starts removing a black object from his right side. And as he pulled the object, all I could see was a top — it looked like the slide of a black gun. My prior experience and training, my prior arrests, dictated to me that this person was pulling a gun."

Carroll yelled out, "Gun! He's got a gun!"

Diallo didn't stop. He continued pulling on something in his pocket, and now he began to raise the black object in the direction of the officers. Carroll opened fire. McMellon instinctively jumped backward off the step and landed on his backside, firing as he flew through the air. As his bullets ricocheted around the vestibule, Carroll assumed that they came from Diallo's gun, and when he saw McMellon flying backward, he assumed that McMellon had been shot by Diallo, so he kept shooting, aiming, as police are taught to do, for "center mass." There were pieces of cement and splinters of wood flying in every direction, and the air was electric with the flash of gun muzzles and the sparks from the bullets.

Boss and Murphy were now out of the car as well, running toward the building. "I saw Ed McMellon," Boss would later testify, when the four officers were brought to trial on charges of first-degree manslaughter and second-degree murder. "He was on the left side of the vestibule and just came flying off that step all the way down. And at the same time, Sean Carroll is on the right-hand side, and he is coming down the stairs. It was frantic. He was running down the stairs, and it was just — it was intense. He was just doing whatever he could to retreat off those stairs. And Ed was on the ground. Shots are still going off. I'm running. I'm moving. And Ed was shot. That's all I could see. Ed was firing his weapon. Sean was firing his weapon into the vestibule. . . . And then I see Mr. Diallo. He is in the rear of the vestibule, in the back, towards the back wall, where that inner door is. He is a little bit off to the side of that door and he is crouched. He is crouched and he has his hand out and I see a gun. And I said, 'My God, I'm going to die.' I fired my weapon. I fired it as I was pushing myself backward and then I jumped off to the left. I was out of the line of fire. . . . His knees were bent. His back was straight up. And what it looked like was somebody trying to make a smaller target. It looked like a combat stance, the same one that I was taught in the police academy."

At that point, the attorney questioning Boss interrupted: "And how was his hand?"

"It was out."

"Straight out?"

"Straight out."

"And in his hand you saw an object. Is that correct?"

"Yeah, I thought I saw a gun in his hand. . . . What I seen was an entire weapon. A square weapon in his hand. It looked to me at that split second, after all the gunshots around me and the gun smoke and Ed McMellon down, that he was holding a gun and that he had just shot Ed and that I was next."

Carroll and McMellon fired sixteen shots each: an entire clip. Boss fired five shots. Murphy fired four shots. There was silence. Guns drawn, they climbed the stairs and approached Diallo. "I seen his right hand," Boss said later. "It was out from his body. His palm was open. And where there should have been a gun, there was a wallet. . . . I said, 'Where's the fucking gun?'"

Boss ran up the street toward Westchester Avenue because he had lost track in the shouting and the shooting of where they were. Later, when the ambulances arrived, he was so distraught, he could not speak.

Carroll sat down on the steps, next to Diallo's bullet-ridden body, and started to cry.

1. Three Fatal Mistakes

Perhaps the most common — and the most important — forms of rapid cognition are the judgments we make and the impressions we form of other people. Every waking minute that we are in the presence of someone, we come up with a constant stream of predictions and inferences about what that person is thinking and feeling. When someone says, "I love you," we look into that person's eyes to judge his or her sincerity. When we meet someone new, we often pick up on subtle signals, so that afterward, even though he or she may have talked in a normal and friendly manner, we may say, "I don't think he liked me," or "I don't think she's very happy." We easily parse complex distinctions in facial expression. If you were to see me grinning, for example, with my eyes twinkling, you'd say I was amused. But if you were to see me nod and smile exaggeratedly, with the corners of my lips tightened, you would take it that I had been teased and was responding sarcastically. If I were to make eye contact with someone, give a small smile, and then look down and avert my gaze, you would think I was flirting. If I were to follow a remark with a quick smile and then nod or tilt my head sideways, you might conclude that I had just said something a little harsh and wanted to take the edge off it. You wouldn't need to hear anything I was saying in order to reach these conclusions. They would just come to you, *blink*. If you were to approach a one-year-old child who sits playing on the floor and do something a little bit puzzling, such as cupping your hands over hers, the child would immediately look up into your eyes. Why? Because what you have done requires explanation, and the child knows that she can find an answer on your face. This practice of inferring the motivations and intentions of others is classic thin-slicing. It is picking up on subtle, fleeting cues in order to read someone's mind — and there is almost no other impulse so basic and so automatic and at which, most of the time, we so effortlessly excel. In the early hours of February 4, 1999, however, the four officers cruising down Wheeler Avenue failed at this most fundamental task. They did not read Diallo's mind.

First, Sean Carroll saw Diallo and said to the others in the car, "What's that guy doing there?" The answer was that Diallo was getting some air. But Carroll sized him up and in that instant decided he looked suspicious. That was mistake number one. Then they backed the car up, and Diallo didn't move. Carroll later said that "amazed" him: *How brazen was this man, who didn't run at the sight of the police?* Diallo wasn't brazen. He was curious. That was mistake number two. Then Carroll and Murphy stepped toward Diallo on the stoop and watched him turn slightly to the side, and make a movement for his pocket. In that split second, they decided he was dangerous. But he was not. He was terrified. That was mistake number three. Ordinarily, we have no difficulty at all distinguishing, in a blink, between someone who is suspicious and someone who is not, between someone brazen and someone curious, and, most easily of all, between someone terrified and someone dangerous; anyone who walks down a city street late at night makes those kinds of instantaneous calculations constantly. Yet, for some reason, that most basic human ability deserted those officers that night. Why?

These kinds of mistakes were not anomalous events. Mind-reading failures happen to all of us. They lie at the root of countless arguments, disagreements, misunderstandings, and hurt feelings. And yet, because these failures are so instantaneous and so mysterious, we don't really know how to understand them. In the weeks and months that followed the Diallo shooting, for example, as the case made headlines around the world, the argument over what happened that night veered back and forth between two extremes. There were those who said that it was just a horrible accident, an inevitable by-product of the fact that police officers sometimes have to make life-or-death decisions in conditions of uncertainty. That's what the jury in the Diallo trial concluded, and Boss, Carroll, McMellon, and Murphy were all acquitted of murder charges. On the other side were those who saw what happened as an open-and-shut case of racism. There were protests and demonstrations throughout the city. Diallo was held up as a martyr. Wheeler Avenue was renamed Amadou Diallo Place. Bruce Springsteen wrote and performed a song in his honor called "41 Shots," with the chorus "You can get killed just for living in your American skin."

Neither of these explanations, however, is particularly satisfying. There was no evidence that the four officers in the Diallo case were bad people, or racists, or out to get Diallo. On the other hand, it seems wrong to call the shooting a simple accident, since this wasn't exactly exemplary police work. The officers made a series of critical misjudgments, beginning with the assumption that a man getting a breath of fresh air outside his own home was a potential criminal.

The Diallo shooting, in other words, falls into a kind of gray area, the middle ground between deliberate and accidental. Mind-reading failures are sometimes like that. They aren't always as obvious and spectacular as other breakdowns in rapid cognition. They are subtle and complex and surprisingly common, and what happened on Wheeler Avenue is a powerful example of how mind reading works — and how it sometimes goes terribly awry.

2. The Theory of Mind Reading

Much of our understanding of mind reading comes from two remarkable scientists, a teacher and his pupil: Silvan Tomkins and Paul Ekman. Tomkins was the teacher. He was born in Philadelphia at the turn of the last century, the son of a dentist from Russia. He was short and thick around the middle, with a wild mane of white hair and huge black plastic-rimmed glasses. He taught psychology at Princeton and Rutgers and was the author of *Affect, Imagery, Consciousness,* a four-volume work so dense that its readers were evenly divided between those who understood it and thought it was brilliant and those who did not understand it and thought it was brilliant. He was a legendary talker. At the end of a cocktail party, a crowd of people would sit rapt at Tomkins's feet. Someone would say, "One more question!" and everyone would stay for another hour and a half as Tomkins held forth on, say, comic books, a television sitcom, the biology of emotion, his problem with Kant, and his enthusiasm for the latest fad diets — all enfolded into one extended riff.

During the Depression, in the midst of his doctoral studies at Harvard, he worked as a handicapper for a horse-racing syndicate and was so successful that he lived lavishly on Manhattan's Upper East Side. At the track, where he sat in the stands for hours staring at the horses through binoculars, he was known as "the professor." "He had a system for predicting how a horse would do, based on what horse was on either side of him, based on their emotional relationship," Ekman remembers. If a male horse, for instance, had lost to a mare in his first or second year, he would be ruined if he went to the gate with a mare next to him in the lineup. (Or something like that — no one really knew for certain.)

Tomkins believed that faces — even the faces of horses — held valuable clues to inner emotions and motivations. He could walk into a post office, it was said, go over to the Wanted posters, and, just by looking at the mug shots, say what crimes the various fugitives had committed. "He would watch the show *To Tell the Truth*, and without fail he could always pick out the people who were lying," his son Mark recalls. "He actually wrote the producer at one point to say it was too easy, and the man invited him to come to New York, go backstage, and show his stuff." Virginia Demos, who teaches psychology at Harvard, recalls having long conversations with Tomkins during the 1988 Democratic National Convention. "We would sit and talk on the phone, and he would turn the sound down while, say, Jesse Jackson was talking to Michael Dukakis. And he would read the faces and give his predictions on what would happen. It was profound."

Paul Ekman first encountered Tomkins in the early 1960s. Ekman was then a young psychologist just out of graduate school, and he was interested in studying faces. Was there a common set of rules, he wondered, that governed the facial expressions that human beings made? Silvan Tomkins said that there was. But most psychologists said that there wasn't. The conventional wisdom at the time held that expressions were culturally determined — that is, we simply used our faces according to a set of learned social conventions. Ekman didn't know which view was right, so, to help him decide, he traveled to Japan, Brazil, and Argentina — and even to remote tribes in the jungles of the Far East — carrying photographs of men and women making a variety of distinctive faces. To his amazement, everywhere he went, people agreed on what those expressions meant. Tomkins, he realized, was right.

Not long afterward, Tomkins visited Ekman at his laboratory in San Francisco. Ekman had tracked down a hundred thousand feet of film that had been shot by the virologist Carleton Gajdusek in the remote jungles of Papua New Guinea. Some of the footage was of a tribe called the South Fore, who were a peaceful and friendly people. The rest was of the Kukukuku, a hostile and murderous tribe with a homosexual ritual in which preadolescent boys were required to serve as courtesans for the male elders of the tribe. For six months, Ekman and his collaborator, Wallace Friesen, had been sorting through the footage, cutting extraneous scenes, focusing just on close-ups of the faces of the tribesmen in order to compare the facial expressions of the two groups.

As Ekman set up the projector, Tomkins waited in the back. He had been told nothing about the tribes involved; all identifying context had been edited out. Tomkins looked on intently, peering through his glasses. At the end of the film, he approached the screen and pointed to the faces of the South Fore. "These are a sweet, gentle people, very indulgent, very peaceful," he said. Then he pointed to the faces of the Kukukuku. "This other group is violent, and there is lots of evidence to suggest homosexuality." Even today, a third of a century later, Ekman cannot get over what Tomkins did. "My God! I vividly remember saying, 'Silvan, how on earth are you doing that?'" Ekman recalls. "And he went up to the screen, and, while we played the film backward in slow motion, he pointed out the particular bulges and wrinkles in the faces that he was using to make his judgment. That's when I realized, 'I've got to unpack the face.' It was a gold mine of information that everyone had ignored. This guy could see it, and if he could see it, maybe everyone else could, too."

Ekman and Friesen decided, then and there, to create a taxonomy of facial expressions. They combed through medical textbooks that outlined the facial muscles, and they identified every distinct muscular movement that the face could make. There were forty-three such movements. Ekman and Friesen called them action units. Then they sat across from each other, for days on end, and began manipulating each action unit in turn, first locating the muscle in their minds and then concentrating on isolating it, watching each other closely as they did, checking their movements in a mirror, making notes on how the wrinkle patterns on their faces would change with each muscle movement, and videotaping the movement for their records. On the few occasions when they couldn't make a particular movement, they went next door to the UCSF anatomy department, where a surgeon they knew would stick them with a needle and electrically stimulate the recalcitrant muscle. "That wasn't pleasant at all," Ekman recalls.

When each of those action units had been mastered, Ekman and Friesen began working action units in combination, layering one movement on top of another. The entire process took seven years. "There are three hundred combinations of two muscles," Ekman says. "If you add in a third, you get over four thousand. We took it up to five muscles, which is over ten thousand visible facial configurations." Most of those ten thousand facial expressions don't mean anything, of course. They are the kind of nonsense faces that children make. But, by working through each action-unit combination, Ekman and Friesen identified about three thousand that did seem to mean something, until they had catalogued the essential repertoire of human facial displays of emotion.

Paul Ekman is now in his sixties. He is clean-shaven, with closely set eyes and thick, prominent eyebrows, and although he is of medium build, he seems much larger: there is something stubborn and substantial in his demeanor. He grew up in Newark, New Jersey, the son of a pediatrician, and entered the University of Chicago at fifteen. He speaks deliberately. Before he laughs, he pauses slightly, as if waiting for permission. He is the sort who makes lists and numbers his arguments. His academic writing has an orderly logic to it; by the end of an Ekman essay, each stray objection and problem has been gathered up and catalogued. Since the mid-1960s, he has been working out of a ramshackle Victorian townhouse at the University of California at San Francisco, where he holds a professorship. When I met Ekman, he sat in his office and began running through the action-unit configurations he had learned so long ago. He leaned forward slightly, placing his hands on his knees. On the wall behind him were photographs of his two heroes, Tomkins and Charles Darwin. "Everybody can do action unit four," he began. He lowered his brow, using his depressor glabellae, depressor supercilii, and corrugator. "Almost everyone can do A.U. nine." He wrinkled his nose, using his levator labii superioris alaeque nasi. "Everybody can do five." He contracted his levator palpebrae superioris, raising his upper eyelid.

I was trying to follow along with him, and he looked up at me. "You've got a very good five," he said generously. "The more deeply set your eyes are, the harder it is to see the five. Then there's seven." He squinted. "Twelve." He flashed a smile, activating the zygomatic major. The inner parts of his eyebrows shot up. "That's A.U. one — distress, anguish." Then he used his frontalis, pars lateralis, to raise the outer half of his eyebrows. "That's A.U. two. It's also very hard, but it's worthless. It's not part of anything except Kabuki theater. Twenty-three is one of my favorites. It's the narrowing of the red margin of the lips. Very reliable anger sign. It's very hard to do voluntarily." He narrowed his lips. "Moving one ear at a time is still one of the hardest things to do. I have to really concentrate. It takes everything I've got." He laughed. "This is something my daughter always wanted me to do for her friends. Here we go." He wiggled his left ear, then his right ear. Ekman does not appear to have a particularly expressive face. He has the demeanor of a psychoanalyst, watchful and impassive, and his ability to transform his face so easily and quickly was astonishing. "There is one I can't do," he went on. "It's A.U. thirty-nine. Fortunately, one of my postdocs can do it. A.U. thirty-eight is dilating the nostrils. Thirty-nine is the opposite. It's the muscle that pulls them down." He shook his head and looked at me again. "Ooh! You've got a fantastic thirty-nine. That's one of the best I've ever seen. It's genetic. There should be other members of your family who have this heretofore unknown talent. You've got it, you've got it." He laughed again. "You're in a position to flash it at people. See, you should try that in a singles bar!"

Ekman then began to layer one action unit on top of another, in order to compose the more complicated facial expressions that we generally recognize as emotions.

Happiness, for instance, is essentially A.U. six and twelve — contracting the muscles that raise the cheek (orbicularis oculi, pars orbitalis) in combination with the zygomatic major, which pulls up the corners of the lips. Fear is A.U. one, two, and four, or, more fully, one, two, four, five, and twenty, with or without action units twenty-five, twenty-six, or twenty-seven. That is: the inner brow raiser (frontalis, pars medialis) plus the outer brow raiser (frontalis, pars lateralis) plus the brow-lowering depressor supercilii plus the levator palpebrae superioris (which raises the upper lid) plus the risorius (which stretches the lips) plus the parting of the lips (depressor labii) plus the masseter (which drops the jaw). Disgust? That's mostly A.U. nine, the wrinkling of the nose (levator labii superioris alaeque nasi), but it can sometimes be ten, and in either case it may be combined with A.U. fifteen or sixteen or seventeen.

Ekman and Friesen ultimately assembled all these combinations — and the rules for reading and interpreting them — into the Facial Action Coding System, or FACS, and wrote them up in a five-hundred-page document. It is a strangely riveting work, full of such details as the possible movements of the lips (elongate, de-elongate, narrow, widen, flatten, protrude, tighten, and stretch); the four different changes of the skin between the eyes and the cheeks (bulges, bags, pouches, and lines); and the critical distinctions between infraorbital furrows and the nasolabial furrow. John Gottman, whose research on marriage I wrote about in chapter 1, has collaborated with Ekman for years and uses the principles of FACS in analyzing the emotional states of couples. Other researchers have em-

ployed Ekman's system to study everything from schizo-
phrenia to heart disease; it has even been put to use by
computer animators at Pixar (*Toy Story*) and DreamWorks
(*Shrek*). FACS takes weeks to master in its entirety, and
only five hundred people around the world have been cer-
tified to use it in research. But those who have mastered it
gain an extraordinary level of insight into the messages we
send each other when we look into one another's eyes.

Ekman recalled the first time he saw Bill Clinton, during the 1992 Democratic primaries. "I was watching his
facial expressions, and I said to my wife, 'This is Peck's
Bad Boy,'" Ekman said. "This is a guy who wants to be
caught with his hand in the cookie jar and have us love
him for it anyway. There was this expression that's one
of his favorites. It's that hand-in-the-cookie-jar, love-me-
Mommy-because-I'm-a-rascal look. It's A.U. twelve, fifteen, seventeen, and twenty-four, with an eye roll." Ekman
paused, then reconstructed that particular sequence of expressions on his face. He contracted his zygomatic major,
A.U. twelve, in a classic smile, then tugged the corners of
his lips down with his triangularis, A.U. fifteen. He flexed
the mentalis, A.U. seventeen, which raises the chin,
slightly pressed his lips together in A.U. twenty-four, and
finally rolled his eyes — and it was as if Slick Willie himself were suddenly in the room.

"I knew someone who was on Clinton's communications staff. So I contacted him. I said, 'Look, Clinton's got
this way of rolling his eyes along with a certain expression,
and what it conveys is "I'm a bad boy." I don't think it's a
good thing. I could teach him how not to do that in two to
three hours.' And he said, 'Well, we can't take the risk that

he's known to be seeing an expert on lying.'" Ekman's voice trailed off. It was clear that he rather liked Clinton and that he wanted Clinton's expression to have been no more than a meaningless facial tic. Ekman shrugged. "Unfortunately, I guess, he needed to get caught — and he got caught."

3. The Naked Face

What Ekman is saying is that the face is an enormously rich source of information about emotion. In fact, he makes an even bolder claim — one central to understanding how mind reading works — and that is that the information on our face is not just a signal of what is going on inside our mind. In a certain sense, it *is* what is going on inside our mind.

The beginnings of this insight came when Ekman and Friesen were first sitting across from each other, working on expressions of anger and distress. "It was weeks before one of us finally admitted feeling terrible after a session where we'd been making one of those faces all day," Friesen says. "Then the other realized that he'd been feeling poorly, too, so we began to keep track." They then went back and began monitoring their bodies during particular facial movements. "Say you do A.U. one, raising the inner eyebrows, and six, raising the cheeks, and fifteen, the lowering of the corner of the lips," Ekman said, and then did all three. "What we discovered is that that expression alone is sufficient to create marked changes in the autonomic nervous system. When this first occurred, we were stunned. We weren't expecting this at all. And it happened to both of us. We felt terrible. What we were generating were sadness, anguish. And when I lower my brows, which is four, and raise the upper eyelid, which is five, and narrow the eyelids, which is seven, and press the lips together, which is twenty-four, I'm generating anger. My heartbeat will go up ten to twelve beats. My hands will get hot. As I do it, I can't disconnect from the system. It's very unpleasant, very unpleasant."

Ekman, Friesen, and another colleague, Robert Levenson (who has also collaborated for years with John Gottman; psychology is a small world) decided to try to document this effect. They gathered a group of volunteers and hooked them up to monitors measuring their heart rate and body temperature — the physiological signals of such emotions as anger, sadness, and fear. Half of the volunteers were told to try to remember and relive a particularly stressful experience. The other half were simply shown how to create, on their faces, the expressions that corresponded to stressful emotions, such as anger, sadness, and fear. The second group, the people who were acting, showed the same physiological responses, the same heightened heart rate and body temperature, as the first group.

A few years later, a German team of psychologists conducted a similar study. They had a group of subjects look at cartoons, either while holding a pen between their lips — an action that made it impossible to contract either of the two major smiling muscles, the risorius and the zygomatic major — or while holding a pen clenched between their teeth, which had the opposite effect and forced them to smile. The people with the pen between their teeth found the cartoons much funnier. These findings may be hard to believe, because we take it as a given that first we experience an emotion, and then we may — or may not — express that emotion on our face. We think of the face as the residue of emotion. What this research showed, though, is that the process works in the opposite direction as well. Emotion can also *start* on the face. The face is not a secondary billboard for our internal feelings. It is an equal partner in the emotional process.

This critical point has enormous implications for the act of mind-reading. Early in his career, for example, Paul Ekman filmed forty psychiatric patients, including a woman named Mary, a forty-two-year-old housewife. She had attempted suicide three times, and she survived the last attempt — an overdose of pills — only because someone found her in time and rushed her to the hospital. Her grown children had left home, and her husband was inattentive, and she was depressed. When she first went to the hospital, she did nothing but sit and cry, but she seemed to respond well to therapy. After three weeks, she told her doctor that she was feeling much better and wanted a weekend pass to see her family. The doctor agreed, but just before Mary was to leave the hospital, she confessed that the real reason she wanted a weekend pass was to make another suicide attempt. Several years later, when a group of young psychiatrists asked Ekman how they could tell when suicidal patients were lying, he remembered the film taken of Mary and decided to see if it held the answer. If the face really was a reliable guide to emotion, he reasoned, shouldn't he be able to look back at the film and see that Mary was lying when she said she was feeling better?

Ekman and Friesen began to analyze the film for clues. They played it over and over for dozens of hours, examining in slow motion every gesture and expression. Finally, they saw what they were looking for: when Mary's doctor asked her about her plans for the future, a look of utter despair flashed across her face so quickly that it was almost imperceptible.

Ekman calls that kind of fleeting look a micro expression, which is a very particular and critical kind of facial expression. Many facial expressions can be made voluntarily. If I'm trying to look stern as I give you a tongue-lashing, I'll have no difficulty doing so, and you'll have no difficulty interpreting my glare. But our faces are also governed by a separate, involuntary system that makes expressions that we have no conscious control over. Few of us, for instance, can voluntarily do A.U. one, the sadness sign. (A notable exception, Ekman points out, is Woody Allen, who uses his frontalis, pars medialis to create his trademark look of comic distress.) Yet we raise our inner eyebrows without thinking when we are unhappy. Watch a baby just as he or she starts to cry, and you'll often see the frontalis, pars medialis shoot up as if it were on a string. Similarly, there is an expression that Ekman has dubbed the Duchenne smile, in honor of the nineteenth-century French neurologist Guillaume Duchenne, who first attempted to document with a camera the workings of the muscles of the face. If I were to ask you to smile, you would flex your zygomatic major. By contrast, if you were to smile spontaneously, in the presence of genuine emotion, you would not only flex your zygomatic but also tighten the orbicularis oculi, pars orbitalis, which is the muscle that encircles the eye. It is almost impossible to tighten the orbicularis oculi, pars orbitalis on demand, and it is equally difficult to stop it from tightening when we smile at something genuinely pleasurable. This kind of smile "does not obey the will," Duchenne wrote. "Its absence unmasks the false friend."

Whenever we experience a basic emotion, that emotion is automatically expressed by the muscles of the face. That response may linger on the face for just a fraction of a second or be detectable only if electrical sensors are attached to the face. But it's always there. Silvan Tomkins once began a lecture by bellowing, "The face is like the penis!" What he meant was that the face has, to a large extent, a mind of its own. This doesn't mean we have no control over our faces. We can use our voluntary muscular system to try to suppress those involuntary responses. But, often, some little part of that suppressed emotion — such as the sense that I'm really unhappy even if I deny it — leaks out. That's what happened to Mary. Our voluntary expressive system is the way we intentionally signal our emotions. But our involuntary expressive system is in many ways even more important: it is the way we have been equipped by evolution to signal our authentic feelings.

"You must have had the experience where somebody comments on your expression and you didn't know you were making it," Ekman says. "Somebody asks you, 'What are you getting upset about?' or 'Why are you smirking?' You can hear your voice, but you can't see your face. If we knew what was on our face, we would be better at concealing it. But that wouldn't necessarily be a good thing. Imagine if there were a switch that all of us had, to turn off the expressions on our face at will. If babies had that switch, we wouldn't know what they were feeling. They'd be in trouble. You could make an argument, if you wanted to, that the system evolved so that parents would be able to take care of kids. Or imagine if you were married to someone with a switch. It would be impossible. I don't think mating and infatuation and friendships and closeness would occur if our faces didn't work that way."

Ekman slipped a tape from the O.J. Simpson trial into the VCR. It showed Kato Kaelin, Simpson's shaggy-haired houseguest, being questioned by Marcia Clark, the lead prosecutor in the case. Kaelin sits in the witness box, with a vacant look on his face. Clark asks a hostile question. Kaelin leans forward and answers her softly. "Did you see that?" Ekman asked me. I saw nothing, just Kato being Kato — harmless and passive. Ekman stopped the tape, rewound it, and played it back in slow motion. On the screen, Kaelin moved forward to answer the question, and in that fraction of a second, his face was utterly transformed. His nose wrinkled, as he flexed his levator labii superioris alaeque nasi. His teeth were bared, his brows lowered. "It was almost totally A.U. nine," Ekman said. "It's disgust, with anger there as well, and the clue to that is that when your eyebrows go down, typically your eyes are not as open as they are here. The raised upper eyelid is a component of anger, not disgust. It's very quick." Ekman stopped the tape and played it again, peering at the screen. "You know, he looks like a snarling dog."

Ekman showed another clip, this one from a press conference given by Harold "Kim" Philby in 1955. Philby had not yet been revealed as a Soviet spy, but two of his colleagues, Donald Maclean and Guy Burgess, had just defected to the Soviet Union. Philby is wearing a dark suit and a white shirt. His hair is straight and parted on the left. His face has the hauteur of privilege.

"Mr. Philby," a reporter asks, "Mr. Macmillan, the foreign secretary, said there was no evidence that you were the so-called third man who allegedly tipped off Burgess and Maclean. Are you satisfied with that clearance that he gave you?"

Philby answers confidently, in the plummy tones of the English upper class. "Yes, I am."

"Well, if there was a third man, were you in fact the third man?"

"No," Philby says, just as forcefully. "I was not."

Ekman rewound the tape and replayed it in slow motion. "Look at this," he said, pointing to the screen. "Twice, after being asked serious questions about whether he's committed treason, he's going to smirk. He looks like the cat who ate the canary." The expression came and went in no more than a few milliseconds. But at quarter speed it was painted on his face: the lips pressed together in a look of pure smugness. "He's enjoying himself, isn't he?" Ekman went on. "I call this 'duping delight,' the thrill you get from fooling other people." Ekman started up the VCR again. "There's another thing he does," he said. On the screen, Philby is answering another question: "In the second place, the Burgess-Maclean affair has raised issues of great" — he pauses — "delicacy." Ekman went back to the pause and froze the tape. "Here it is," he said. "A very subtle microexpression of distress or unhappiness. It's only in the eyebrows — in fact, just in one eyebrow." Sure enough, Philby's right inner eyebrow was raised in an unmistakable A.U. one. "It's very brief," Ekman said. "He's not doing it voluntarily. And it totally contradicts all his confidence and assertiveness. It comes when he's talking about Burgess and Maclean, whom he had tipped off. It's a hot spot that suggests, 'You shouldn't trust what you hear.'"

What Ekman is describing, in a very real sense, is the physiological basis of how we thin-slice other people. We can all mind-read effortlessly and automatically because the clues we need to make sense of someone or some social situation are right there on the faces of those in front of us. We may not be able to read faces as brilliantly as someone like Paul Ekman or Silvan Tomkins can, or pick up moments as subtle as Kato Kaelin's transformation into a snarling dog. But there is enough accessible information on a face to make everyday mind reading possible. When someone tells us "I love you," we look immediately and directly at him or her because by looking at the face, we can *know* — or, at least, we can know a great deal more — about whether the sentiment is genuine. Do we see tenderness and pleasure? Or do we catch a fleeting microexpression of distress and unhappiness flickering across his or her face? A baby looks into your eyes when you cup your hands over hers because she knows she can find an explanation in your face. Are you contracting action units six and twelve (the orbicularis oculi, pars orbitalis in combination with the zygomatic major) in a sign of happiness? Or are you contracting action units one, two, four, five, and twenty (the frontalis, pars medialis; the frontalis, pars lateralis; the depressor supercilii; the levator palpebrae superioris; and the risorius) in what even a child intuitively understands as the clear signal of fear? We make these kinds of complicated, lightning-fast calculations very well. We make them every day, and we make them without thinking. And this is the puzzle of the Amadou Diallo case, because in the early hours of February 4, 1999, Sean Carroll and his fellow officers for some reason could not do this at all. Diallo was innocent, curious, and terrified — and every one of those emotions must have been written all over his face. Yet they saw none of it. Why?

4. A Man, a Woman, and a Light Switch

The classic model for understanding what it means to lose the ability to mind-read is the condition of autism. When someone is autistic, he or she is, in the words of the British psychologist Simon Baron-Cohen, "mind-blind." People with autism find it difficult, if not impossible, to do all of the things that I've been describing so far as natural and automatic human processes. They have difficulty interpreting nonverbal cues, such as gestures and facial expressions or putting themselves inside someone else's head or drawing understanding from anything other than the literal meaning of words. Their first-impression apparatus is fundamentally disabled, and the way that people with autism see the world gives us a very good sense of what happens when our mind-reading faculties fail.

One of the country's leading experts on autism is a man named Ami Klin. Klin teaches at Yale University's Child Study Center in New Haven, where he has a patient whom he has been studying for many years whom I'll call Peter. Peter is in his forties. He is highly educated and works and lives independently. "This is a very high-functioning individual. We meet weekly, and we talk," Klin explains. "He's very articulate, but he has no intuition about things, so he needs me to define the world for him." Klin, who bears a striking resemblance to the actor Martin Short, is half Israeli and half Brazilian, and he speaks with an understandably peculiar accent. He has been seeing Peter for years, and he speaks of his condition not with condescension or detachment but matter-of-factly, as if describing a minor character tic. "I talk to him every week, and the sense that I have in talking to him is that I could do anything. I could pick my nose. I could take my pants down. I could do some work here. Even though he is looking at me, I don't have the sense of being scrutinized or monitored. He focuses very much on what I say. The words mean a great deal to him. But he doesn't focus at all on the way my words are contextualized with facial expressions and nonverbal cues. Everything that goes on inside the mind — that he cannot observe directly — is a problem for him. Am I his therapist? Not really. Normal therapy is based on people's ability to have insight into their own motivations. But with him, insight wouldn't take you very far. So it's more like problem solving."

One of the things that Klin wanted to discover, in talking to Peter, was how someone with his condition makes sense of the world, so he and his colleagues devised an ingenious experiment. They decided to show Peter a movie and then follow the direction of his eyes as he looked at the screen. The movie they chose was the 1966 film version of the Edward Albee play *Who's Afraid of Virginia Woolf?*

starring Richard Burton and Elizabeth Taylor as a husband and wife who invite a much younger couple, played
by George Segal and Sandy Dennis, for what turns out to
be an intense and grueling evening. "It's my favorite play
ever, and I love the movie. I love Richard Burton. I love
Elizabeth Taylor," Klin explains, and for what Klin was
trying to do, the film was perfect. People with autism are
obsessed with mechanical objects, but this was a movie
that followed very much the spare, actor-focused design of
the stage. "It's tremendously contained," Klin says. "It's
about four people and their minds. There are very few
inanimate details in that movie that would be distracting
to someone with autism. If I had used *Terminator Two,*
where the protagonist is a gun, I wouldn't have got those
results. It's all about intensive, engaging social interaction
at multiple levels of meaning, emotion, and expression.
What we are trying to get at is people's search for meaning.
So that's why I chose *Who's Afraid of Virginia Woolf?* I
was interested in getting to see the world through the eyes
of an autistic person."

Klin had Peter put on a hat with a very simple, but
powerful, eye-tracking device composed of two tiny cameras. One camera recorded the movement of Peter's
fovea — the centerpiece of his eye. The other camera
recorded whatever it was Peter was looking at, and then
the two images were superimposed. This meant that on
every frame of the movie, Klin could draw a line showing
where Peter was looking at that moment. He then had
people without autism watch the movie as well, and he
compared Peter's eye movements with theirs. In one

scene, for example, Nick (George Segal) is making polite conversation, and he points to the wall of host George's (Richard Burton's) study and asks, "Who did the painting?" The way you and I would look at that scene is straightforward: our eyes would follow in the direction that Nick is pointing, alight on the painting, swivel back to George's eyes to get his response, and then return to Nick's face, to see how he reacts to the answer. All of that takes place in a fraction of a second, and on Klin's visual-scanning pictures, the line representing the gaze of the normal viewer forms a clean, straight-edged triangle from Nick to the painting to George and back again to Nick. Peter's pattern, though, is a little different. He starts somewhere around Nick's neck. But he doesn't follow the direction of Nick's arm, because interpreting a pointing gesture requires, if you think about it, that you instantaneously inhabit the mind of the person doing the pointing. You need to read the mind of the pointer, and, of course, people with autism can't read minds. "Children respond to pointing gestures by the time they are twelve months old," Klin said. "This is a man who is forty-two years old and very bright, and he's not doing that. Those are the kinds of cues that children are learning naturally — and he just doesn't pick up on them."

So what does Peter do? He hears the words "painting" and "wall," so he looks for paintings on the wall. But there are three in the general vicinity. Which one is it? Klin's visual-scanning pictures show Peter's gaze moving frantically from one picture to the other. Meanwhile, the conversation has already moved on. The only way Peter could have made sense of that scene is if Nick had been perfectly, verbally explicit — if he had said, "Who did that painting to the left of the man and the dog?" In anything less than a perfectly literal environment, the autistic person is lost.

There's another critical lesson in that scene. The normal viewers looked at the eyes of George and Nick when they were talking, and they did that because when people talk, we listen to their words and watch their eyes in order to pick up on all those expressive nuances that Ekman has so carefully catalogued. But Peter didn't look at anyone's eyes in that scene. At another critical moment in the movie, when, in fact, George and Martha (Elizabeth Taylor) are locked in a passionate embrace, Peter looked not at the eyes of the kissing couple — which is what you or I would do — but at the light switch on the wall behind them. That's not because Peter objects to people or finds the notion of intimacy repulsive. It's because if you cannot mind-read — if you can't put yourself in the mind of someone else — then there's nothing special to be gained by looking at eyes and faces.

One of Klin's colleagues at Yale, Robert T. Schultz, once did an experiment with what is called an FMRI (functional magnetic resonance imagery), a highly sophisticated brain scanner that shows where the blood is flowing in the brain at any given time — and hence, which part of the brain is in use. Schultz put people in the FMRI machine and had them perform a very simple task in which they were given either pairs of faces or pairs of objects (such as chairs or hammers) and they had to press a button indicating whether the pairs were the same or different.

Normal people, when they were looking at the faces, used a part of their brain called the fusiform gyrus, which is an incredibly sophisticated piece of brain software that allows us to distinguish among the literally thousands of faces that we know. (Picture in your mind the face of Marilyn Monroe. Ready? You just used your fusiform gyrus.) When the normal participants looked at the chair, however, they used a completely different and less powerful part of the brain — the inferior temporal gyrus — which is normally reserved for objects. (The difference in the sophistication of those two regions explains why you can recognize Sally from the eighth grade forty years later but have trouble picking out your bag on the airport luggage carousel.) When Schultz repeated the experiment with autistic people, however, he found that they used their object-recognition area for both the chairs and the faces. In other words, on the most basic neurological level, for someone with autism, a face is just another object. Here is one of the earliest descriptions of an autistic patient in the medical literature: "He never looked up at people's faces. When he had any dealings with persons at all, he treated them, or rather parts of them, as if they were objects. He would use a hand to lead him. He would, in playing, butt his head against his mother as at other times he did against a pillow. He allowed his boarding mother's hand to dress him, paying not the slightest attention to her."

So, when Peter looked at the scene of Martha and George kissing, their two faces did not automatically command his attention. What he saw were three objects — a man, a woman, and a light switch. And what did he prefer? As it happens, the light switch. "I know for [Peter] that light switches have been important in his life," says Klin. "He sees a light switch, and he gravitates toward it. It's like if you were a Matisse connoisseur, and you look at a lot of pictures, and then you'd go, ahh, *there* is the Matisse. So he goes, *there* is the light switch. He's seeking meaning, organization. He doesn't like confusion. All of us gravitate toward things that mean something to us, and for most of us, that's people. But if people don't anchor meaning for you, then you seek something that does."

Perhaps the most poignant scene Klin studied comes at a point in the movie when Martha is sitting next to Nick, flirting outrageously, even putting a hand on his thigh. In the background, his back slightly turned to them, lurks an increasingly angry and jealous George. As the scene unfolds, the normal viewer's eyes move in an almost perfect triangle from Martha's eyes to Nick's eyes to George's eyes and then back to Martha's, monitoring the emotional states of all three as the temperature in the room rises. But Peter? He starts at Nick's mouth, and then his eyes drop to the drink in Nick's hand, and then his gaze wanders to a brooch on Martha's sweater. *He never looks at George at all,* so the entire emotional meaning of the scene is lost on him.

"There's a scene where George is about to lose his temper," says Warren Jones, who worked with Klin on the experiment. "He goes to the closet and pulls a gun down from the shelf, and points it directly at Martha and pulls the trigger. And when he does, an umbrella pops out the front of the barrel. But we have no idea until it comes out that it's a ruse — so there is this genuine moment of fear. And one of the most telltale things is that the classic autistic individual will laugh out loud and find it to be this moment of real physical comedy. They've missed the emotional basis for the act. They read only the superficial aspect that he pulls the trigger, an umbrella pops out, and they walk away thinking, those people were having a good time."

Peter's movie-watching experiment is a perfect example of what happens when mind reading fails. Peter is a highly intelligent man. He has graduate degrees from a prestigious university. His IQ is well above normal, and Klin speaks of him with genuine respect. But because he lacks one very basic ability — the ability to mind-read — he can be presented with that scene in *Who's Afraid of Virginia Woolf?* and come to a conclusion that is socially completely and catastrophically wrong. Peter, understandably, makes this kind of mistake often: he has a condition that makes him permanently mind-blind. But I can't help but wonder if, under certain circumstances, the rest of us could momentarily think like Peter as well. What if it were possible for autism — for mind-blindness — to be a temporary condition instead of a chronic one? Could that explain why sometimes otherwise normal people come to conclusions that are completely and catastrophically wrong?

5. Arguing with a Dog

In the movies and in detective shows on television, people fire guns all the time. They shoot and shoot and run after people, and sometimes they kill them, and when they do, they stand over the body and smoke a cigarette and then go and have a beer with their partner. To hear Hollywood tell it, shooting a gun is a fairly common and straightforward act. The truth is, though, that it isn't. Most police officers — well over 90 percent — go their whole career without ever firing at anyone, and those who do describe the experience as so unimaginably stressful that it seems reasonable to ask if firing a gun could be the kind of experience that could cause temporary autism.

Here, for example, are excerpts of interviews that the University of Missouri criminologist David Klinger did with police officers for his fascinating book *Into the Kill Zone.* The first is with an officer who fired on a man who was threatening to kill his partner, Dan:

> He looked up, saw me, and said, "Oh, shit." Not like "Oh, shit, I'm scared." But like "Oh, shit, now here's somebody else I gotta kill" — real aggressive and mean. Instead of continuing to push the gun at Dan's head, he started to try to bring it around on me. This all happened real fast — in milliseconds — and at the same time, I was bringing my gun up. Dan was still fighting with him, and the only thought that came through my mind was "Oh, dear God, don't let me hit Dan." I fired five rounds. My vision changed as soon as I started to shoot. It went from seeing the whole picture to just the suspect's head. Everything else just disappeared. I didn't see Dan anymore, didn't see anything else. All I could see was the suspect's head.
>
> I saw four of my five rounds hit. The first one hit him on his left eyebrow. It opened up a hole and the guy's head snapped back and he said, "Ooh," like, "Ooh, you got me." He still continued to turn the gun toward me,

and I fired my second round. I saw a red dot right below the base of his left eye, and his head kind of turned sideways. I fired another round. It hit on the outside of his left eye, and his eye exploded, just ruptured and came out. My fourth round hit just in front of his left ear. The third round had moved his head even further sideways to me, and when the fourth round hit, I saw a red dot open on the side of his head, then close up. I didn't see where my last round went. Then I heard the guy fall backwards and hit the ground.

Here's another:

When he started toward us, it was almost like it was in slow motion and everything went into a tight focus. . . . When he made his move, my whole body just tensed up. I don't remember having any feeling from my chest down. Everything was focused forward to watch and react to my target. Talk about an adrenaline rush! Everything tightened up, and all my senses were directed forward at the man running at us with a gun. My vision was focused on his torso and the gun. I couldn't tell you what his left hand was doing. I have no idea. I was watching the gun. The gun was coming down in front of his chest area, and that's when I did my first shots.

I didn't hear a thing, not one thing. Alan had fired one round when I shot my first pair, but I didn't hear him shoot. He shot two more rounds when I fired the second time, but I didn't hear any of those rounds, either. We stopped shooting when he hit the floor and slid into me. Then I was on my feet standing over the guy. I don't even remember pushing myself up. All I know is the next thing I knew I was standing on two feet looking down at the guy. I don't know how I got there, whether I pushed up with my hands, or whether I pulled my knees up underneath. I don't know, but once I was up, I was hearing things again because I could hear brass still clinking on the tile floor. Time had also returned to normal by then, because it had slowed down during the shooting. That started as soon as he started toward us. Even though I knew he was running at us, it looked like he was moving in slow motion. Damnedest thing I ever saw.

I think you'll agree that these are profoundly strange stories. In the first instance, the officer appears to be describing something that is quite impossible. How can someone watch his bullets hit someone? Just as strange is the second man's claim not to have heard the sound of his gun going off. How can that be? Yet, in interviews with police officers who have been involved with shootings, these same details appear again and again: extreme visual clarity, tunnel vision, diminished sound, and the sense that time is slowing down. This is how the human body reacts to extreme stress, and it makes sense. Our mind, faced with a life-threatening situation, drastically limits the range and amount of information that we have to deal with. Sound and memory and broader social understanding are sacrificed in favor of heightened awareness of the threat directly in front of us. In a critical sense, the police officers whom Klinger describes performed better because their senses narrowed: that narrowing allowed them to focus on the threat in front of them.

But what happens when this stress response is taken to an extreme? Dave Grossman, a former army lieutenant colonel and the author of *On Killing*, argues that the optimal state of "arousal" — the range in which stress improves performance — is when our heart rate is between 115 and 145 beats per minute. Grossman says that when he measured the heart rate of champion marksman Ron Avery, Avery's pulse was at the top of that range when he was performing in the field. The basketball superstar Larry Bird used to say that at critical moments in the game, the court would go quiet and the players would seem to be moving in slow motion. He clearly played basketball in that same optimal range of arousal in which Ron Avery performed. But very few basketball players see the court as clearly as Larry Bird did, and that's because very few people play in that optimal range. Most of us, under pressure, get *too* aroused, and past a certain point, our bodies begin shutting down so many sources of information that we start to become useless.

"After 145," Grossman says, "bad things begin to happen. Complex motor skills start to break down. Doing something with one hand and not the other becomes very difficult. . . . At 175, we begin to see an absolute breakdown of cognitive processing. . . . The forebrain shuts down, and the mid-brain — the part of your brain that is the same as your dog's (all mammals have that part of the brain) — reaches up and hijacks the forebrain. Have you ever tried to have a discussion with an angry or frightened human being? You can't do it. . . . You might as well try to argue with your dog." Vision becomes even more restricted. Behavior becomes inappropriately aggressive. In an extraordinary number of cases, people who are being fired upon void their bowels because at the heightened level of threat represented by a heart rate of 175 and above, the body considers that kind of physiological control a nonessential activity. Blood is withdrawn from our outer muscle layer and concentrated in core muscle mass. The evolutionary point of that is to make the muscles as hard as possible — to turn them into a kind of armor and limit bleeding in the event of injury. But that leaves us clumsy and helpless. Grossman says that everyone should practice dialing 911 for this very reason, because he has heard of too many situations where, in an emergency, people pick up the phone and cannot perform this most basic of functions. With their heart rate soaring and their motor coordination deteriorating, they dial 411 and not 911 because that's the only number they remember, or they forget to press "send" on their cell phone, or they simply cannot pick out the individual numbers at all. "You must rehearse it," Grossman says, "because only if you have rehearsed it will it be there."

This is precisely the reason that many police departments in recent years have banned high-speed chases. It's not just because of the dangers of hitting some innocent bystander *during* the chase, although that is clearly part of the worry, since about three hundred Americans are killed accidentally every year during chases. It's also because of what happens *after* the chase, since pursuing a suspect at high speed is precisely the kind of activity that pushes police officers into this dangerous state of high arousal. "The L.A. riot was started by what cops did to Rodney King at the end of the high-speed chase," says James Fyfe, head of training for the NYPD, who has testified in many police brutality cases. "The Liberty City riot in Miami in 1980 was started by what the cops did at the end of a chase. They beat a guy to death. In 1986, they had another riot in Miami based on what cops did at the end of the chase. Three of the major race riots in this country over the past quarter century have been caused by what cops did at the end of a chase."

"When you get going at high speeds, especially through residential neighborhoods, that's scary," says Bob Martin, a former high-ranking LAPD officer. "Even if it is only fifty miles per hour. Your adrenaline and heart start pumping like crazy. It's almost like a runner's high. It's a very euphoric kind of thing. You lose perspective. You get wrapped up in the chase. There's that old saying — 'a dog in the hunt doesn't stop to scratch its fleas.' If you've ever listened to a tape of an officer broadcasting in the midst of pursuit, you can hear it in the voice. They almost yell. For new officers, there's almost hysteria. I remember my first pursuit. I was only a couple of months out of the academy. It was through a residential neighborhood. A couple of times we even went airborne. Finally we captured him. I went back to the car to radio in and say we were okay, and I couldn't even pick up the radio, I was shaking so badly." Martin says that the King beating was precisely what one would expect when two parties — both with soaring heartbeats and predatory cardiovascular reactions — encounter each other after a chase. "At a key point, Stacey Koon" — one of the senior officers at the scene of the arrest — "told the officers to back off," Martin says. "But they ignored him. Why? Because they didn't hear him. They had shut down."

Fyfe says that he recently gave a deposition in a case in Chicago in which police officers shot and killed a young man at the end of a chase, and unlike Rodney King, he wasn't resisting arrest. He was just sitting in his car. "He was a football player from Northwestern. His name was Robert Russ. It happened the same night the cops there shot another kid, a girl, at the end of a vehicle pursuit, in a case that Johnnie Cochran took and got over a $20 million settlement. The cops said he was driving erratically. He led them on a chase, but it wasn't even that high-speed. They never got above seventy miles per hour. After a while, they ran him off the road. They spun his car out on the Dan Ryan Expressway. The instructions on vehicle stops like that are very detailed. You are not supposed to approach the car. You are supposed to ask the driver to get out. Well, two of the cops ran up ahead and opened the passenger side door. The other asshole was on the other side, yelling at Russ to open the door. But Russ just sat there. I don't know what was going through his head. But he didn't respond. So this cop smashes the left rear window of the car and fires a single shot, and it hits Russ in the hand and chest. The cop says that he said, 'Show me your hands, show me your hands,' and he's claiming now that Russ was trying to grab his gun. I don't know if that was the case. I have to accept the cop's claim. But it's beside the point. It's still an unjustified shooting because he shouldn't have been anywhere near the car, and he shouldn't have broken the window."

Was this officer mind-reading? Not at all. Mind-reading allows us to adjust and update our perceptions of the intentions of others. In the scene in *Who's Afraid of Virginia Woolf?* where Martha is flirting with Nick while George lurks jealously in the background, our eyes bounce from Martha's eyes to George's to Nick's and around and around again because we don't know what George is going to do. We keep gathering information on him because we want to find out. But Ami Klin's autistic patient looked at Nick's mouth and then at his drink and then at Martha's brooch. In his mind he processed human beings and objects in the same way. He didn't see individuals, with their own emotions and thoughts. He saw a collection of inanimate objects in the room and constructed a system to explain them — a system that he interpreted with such rigid and impoverished logic that when George fires his shotgun at Martha and an umbrella pops out, he laughed out loud. This, in a way, is what that officer on the Dan Ryan Expressway did as well. In the extreme excitement of the chase, he stopped reading Russ's mind. His vision and his thinking narrowed. He constructed a rigid system that said that a young black man in a car running from the police had to be a dangerous criminal, and all evidence to the contrary that would ordinarily have been factored into his thinking — the fact that Russ was just sitting in his car and that he had never gone above seventy miles per hour — did not register at all. Arousal leaves us mind-blind.

6. Running Out of White Space

Have you ever seen the videotape of the assassination attempt on Ronald Reagan? It's the afternoon of March 30, 1981. Reagan has just given a speech at the Washington

Hilton Hotel and is walking out a side door toward his limousine. He waves to the crowd. Voices cry out: "President Reagan! President Reagan!" Then a young man named John Hinckley lunges forward with a .22-caliber pistol in his hand and fires six bullets at Reagan's entourage at point-blank range before being wrestled to the ground. One of the bullets hits Reagan's press secretary, James Brady, in the head. A second bullet hits a police officer, Thomas Delahanty, in the back. A third hits Secret Service agent Timothy McCarthy in the chest, and a fourth ricochets off the limousine and pierces Reagan's lung, missing his heart by inches. The puzzle of the Hinckley shooting, of course, is how he managed to get at Reagan so easily. Presidents are surrounded by bodyguards, and bodyguards are supposed to be on the lookout for people like John Hinckley. The kind of people who typically stand outside a hotel on a cold spring day waiting for a glimpse of their President are well-wishers, and the job of the bodyguard is to scan the crowd and look for the person who doesn't fit, the one who doesn't wish well at all. Part of what bodyguards have to do is read faces. They have to mind-read. So why didn't they read Hinckley's mind? The answer is obvious if you watch the video — and it's the second critical cause of mind-blindnesss: there is no time.

Gavin de Becker, who runs a security firm in Los Angeles and is the author of the book *The Gift of Fear*, says that the central fact in protection is the amount of "white space," which is what he calls the distance between the target and any potential assailant. The more white space there is, the more time the bodyguard has to react. And the more time the bodyguard has, the better his ability to read the mind of any potential assailant. But in the Hinckley shooting, there was no white space. Hinckley was in a knot of reporters who were standing within a few feet of the President. The Secret Service agents became aware of him only when he starting firing. From the first instance when Reagan's bodyguards realized that an attack was under way — what is known in the security business as the moment of recognition — to the point when no further harm was done was 1.8 seconds. "The Reagan attack involves heroic reactions by several people," de Becker says. "Nonetheless, every round was still discharged by Hinckley. In other words, those reactions didn't make one single difference, because he was too close. In the videotape you see one bodyguard. He gets a machine gun out of his briefcase and stands there. Another has his gun out, too. What are they going to shoot at? It's over." In those 1.8 seconds, all the bodyguards could do was fall back on their most primitive, automatic (and, in this case, useless) impulse — to draw their weapons. They had no chance at all to understand or anticipate what was happening. "When you remove time," de Becker says, "you are subject to the lowest-quality intuitive reaction."

We don't often think about the role of time in life-or-death situations, perhaps because Hollywood has distorted our sense of what happens in a violent encounter. In the movies, gun battles are drawn-out affairs, where one cop has time to whisper dramatically to his partner, and the villain has time to call out a challenge, and the gunfight builds slowly to a devastating conclusion. Just telling the story of a gun battle makes what happened seem to have taken much longer than it did. Listen to de Becker describe the attempted assassination a few years ago of the president of South Korea: "The assassin stands up, and he shoots himself in the leg. That's how it starts. He's nervous out of his mind. Then he shoots at the president and he misses. Instead he hits the president's wife in the head. Kills the wife. The bodyguard gets up and shoots back. He misses. He hits an eight-year-old boy. It was a screw-up on all sides. Everything went wrong." How long do you think that whole sequence took? Fifteen seconds? Twenty seconds? No, three-point-five seconds.

I think that we become temporarily autistic also in situations when we run out of time. The psychologist Keith Payne, for instance, once sat people down in front of a computer and primed them — just like John Bargh did in the experiments described in chapter 2 — by flashing either a black face or a white face on a computer screen. Then Payne showed his subjects either a picture of a gun or a picture of a wrench. The image was on the screen for 200 milliseconds, and everyone was supposed to identify what he or she had just seen on the screen. It was an experiment inspired by the Diallo case. The results were what you might expect. If you are primed with a black face first, you'll identify the gun as a gun a little more quickly than if you are primed with a white face first. Then Payne redid his experiment, only this time he sped it up. Instead of letting people respond at their own pace, he forced them to make a decision within 500 milliseconds — half a second. Now people began to make errors. They were quicker to call a gun a gun when they saw a black face first. But when they saw a black face first, they were also quicker to call a wrench a gun. Under time pressure, they began to behave just as people do when they are highly aroused. They stopped relying on the actual evidence of their senses and fell back on a rigid and unyielding system, a stereotype.

"When we make a split-second decision," Payne says, "we are really vulnerable to being guided by our stereotypes and prejudices, even ones we may not necessarily endorse or believe." Payne has tried all kinds of techniques to reduce this bias. To try to put them on their best behavior, he told his subjects that their performance would be scrutinized later by a classmate. It made them even more biased. He told some people precisely what the experiment was about and told them explicitly to avoid stereotypes based on race. It didn't matter. The only thing that made a difference, Payne found, was slowing the experiment down and forcing people to wait a beat before identifying the object on the screen. Our powers of thin-slicing and snap judgments are extraordinary. But even the giant computer in our unconscious needs a moment to do its work. The art experts who judged the Getty kouros needed to *see* the kouros before they could tell whether it was a fake. If they had merely glimpsed the statue through a car window at sixty miles per hour, they could only have made a wild guess at its authenticity.

For this very reason, many police departments have moved, in recent years, toward one-officer squad cars instead of two-. That may sound like a bad idea, because surely having two officers work together makes more sense. Can't they provide backup for each other? Can't they more easily and safely deal with problematic situations? The answer in both cases is no. An officer with a partner is no safer than an officer on his own. Just as important, two-officer teams are more likely to have complaints filed against them. With two officers, encounters with citizens are far more likely to end in an arrest or an injury to whomever they are arresting or a charge of assaulting a police officer. Why? *Because when police officers are by themselves, they slow things down, and when they are with someone else, they speed things up.* "All cops want two-man cars," says de Becker. "You have a buddy, someone to talk to. But one-man cars get into less trouble because you reduce bravado. A cop by himself makes an approach that is entirely different. He is not as prone to ambush. He doesn't charge in. He says, 'I'm going to wait for the other cops to arrive.' He acts more kindly. He allows more time."

Would Russ, the young man in the car in Chicago, have ended up dead if he had been confronted by just one officer? It's hard to imagine that he would have. A single officer — even a single officer in the heat of the chase — would have had to pause and wait for backup. It was the false safety of numbers that gave the three officers the bravado to rush the car. "You've got to slow the situation down," Fyfe says. "We train people that time is on their side. In the Russ case, the lawyers for the other side were saying that this was a fast-breaking situation. But it was only fast-breaking because the cops let it become one. He was stopped. He wasn't going anywhere."

What police training does, at its best, is teach officers how to keep themselves out of this kind of trouble; to avoid the risk of momentary autism. In a traffic stop, for instance, the officer is trained to park behind the car. If it's at night, he shines his brights directly into the car. He walks toward the car on the driver's side, then stops and stands just behind the driver, shining his flashlight over the shoulder onto his or her lap. I've had this happen to me, and I always feel a bit like I'm being disrespected. Why can't the officer stand and talk to me face-to-face, like a normal human being? The reason is that it would be virtually impossible for me to pull a gun on the officer if he's standing behind me. First of all, the officer is shining his flashlight on my lap, so he can see where my hands are and whether I'm going for a gun. And even if I get my hands on the gun, I have to twist almost entirely around in my seat, lean out the window, and fire around the door pillar at the officer (and remember, I'm blinded by his brights) — and all this in his full view. The police procedure, in other words, is for my benefit: it means that the only way the officer will ever draw his gun on me is if I engage in a drawn-out and utterly unambiguous sequence of actions.

Fyfe once ran a project in Dade County, Florida, where there was an unusually high number of violent incidents between police officers and civilians. You can imagine the kind of tension that violence caused. Community groups accused the police of being insensitive and racist. The police responded with anger and defensiveness; violence, they said, was a tragic but inevitable part of police work. It was an all-too-familiar script. Fyfe's response, though, was to sidestep that controversy and conduct a study. He put observers in squad cars and had them keep a running score of how the officers' behavior matched up with proper training techniques. "It was things like, did the officer take advantage of available cover?" he said. "We train officers to make themselves the smallest possible target, so you leave it to the bad guy to decide whether they'll be shooting or not. So we were looking at things like, did the officer take advantage of available cover or did he just walk in the front door? Did he keep his gun away from the individual at all times? Did he keep his flashlight in his weak hand? In a burglary call, did they call back for more information or did they just say ten-four? Did they ask for backup? Did they coordinate their approach? — you know, you be the shooter, I'll cover you. Did they take a look around the neighborhood? Did they position another car at the back of the building? When they were inside the place, did they hold their flashlights off to the side? — because if the guy happens to be armed, he's going to shoot at the flashlight. On a traffic stop, did they look at the back of the car before approaching the driver? These kind of things."

What Fyfe found was that the officers were really good when they were face-to-face with a suspect and when they had the suspect in custody. In those situations, they did the "right" thing 92 percent of the time. But in their approach to the scene they were terrible, scoring just 15 percent. That was the problem. They didn't take the necessary steps to steer clear of temporary autism. And when Dade County zeroed in on improving what officers did *before they encountered the suspect,* the number of complaints against officers and the number of injuries to officers and civilians plummeted. "You don't want to put yourself in a position where the only way you have to defend yourself is to shoot someone," Fyfe says. "If you have to rely on your reflexes, someone is going to get hurt — and get hurt unnecessarily. If you take advantage of intelligence and cover, you will almost never have to make an instinctive decision."

7. "Something in My Mind Just Told Me I Didn't Have to Shoot Yet"

What is valuable about Fyfe's diagnosis is how it turns the usual discussion of police shootings on its head. The critics of police conduct invariably focus on the intentions of individual officers. They talk about racism and conscious bias. The defenders of the police, on the other hand, invariably take refuge in what Fyfe calls the split-second syndrome: An officer goes to the scene as quickly as possible. He sees the bad guy. There is no time for thought. He acts. That scenario requires that mistakes be accepted as unavoidable. In the end, both of these perspectives are defeatist. They accept as a given the fact that once any critical incident is in motion, there is nothing that can be done to stop or control it. And when our instinctive reactions are involved, that view is all too common. But that assumption is wrong. Our unconscious thinking is, in one critical respect, no different from our conscious thinking: in both, we are able to develop our rapid decision making with training and experience.

Are extreme arousal and mind-blindness inevitable under conditions of stress? Of course not. De Becker, whose firm provides security for public figures, puts his bodyguards through a program of what he calls stress inoculation. "In our test, the principal [the person being guarded] says, 'Come here, I hear a noise,' and as you come around the corner — boom! — you get shot. It's not with a real gun. The round is a plastic marking capsule, but you *feel* it. And then you have to continue to function. Then we say, 'You've got to do it again,' and this time, we shoot you as you are coming into the house. By the fourth or fifth time you get shot in simulation, you're okay." De Becker does a similar exercise where his trainees are required to repeatedly confront a ferocious dog. "In the beginning, their heart rate is 175. They can't see straight. Then the second or third time, it's 120, and then it's 110, and they can function." That kind of training, conducted over and over again, in combination with real-world experience, fundamentally changes the way a police officer reacts to a violent encounter.

Mind reading, as well, is an ability that improves with practice. Silvan Tomkins, maybe the greatest mind reader of them all, was compulsive about practicing. He took a sabbatical from Princeton when his son Mark was born and stayed in his house at the Jersey Shore, staring into his son's face long and hard, picking up the patterns of emotion — the cycles of interest, joy, sadness, and anger — that flash across an infant's face in the first few months of life. He put together a library of thousands of photographs of human faces in every conceivable expression and taught himself the logic of the furrows and the wrinkles and the creases, the subtle differences between the pre-smile and the pre-cry face.

Paul Ekman has developed a number of simple tests of people's mind-reading abilities; in one, he plays a short clip of a dozen or so people claiming to have done something that they either have or haven't actually done, and the test taker's task is to figure out who is lying. The tests are surprisingly difficult. Most people come out right at the level of chance. But who does well? People who have practiced. Stroke victims who have lost the ability to speak, for example, are virtuosos, because their infirmity has forced them to become far more sensitive to the information written on people's faces. People who have had highly abusive childhoods also do well; like stroke victims, they've had to practice the difficult art of reading minds, in their case the minds of alcoholic or violent parents. Ekman actually runs seminars for law-enforcement agencies in which he teaches people how to improve their mind-reading skills. With even half an hour of practice, he says, people can become adept at picking up microexpressions. "I have a training tape, and people love it," Ekman says. "They start it, and they can't see any of these expressions. Thirty-five minutes later, they can see them all. What that says is that this is an accessible skill."

In one of David Klinger's interviews, he talks to a veteran police officer who had been in violent situations many times in his career and who had on many occasions been forced to read the minds of others in moments of stress. The officer's account is a beautiful example of how a high-stress moment — in the right hands — can be utterly transformed: It was dusk. He was chasing a group of three teenaged gang members. One jumped the fence, the second ran in front of the car, and the third stood

stock-still before him, frozen in the light, no more than
ten feet away. "As I was getting out of the passenger side,"
the officer remembers, the kid:

> started digging in his waistband with his right hand.
> Then I could see that he was reaching into his crotch
> area, then that he was trying to reach toward his left thigh
> area, as if he was trying to grab something that was falling
> down his pants leg.
>
> He was starting to turn around toward me as he was
> fishing around in his pants. He was looking right at me
> and I was telling him not to move: "Stop! Don't move!
> Don't move! Don't move!" My partner was yelling at
> him too: "Stop! Stop! Stop!" As I was giving him com-
> mands, I drew my revolver. When I got about five feet
> from the guy, he came up with a chrome .25 auto. Then,
> as soon as his hand reached his center stomach area, he
> dropped the gun right on the sidewalk. We took him into
> custody, and that was that.
>
> I think the only reason I didn't shoot him was his
> age. He was fourteen, looked like he was nine. If he was
> an adult I think I probably would have shot him. I sure
> perceived the threat of that gun. I could see it clearly, that
> it was chrome and that it had pearl grips on it. But I knew
> that I had the drop on him, and I wanted to give him just
> a little more benefit of a doubt because he was so young
> looking. I think the fact that I was an experienced officer
> had a lot to do with my decision. I could see a lot of fear
> in his face, which I also perceived in other situations, and
> that led me to believe that if I would just give him just a
> little bit more time that he might give me an option to not
> shoot him. The bottom line was that I was looking at

him, looking at what was coming out of his pants leg, identifying it as a gun, seeing where that muzzle was gonna go when it came up. If his hand would've come out a little higher from his waistband, if the gun had just cleared his stomach area a little bit more, to where I would have seen that muzzle walk my way, it would've been over with. But the barrel never came up, and something in my mind just told me I didn't have to shoot yet.

How long was this encounter? Two seconds? One and a half seconds? But look at how the officer's experience and skill allowed him to stretch out that fraction of time, to slow the situation down, to keep gathering information until the last possible moment. He watches the gun come out. He sees the pearly grip. He tracks the direction of the muzzle. He waits for the kid to decide whether to pull the gun up or simply to drop it — and all the while, even as he tracks the progress of the gun, he is also watching the kid's face, to see whether he is dangerous or simply frightened. Is there a more beautiful example of a snap judgment? This is the gift of training and expertise — the ability to extract an enormous amount of meaningful information from the very thinnest slice of experience. To a novice, that incident would have gone by in a blur. But it wasn't a blur at all. Every moment — every blink — is composed of a series of discrete moving parts, and every one of those parts offers an opportunity for intervention, for reform, and for correction.

8. Tragedy on Wheeler Avenue

So there they were: Sean Carroll, Ed McMellon, Richard
Murphy, and Ken Boss. It was late. They were in the South
Bronx. They saw a young black man, and he seemed to be
behaving oddly. They were driving past, so they couldn't
see him well, but right away they began to construct a system to explain his behavior. He's not a big man, for instance. He's quite small. "What does small mean? It means
he's got a gun," says de Becker, imagining what flashed
through their minds. "He's out there alone. At twelve-
thirty in the morning. In this lousy neighborhood. Alone.
A black guy. He's got a gun; otherwise he wouldn't be
there. And he's little, to boot. Where's he getting the balls
to stand out there in the middle of the night? He's got a
gun. That's the story you tell yourself." They back the car
up. Carroll said later he was "amazed" that Diallo was still
standing there. Don't bad guys run at the sight of a car full
of police officers? Carroll and McMellon get out of the
car. McMellon calls out, "Police. Can we have a word?"
Diallo pauses. He is terrified, of course, and his terror is
written all over his face. Two towering white men, utterly
out of place in that neighborhood and at that time of night,
have confronted him. But the mind-reading moment is
lost because Diallo turns and runs back into the building.
Now it's a pursuit, and Carroll and McMellon are not experienced officers like the officer who watched the pearl-
handled revolver rise toward him. They are raw. They are
new to the Bronx and new to the Street Crime Unit and
new to the unimaginable stresses of chasing what they
think is an armed man down a darkened hallway. Their

heart rates soar. Their attention narrows. Wheeler Avenue is an old part of the Bronx. The sidewalk is flush with the curb, and Diallo's apartment building is flush with the sidewalk, separated by just a four-step stoop. There is no white space here. When they step out of the squad car and stand on the street, McMellon and Carroll are no more than ten or fifteen feet from Diallo. Now Diallo runs. It's a chase! Carroll and McMellon were just a little aroused before. What is their heart rate now? 175? 200? Diallo is now inside the vestibule, up against the inner door of his building. He twists his body sideways and digs at something in his pocket. Carroll and McMellon have neither cover nor concealment: there is no car door pillar to shield them, to allow them to slow the moment down. They are in the line of fire, and what Carroll sees is Diallo's hand and the tip of something black. As it happens, it is a wallet. But Diallo is black, and it's late, and it's the South Bronx, and time is being measured now in milliseconds, and under those circumstances we know that wallets invariably look like guns. Diallo's face might tell him something different, but Carroll isn't looking at Diallo's face — and even if he were, it isn't clear that he would understand what he saw there. He's not mind-reading now. He's effectively autistic. He's locked in on whatever it is coming out of Diallo's pocket, just as Peter was locked in on the light switch in George and Martha's kissing scene. Carroll yells out, "He's got a gun!" And he starts firing. McMellon falls backward and starts firing — and a man falling backward in combination with the report of a gun seems like it can mean only one thing. *He's been shot.* So Carroll keeps firing, and McMellon sees Carroll firing, so he keeps firing, and Boss and Murphy see Carroll and McMellon firing, so they jump out of the car and start firing, too. The papers the next day will make much of the fact that forty-one bullets were fired, but the truth is that four people with semiautomatic pistols can fire forty-one bullets in about two and a half seconds. The entire incident, in fact, from start to finish, was probably over in less time than it has taken you to read this paragraph. But packed inside those few seconds were enough steps and decisions to fill a lifetime. Carroll and McMellon call out to Diallo. *One thousand and one*. He turns back into the house. *One thousand and two*. They run after him, across the sidewalk and up the steps. *One thousand and three*. Diallo is in the hallway, tugging at something in his pocket. *One thousand and four*. Carroll yells out, "He's got a gun!" The shooting starts. *One thousand and five. One thousand and six.* Bang! Bang! Bang! *One thousand and seven.* Silence. Boss runs up to Diallo, looks down at the floor, and yells out, "Where's the fucking gun?" and then runs up the street toward Westchester Avenue, because he has lost track in the shouting and the shooting of where he is. Carroll sits down on the steps next to Diallo's bullet-ridden body and starts to cry.

Conclusion
Listening with Your Eyes:
The Lessons of Blink

At the beginning of her career as a professional musician, Abbie Conant was in Italy, playing trombone for the Royal Opera of Turin. This was in 1980. That summer, she applied for eleven openings for various orchestra jobs throughout Europe. She got one response: The Munich Philharmonic Orchestra. "Dear Herr Abbie Conant," the letter began. In retrospect, that mistake should have tripped every alarm bell in Conant's mind.

The audition was held in the Deutsches Museum in Munich, since the orchestra's cultural center was still under construction. There were thirty-three candidates, and each played behind a screen, making them invisible to the selection committee. Screened auditions were rare in Europe at that time. But one of the applicants was the son of someone in one of the Munich orchestras, so, for the sake of fairness, the Philharmonic decided to make the first round of auditions blind. Conant was number sixteen. She played Ferdinand David's Konzertino for Trombone, which is the warhorse audition piece in Germany, and missed one note (she cracked a G). She said to herself, "That's it," and went backstage and started packing up her belongings to go home. But the committee thought otherwise. They were floored. Auditions are classic thin-slicing moments. Trained classical musicians say that they can tell whether a player is good or not almost instantly — sometimes in just the first few bars, sometimes even with just the first note — and with Conant they knew. After she left the audition room, the Philharmonic's music director, Sergiu Celibidache, cried out, "That's who we want!" The remaining seventeen players, waiting their turn to audition, were sent home. Somebody went backstage to find Conant. She came back into the audition room, and when she stepped out from behind the screen, she heard the Bavarian equivalent of whoa. *"Was ist'n des? Sacra di! Meine Goetter! Um Gottes willen!"* They were expecting Herr Conant. This was Frau Conant.

It was an awkward situation, to say the least. Celibidache was a conductor from the old school, an imperious and strong-willed man with very definite ideas about how music ought to be played — and about who ought to play music. What's more, this was Germany, the land where classical music was born. Once, just after the Second World War, the Vienna Philharmonic experimented with an audition screen and ended up with what the orchestra's former chairman, Otto Strasser, described in his memoir as a "grotesque situation": "An applicant qualified himself as the best, and as the screen was raised, there stood a Japanese before the stunned jury." To Strasser, someone who was Japanese simply could not play with any soul or fidelity music that was composed by a European. To Celibidache, likewise, a woman could not play the trombone. The Munich Philharmonic had one or two women on the violin and the oboe. But those were "feminine" instruments. The trombone is masculine. It is the instrument that men played in military marching bands. Composers of operas used it to symbolize the underworld. In the Fifth and Ninth symphonies, Beethoven used the trombone as a noisemaker. "Even now if you talk to your typical professional trombonist," Conant says, "they will ask, 'What kind of *equipment* do you play?' Can you imagine a violinist saying, 'I play a Black and Decker'?"

There were two more rounds of auditions. Conant passed both with flying colors. But once Celibidache and the rest of the committee saw her in the flesh, all those long-held prejudices began to compete with the winning first impression they had of her performance. She joined the orchestra, and Celibidache stewed. A year passed. In May of 1981, Conant was called to a meeting. She was to be demoted to second trombone, she was told. No reason was given. Conant went on probation for a year, to prove herself again. It made no difference. "You know the problem," Celibidache told her. "We need a man for the solo trombone."

Conant had no choice but to take the case to court. In its brief, the orchestra argued, "The plaintiff does not possess the necessary physical strength to be a leader of the trombone section." Conant was sent to the Gautinger Lung Clinic for extensive testing. She blew through special machines, had a blood sample taken to measure her capacity for absorbing oxygen, and underwent a chest exam. She scored well above average. The nurse even asked if she was an athlete. The case dragged on. The orchestra claimed that Conant's "shortness of breath was overhearable" in her performance of the famous trombone solo in Mozart's *Requiem,* even though the guest conductor of those performances had singled out Conant for praise. A special audition in front of a trombone expert was set up. Conant played seven of the most difficult passages in the trombone repertoire. The expert was effusive. The orchestra claimed that she was unreliable and unprofessional. It was a lie. After eight years, she was reinstated as first trombone.

But then another round of battles began — that would last another five years — because the orchestra refused to pay her on par with her male colleagues. She won, again. She prevailed on every charge, and she prevailed because she could mount an argument that the Munich Philharmonic could not rebut. Sergiu Celibidache, the man complaining about her ability, had listened to her play Ferdinand David's Konzertino for Trombone under conditions of perfect objectivity, and in that unbiased moment, he had said, *"That's who we want!"* and sent the remaining trombonists packing. Abbie Conant was saved by the screen.

1. A Revolution in Classical Music

The world of classical music — particularly in its European home — was until very recently the preserve of white men. Women, it was believed, simply could not play like men. They didn't have the strength, the attitude, or the resilience for certain kinds of pieces. Their lips were different. Their lungs were less powerful. Their hands were smaller. That did not seem like a prejudice. It seemed like a fact, because when conductors and music directors and maestros held auditions, the men always seemed to sound better than the women. No one paid much attention to how auditions were held, because it was an article of faith that one of the things that made a music expert a music expert was that he could listen to music played under any circumstances and gauge, instantly and objectively, the quality of the performance. Auditions for major orchestras were sometimes held in the conductor's dressing room, or in his hotel room if he was passing through town. Performers played for five minutes or two minutes or ten minutes. What did it matter? Music was music. Rainer Kuchl, the concertmaster of the Vienna Philharmonic, once said he could instantly tell the difference with his eyes closed between, say, a male and female violinist. The trained ear, he believed, could pick up the softness and flexibility of the female style.

But over the past few decades, the classical music world has undergone a revolution. In the United States, orchestra musicians began to organize themselves politically. They formed a union and fought for proper contracts, health benefits, and protections against arbitrary firing, and along with that came a push for fairness in hiring. Many musicians thought that conductors were abusing their power and playing favorites. They wanted the audition process to be formalized. That meant an official audition committee was established instead of a conductor making the decision all by himself. In some places, rules were put in place forbidding the judges from speaking among themselves during auditions, so that one person's opinion would not cloud the view of another. Musicians were identified not by name but by number. Screens were erected between the committee and the auditioner, and if the person auditioning cleared his or her throat or made any kind of identifiable sound — if they were wearing heels, for example, and stepped on a part of the floor that wasn't carpeted — they were ushered out and given a new number. And as these new rules were put in place around the country, an extraordinary thing happened: orchestras began to hire women.

In the past thirty years, since screens became commonplace, the number of women in the top U.S. orchestras has increased fivefold. "The very first time the new rules for auditions were used, we were looking for four new violinists," remembers Herb Weksleblatt, a tuba player for the Metropolitan Opera in New York, who led the fight for blind auditions at the Met in the mid-1960s. "And all of the winners were women. That would simply never have happened before. Up until that point, we had maybe three women in the whole orchestra. I remember that after it was announced that the four women had won, one guy was absolutely furious at me. He said, 'You're going to be remembered as the SOB who brought women into this orchestra.'"

What the classical music world realized was that what they had thought was a pure and powerful first impression — listening to someone play — was in fact hopelessly corrupted. "Some people look like they sound better than they actually sound, because they look confident and have good posture," one musician, a veteran of many auditions, says. "Other people look awful when they play but sound great. Other people have that belabored look when they play, but you can't hear it in the sound. There is always this dissonance between what you see and hear. The audition begins the first second the person is in view. You think, Who is this nerd? Or, Who does this guy think he is? — just by the way they walk out with their instrument."

Julie Landsman, who plays principal French horn for the Metropolitan Opera in New York, says that she's found herself distracted by the position of someone's mouth. "If they put their mouthpiece in an unusual position, you might immediately think, Oh my God, it can't possibly work. There are so many possibilities. Some horn players use a brass instrument, and some use nickel-silver, and the kind of horn the person is playing tells you something about what city they come from, their teacher, and their school, and that pedigree is something that influences your opinion. I've been in auditions without screens, and I can assure you that I was prejudiced. I began to listen with my eyes, and there is no way that your eyes don't affect your judgment. The only true way to listen is with your ears and your heart."

In Washington, D.C., the National Symphony Orchestra hired Sylvia Alimena to play the French horn. Would she have been hired before the advent of screens? Of course not. The French horn — like the trombone — is a "male" instrument. More to the point, Alimena is tiny.

She's five feet tall. In truth, that's an irrelevant fact. As another prominent horn player says, "Sylvia can blow a house down." But if you were to look at her before you really listened to her, you would not be able to hear that power, because what you saw would so contradict what you heard. There is only one way to make a proper snap judgment of Sylvia Alimena, and that's from behind a screen.

2. A Small Miracle

There is a powerful lesson in classical music's revolution. Why, for so many years, were conductors so oblivious to the corruption of their snap judgments? Because we are often careless with our powers of rapid cognition. We don't know where our first impressions come from or precisely what they mean, so we don't always appreciate their fragility. Taking our powers of rapid cognition seriously means we have to acknowledge the subtle influences that can alter or undermine or bias the products of our unconscious. Judging music sounds like the simplest of tasks. It is not, any more than sipping cola or rating chairs or tasting jam is easy. Without a screen, Abbie Conant would have been dismissed before she played a note. With a screen, she was suddenly good enough for the Munich Philharmonic.

And what did orchestras do when confronted with their prejudice? They solved the problem, and that's the second lesson of *Blink*. Too often we are resigned to what happens in the blink of an eye. It doesn't seem like we have much control over whatever bubbles to the surface from our unconscious. But we do, and if we can control the environment in which rapid cognition takes place, then we can control rapid cognition. We can prevent the people fighting wars or staffing emergency rooms or policing the streets from making mistakes.

"If I was coming to see a work of art, I used to ask dealers to put a black cloth over it, and then whip it off when I walked in, and *blam*, so I could have total concentration on that particular thing," says Thomas Hoving. "At the Met, I'd have my secretary or another curator take a new thing we were thinking of buying and stick it somewhere where I'd be surprised to see it, like a coat closet, so I'd open the door and there it would be. And I'd either feel good about it or suddenly I'd see something that I hadn't noticed before." Hoving valued the fruits of spontaneous thinking so much that he took special steps to make sure his early impressions were as good as possible. He did not look at the power of his unconscious as a magical force. He looked at it as something he could protect and control and educate — and when he caught his first glimpse of the kouros, Hoving was ready.

The fact that there are now women playing for symphony orchestras is not a trivial change. It matters because it has opened up a world of possibility for a group that had been locked out of opportunity. It also matters because by fixing the first impression at the heart of the audition — by judging purely on the basis of ability — orchestras now hire better musicians, and better musicians mean better music. And how did we get better music? Not by rethinking the entire classical music enterprise or building new concert halls or pumping in millions of new dollars, but by paying attention to the tiniest detail, the first two seconds of the audition.

When Julie Landsman auditioned for the role of principal French horn at the Met, the screens had just gone up in the practice hall. At the time, there were no women in the brass section of the orchestra, because everyone "knew" that women could not play the horn as well as men. But Landsman came and sat down and played — and she played well. "I knew in my last round that I had won before they told me," she says. "It was because of the way I performed the last piece. I held on to the last high C for a very long time, just to leave no doubt in their minds. And they started to laugh, because it was above and beyond the call of duty." But when they declared her the winner and she stepped out from behind the screen, there was a gasp. It wasn't just that she was a woman, and female horn players were rare, as had been the case with Conant. And it wasn't just that bold, extended high C, which was the kind of macho sound that they expected from a man only. It was because they *knew* her. Landsman had played for the Met before as a substitute. Until they listened to her with just their ears, however, they had no idea she was so good. When the screen created a pure *Blink* moment, a small miracle happened, the kind of small miracle that is always possible when we take charge of the first two seconds: they saw her for who she truly was.

Afterword

1. The Lesson of Chancellorsville

One of the most famous battles of the American Civil War took place in the spring of 1863 in the northern Virginia town of Chancellorsville. It pitted the legendary Confederate general Robert E. Lee against "Fighting Joe" Hooker, commander of the Union's Army of the Potomac. Lee was by then well into his fifties and of uncertain health. He was a devout and principled man, with a long, somber face and a full gray beard. He was revered by his troops and had demonstrated by that point in the war an unmatched tactical genius. His opponent, Hooker, was his antithesis. Hooker was young, tall, and fair. "He was a bachelor and liked the company of women," the historian Gary Gallagher says. "Charles Francis Adams has a famous quotation that Hooker's headquarters was part barroom and part brothel and no decent person would have business there." Under his command, the Army of the Potomac had been transformed from a ragged, ill-disciplined group into what Hooker called "the finest body of soldiers the sun ever shone on." That was typical Hooker. He did not lack for self-confidence. "It is no vanity in me to say I am a damned sight better general than you had on that field," he told Lincoln after the Battle of Bull Run. And when he confronted Lee in the spring of 1863, he was even more sure of himself. "My plans are perfect," he said before committing his troops to battle. "And when I start to carry them out, may God have mercy on Bobby Lee, for I shall have none."

The situation at Chancellorsville was quite simple. The top half of Virginia is bisected by the Rappahannock River, which meanders from the Blue Ridge Mountains in the north and empties into Chesapeake Bay. In 1863, in the third year of the Civil War, Lee had dug in along the southern banks of the Rappahannock, midway between Richmond, the capital of the Confederacy, and, to the north, Washington, D.C., where President Lincoln anxiously awaited news of the war's progress. Lee had 61,000 men in his army and was assisted by another of the Confederacy's legendary commanders, Stonewall Jackson. Hooker faced Lee across the river, and he had under his command 134,000 men and twice as many artillery pieces. One obvious option for Hooker would have been to charge across the river at Lee directly, hoping to overwhelm him with superior numbers. But Hooker decided on something far more elegant. He took about half of his troops and had them march fifteen miles upriver, then stealthily cross the Rappahannock and march back, until they were massed directly behind Lee's army at a cross-roads known as Chancellorsville. Hooker's position was unassailable. He had Lee in a vise: Lee had a larger army in front of him and a larger army behind him.

Hooker also had intelligence that was vastly superior to Lee's. He had a network of spies throughout the Confederate army, whose intelligence allowed him to do what even today seems extraordinary — that is, move 70,000 troops into position behind his enemy's army without his enemy's knowledge. What's more, he had two hot-air balloons at his disposal, which he sent up periodically to provide almost perfect aerial reconnaissance of Lee's positions. The Battle of Chancellorsville was a fight that, by any normal measure, ought to have been won by the Union army in a rout. When Hooker joined his troops at Chancellorsville, he gathered them around and read to them his final orders: "It is with heartfelt satisfaction that the commanding general announces to the army that the operations of the last three days have determined that our enemy must either ingloriously fly, or come out from behind his own defenses and give us battle on our own ground, where certain destruction awaits."

But when the battle began, what had seemed perfectly clear-cut in the planning stage quickly turned murky. Hooker thought that Lee, faced with such a dire situation, would retreat in the only direction he could — back to Richmond — and that in the chaos of retreat, his army would be a sitting duck for the pursuing Union forces. This is the scenario that he had thought about and talked about and that had hardened in his mind. But Lee did not

retreat. Instead, he divided his forces and turned, unexpectedly, to face Hooker at Chancellorsville. Hooker had
the advantage of position and numbers. But now he was
thrown into confusion. Lee was not acting like a man
heavily outnumbered. He was acting like a man with a nu-
merical advantage. A number of Confederate deserters
were captured by the Union forces, and they said that
another Confederate general, James Longstreet, had come
to Lee's defense with massive reinforcements. Was this
true? The fact is that it wasn't, but Hooker was confused.
On paper, he had an insurmountable advantage over Lee.
But the battle was not being fought on paper. It was being
fought in the moment. He told his troops to halt, then
to withdraw. He ceded his battlefield advantage. "It's all
right," Hooker told Darius Couch, one of his generals, in
an attempt to put a brave face on the situation. "I've got
Lee just where I want him. He must fight me on my own
ground." But Couch was not fooled. "I retired from his
presence," he would say later, "with the belief that my
commander was a whipped man."

Lee sensed that weakness as well. So he acted without
hesitation. He divided his army again and set Stonewall
Jackson, under cover of darkness and fog, to creep far
around Hooker's flank and attack at the farthest edge of
Hooker's position, where the Union army felt it was most
invulnerable. At just after five o'clock in the afternoon,
Lee's forces attacked. Hooker's troops were eating supper.
Their rifles were off to the side, stacked in piles. Lee's
troops came screaming out of the surrounding forest, bay-
onets drawn, and Hooker's army turned and ran. It was
one of the most devastating defeats of the Civil War.

2. *Paul Van Riper's War*

Of all the interviews I conducted while researching *Blink*, the one that made the most lasting impression on me was my interview with General Paul Van Riper — the hero (or villain) of the Pentagon's Millennium Challenge war game. Van Riper lives just outside Williamsburg, in Virginia, in the kind of immaculate, orderly house that one would expect of a career military man. I remember being surprised when he took me on a tour of his house by the number of books in his study. In retrospect, of course, that's a silly thing to find surprising. Why shouldn't a Marine Corps general have as many books as an English professor? I suppose that I had blithely assumed that generals were people who charged around and "did" things; that they were men of action, men of the moment. But one of the things that Van Riper taught me was that being able to act intelligently and instinctively in the moment is possible only after a long and rigorous course of education and experience. Van Riper beat Blue Team because of what he had learned about waging war in the jungles of Vietnam. And he also beat Blue Team because of what he had learned in that library of his. Van Riper was a student of military history. And what was the student's favorite battle? Chancellorsville.

Van Riper brought up Chancellorsville when I met him at his house, and then again later, when we talked on the phone. But it wasn't until my book was finished and about to come out that I actually went to the library and read histories of that battle for myself. Almost immediately I understood why Van Riper was so taken by the showdown between Hooker and Lee. Here was a battle between two armies, and we think we know how to make sense of contests like this. We count the number of soldiers on each side. We compare the size and quality of each army's arsenal. We compare strategy; the quality of each side's military intelligence; the strength of their positions — and then we total up each side's advantages and disadvantages like we're doing an arithmetic problem. What Chancellorsville tells us, though, is that in the real world — when it comes to fast-moving, high-stakes situations like battlefields (or emergency rooms, or auditions, or late-night shoot-outs in the Bronx) — that kind of formal, conventional analysis doesn't help that much. Chancellorsville came down to some ineffable, magical decision-making ability that Lee possessed and Hooker did not.

What was that magical thing? It's the same thing that Evelyn Harrison and Tom Hoving had when they looked at the kouros, and that Vic Braden had when he watched someone serving and knew if the ball was going to go out. It's the kind of wisdom that someone acquires after a lifetime of learning and watching and doing. It's *judgment*. And what *Blink* is — what all the stories and studies and arguments add up to — is an attempt to understand this magical and mysterious thing called judgment.

Think about Lee. His ability to sense Hooker's indecision, to act on the spur of the moment, to conjure up a battle plan that would take Hooker by surprise — his ability, in other words, to move quickly and instinctively on the field of battle — was so critical that it is what made it possible for him to defeat an army twice the size of his. Judgment *matters:* it is what separates winners from losers. Now think about Hooker. He wasn't a fool, and he wasn't a coward.

He was an experienced general. So, what happened to him? Why, on the brink of victory, did he falter? This is a question that many historians have considered. Here is Harry Hansen's view, from his magisterial history, *The Civil War*:

> Perhaps Hooker at last had recalled Lincoln's admonition, "Beware of rashness." Perhaps at this critical juncture he missed the artificial stimulus of whiskey, which formerly had been part of his daily ration but which he had abjured on taking command. Perhaps he mistrusted his already considerable accomplishment in putting more than 70,000 soldiers in Lee's immediate rear, with practically no losses because he had met practically no resistance. It had been altogether too easy; Lee must have wanted him where he was, or at any rate where he had been headed before he called a halt and ordered a pullback. Or perhaps it was simpler than that. Perhaps he was badly frightened (not physically frightened — Hooker was never that — but morally frightened) after the manner of the bullfighter Gallo who, according to Hemingway, "was the inventor of refusing to kill the bull if the bull looked at him in a certain way." This Gallo had a long career, featuring many farewell performances, and at the first of these, having fought the animal bravely and well, when the time came for killing . . . he turned, sword in hand, and approached the bull, which was standing there, head down, looking at him. Gallo returned to the *barerra*. "You take him, Paco," he told a fellow matador; "I don't like the way he looks at me." So it was with Hooker, perhaps, when he heard that Lee had turned in his direction and was, so to speak, looking at him.

Hansen is saying that, as a sports fan would put it, Hooker choked, and I hope that after reading this far, you recognize the characteristic signs of judgment's fragility. From experience, we gain a powerful gift, the ability to act instinctively, in the moment. But — and this is one of the lessons I tried very hard to impart in *Blink* — it is easy to disrupt this gift. The four officers in the Amadou Diallo case had their judgment derailed by the color of Diallo's skin and the lack of white space and the physiologically disruptive trajectory of those seven seconds. Were they bad people, or bad police officers? I don't think so. But I do think that they were in a situation that brought out the absolute worst in their decision making. So was Hooker. Can you imagine the pressure he was under? He had Abraham Lincoln, back in the White House, counting on him to hold off the Confederate march toward Washington. And there he was, face-to-face with the most legendary military mind of his generation.

"It's a classic example of two army commanders reaching a point of crisis, and one giving way," says Gallagher. "It's an instance of Hooker being overawed by Lee. Lee had this effect on everyone. You play hoping you'll look good en route to defeat. I don't think there was an expectation of victory in Hooker's heart of hearts. He suspected he would not win a battle with Lee. He hoped Lee would retreat and simplify his life, and Lee didn't simplify anyone's life."

After I read the historical accounts of Chancellorsville, I felt about Hooker the same way I felt about the four officers in the Diallo case when I first read through the testimony about that night in the Bronx. I felt sorry for him. This is the second lesson of *Blink:* understanding the true nature of instinctive decision making requires us to be forgiving of those people trapped in circumstances where good judgment is imperiled.

There's a third lesson in the Chancellorsville story, and in the time since *Blink* was published I've come to think that it is the most important lesson of all. Lee outthought Hooker, even though he knew far less about Hooker's army than Hooker knew about his. Hooker was the one who knew exactly how many soldiers his enemy had. Hooker was the one who had two hot-air balloons up in the sky giving him perfect aerial reconnaissance of his enemy's positions. Lee won the battle despite knowing less than Hooker. But now that you've read *Blink*, you'll know that I think we ought to turn that sentence around, and say that probably Lee won the battle *because* he knew less than Hooker.

Remember the Getty? The people at the museum "knew" far more about the kouros than Thomas Hoving and Evelyn Harrison did. But all the pages and pages of documentation they had gathered from the lawyers and geologists and archeologists didn't help them in the end. It hurt them. In the case of the classical musicians' auditions, the maestros were incapable of making a fair judgment about how well someone was playing if they could see them. It was only when the screen went up that the maestros' judgment was restored. Think about it. How much of the "information" in an audition is visual? Seventy percent? Eighty percent? It's mostly visual. An audition is supposed to be an exercise in listening. But mostly what we do is look. How is the musician dressed? Is she tall or short? How does she hold her instrument? How does she carry herself while she's playing? In the classical music world, 80 percent of the information available to the maestros was removed, and lo and behold, the maestros suddenly exercised much better judgment.

As I've talked to people about *Blink* over the past few years, I've been amazed at how often this point has come up. In fact, I would venture to say that no argument in the book has resonated more with readers than this one. We live in a world saturated with information. We have virtually unlimited amounts of data at our fingertips at all times, and we're well versed in the arguments about the dangers of not knowing enough and not doing our homework. But what I have sensed is an enormous frustration with the unexpected costs of knowing too much, of being inundated with information. We have come to confuse information with understanding.

I recently ran across a marvelous book by the historian Roberta Wohlstetter called *Pearl Harbor: Warning and Decision*. At Pearl Harbor, the American intelligence community was taken completely by surprise by the Japanese military. But as Wohlstetter points out, that wasn't because the American military didn't know enough about Japan's intentions. On the contrary, it knew an enormous amount. The U.S. military had, in fact, broken many of the key Japanese codes. *They were reading the Japanese military's mail.* And that, she argues, was the problem. The military's analysts were overwhelmed with information. They would come in in the morning and there would be a stack of reports in their in-boxes a foot high. They couldn't see the forest for the trees. Meanwhile, who did the best job in predicting what the Japanese were up to in the summer and fall of 1941? Journalists. If all you had done was read the *New York Times,* you would have been in a better position to understand Japan's intentions than if you had had access to all of the military's secret reports. That's not because journalists knew more about Japan. It's because they knew less: they had the ability to sort through what they knew and find a pattern.

I read Wohlstetter's book right around the time that all of the 9/11 postmortems were being conducted. Everyone in Congress was standing up and complaining that the Central Intelligence Agency and the Federal Bureau of Investigation and the National Security Agency didn't know enough about terrorist activity, and proposing that we needed to expand and strengthen our intelligence-gathering capability. Really? All I could think of was Pearl Harbor and Millennium Challenge and, of course, Chancellorsville. Hooker knew everything he could possibly know about his enemy. But it didn't help him. The key to good decision making is not knowledge. It is understanding. We are swimming in the former. We are desperately lacking in the latter.

One last thing about Paul Van Riper. I met him before the start of the Iraq War. Neither of us had any idea about what was going to happen over the next few years. But the storm clouds were already brewing in the Middle East, and I will always remember what Van Riper said. The prospect of fighting a war in Iraq made him nervous, he told me. People in Washington at that point were talking about a short and triumphant war, one that could be fought and won quickly and easily. But nothing in Van Riper's experience made him think that was possible, and he believed that before we set off to conquer Baghdad, we ought to be honest about how long and hard the war would be. Van Riper told me that many of his retired compatriots from the Army and the Marine Corps felt the same way. He and the other old military hands had looked at Iraq and knew what was coming in the same way that Evelyn Harrison and Tom Hoving had only had to look at the kouros to see the truth. Thinking back on my visit with Van Riper, I wish that he could have shared his gut instinct about Iraq with the rest of America as well.

3. When to Blink — And When to Think

About a year after *Blink* was published, *Science* — one of the most prestigious academic journals in the world — published the results of an experiment conducted by the psychologist Ap Dijksterhuis and a number of his colleagues at the University of Amsterdam. Dijksterhuis drew up a description of four hypothetical cars and gave the performance of each of them in four different categories. So, for example, car number one was described as having good mileage, good handling, a large trunk, and a poor sound system, while car number two was described as having good mileage and a large trunk but was old and handled poorly. Of the four, one was clearly the best. The question was: How often would consumers, asked to choose among the four alternatives, pick the right car? Dijksterhuis gave the test to eighty volunteers, flashing the car's characteristics on a screen in front of them. Each test taker was given four minutes to puzzle over the problem and then was asked for an answer. Well over half of the test takers chose the right car.

Then he had another group of people take the same test, except that this time, after giving them all of the information, he distracted them by having them do anagrams.

After a four-minute interval, he posed to them the same question, seemingly out of the blue: Which car do you want? Well under half of the test takers chose the right car. In other words, if you have to make a decision, you've got to take your time and think about it first. Otherwise, you'll make the wrong choice. Right?

Not quite. Dijksterhuis went back and redid his experiment, only this time he classified the cars in twelve different categories. What was once a simple choice was now a complicated one. And what happened? The people given four minutes to deliberate got the right answer a mere 20 percent of the time. Those who were distracted by doing anagrams — those who were forced to make an unconscious, spontaneous gut decision — chose the best car 60 percent of the time.

One of the questions that I've been asked over and over again since *Blink* came out is, When should we trust our instincts, and when should we consciously think things through? Well, here is a partial answer. On straightforward choices, deliberate analysis is best. When questions of analysis and personal choice start to get complicated — when we have to juggle many different variables — then our unconscious thought processes may be superior. Now, I realize that this is exactly contrary to conventional wisdom. We typically regard our snap judgment as best on immediate trivial questions. Is that person attractive? Do I want that candy bar? But Dijksterhuis is suggesting the opposite: that maybe that big computer in our brain that handles our unconscious is at its best when it has to juggle many competing variables.

Dijksterhuis did another similar experiment, only this time in the real world. He questioned shoppers coming out of a Dutch department store called De Bijenkorf, which sells relatively low-cost items, like kitchen accessories. He asked them how long they had deliberated before they bought what they bought. Then he called all the shoppers a few weeks later to find out how happy they were with their purchases. Sure enough, the people who had thought the most before buying were the most satisfied, and those who had made impulse purchases more often regretted their decision. For the second half of the experiment, Dijksterhuis went to the furniture store IKEA, where people were making much more complicated and expensive purchases. Now the reverse was true. A few weeks later, the thinkers were least happy, and those who had gone with their gut instinct were the happiest. Dijksterhuis argues that his findings represent a fundamental principle of human cognition, and that "there is no a priori reason to assume that [it] does not generalize to other types of choices — political, managerial, or otherwise." Not long after I read the *Science* study, a reader sent me the following quotation from Sigmund Freud. It seems that the father of the unconscious agreed: "When making a decision of minor importance, I have always found it advantageous to consider all the pros and cons. In vital matters, however, such as the choice of a mate or a profession, the decision should come from the unconscious, from somewhere within ourselves. In the important decisions of personal life, we should be governed, I think, by the deep inner needs of our nature."

You may have noticed that I called the Dijksterhuis study a "partial answer" to the question of when to draw on our instincts and when to rely on conscious analysis. The truth is that this is not a question that I — or anyone else, for that matter — can answer definitively. It's just too complicated. The best we can do, I think, is try to puzzle out the right mix of conscious and unconscious analysis on a case-by-case basis.

Take, for instance, the efforts at Cook County Hospital to help emergency room doctors better diagnose chest pain. There, the initial instincts of physicians about who was suffering a heart attack weren't very good. So, what happened? Lee Goldman sat down with a powerful computer program and plowed through mountains of data on heart attack victims until he managed to identify a few key factors that seemed to be most diagnostic of chest pain. Then Brendan Reilly took that research and used it to reeducate the instincts of his doctors. It is important to note that Reilly wasn't looking to replace the instincts of his physicians. He still needed them to make a thousand instant judgments about who the patient was, what he or she needed, what was wrong if the patient wasn't having a heart attack, what the best treatment was, and so on. Reilly was simply saying that in this particular instance, the best decision making came from using rational computer analysis to do what rational analysis does best — find statistical patterns in mountains of data — and using human clinical judgment to do what clinical judgment does best — apply general statistical lessons to the particulars of a situation and a person.

I think that the task of figuring out how to combine the best of conscious deliberation and instinctive judgment is one of the great challenges of our time. If you're a teacher and you want to make a decision about how to treat a student, how much do you weigh the results of standardized tests, and how much do you weigh your own judgment about the student's motivation and attitude and prospects? If you're an entrepreneur gambling on a new product, how do you weigh the intelligence you get from rational analysis of the existing marketplace against your own instincts about the potential of your new idea?

Not long ago, I reviewed a fascinating book for *The New Yorker* magazine. It was called *The Wages of Wins*, and it was an attempt by three economists (David Berri, Martin Schmidt, and Stacey Brook) to come up with a more sophisticated statistical measure for rating professional basketball players. The trio developed what they called a Win Score, which was a rating system based on combining points and assists and rebounds and turnovers and shooting percentages in a complicated equation. And what they found was that when you run the Win Score equation for professional basketball players, a number of people who are thought to be really good end up looking pretty mediocre, and a number of players thought to be mediocre turn out to look surprisingly good. One of their most prominent examples was the former Philadelphia 76er Allen Iverson, the perennial all-star and one-time NBA Most Valuable Player. The consensus among fans is that Iverson is one of the top players in the league. The economists' analysis was that he wasn't even in the top fifty. Using a tool based on rational analysis turns our intuitions upside down.

In the aftermath of my article, I was inundated with skeptical e-mails. A large number of sports fans, it turned out, refused to believe that a set of statistical tools could help them understand how good a basketball player someone was. They thought that their instincts were a much better guide to that question. And isn't that what the author of *Blink* ought to believe as well?

Not quite. In fact, evaluating basketball players is a very good example of what I've been talking about here — the necessity of understanding when to rely on our instincts and when not to. If you think about it, there are two very different ways to evaluate an athlete. The first is the athlete's performance: that is, how well he or she has played in a specific game, or series, or season. To make this kind of assessment, it's very hard to rely on instinctive judgments. For one thing, instinctive judgments rely on experience, and we don't experience everything that happens on a basketball court or a baseball diamond. We miss things. We can't see every game or even everything that happens in one game. Furthermore, a lot of the things that we try to measure are awfully subtle. As the economists point out, the baseball legend Ty Cobb had a lifetime batting average of .366, almost thirty points higher than the former San Diego Padres outfielder Tony Gwynn, who had a lifetime batting average of .338: "So Cobb hit safely 37 percent of the time while Gwynn hit safely on 34 percent of his at bats. If all you did was watch these players, could you say who was a better hitter? Can one really tell the difference between 37 percent and 34 percent just staring at the players' play? To see the problem with the non-numbers approach to player evaluation, consider that out of every 100 at bats, Cobb got three more hits than Gwynn. That's it, three hits." This is why we keep statistics in sports, and why it makes sense to do a computer analysis of all the factors that go into diagnosing heart attacks. There are some situations where the human mind needs a little help.

But understanding someone's statistical performance in a game is only one small part of understanding how good an athlete that person is. There is also the broader issue of ability. How good is he at the myriad of skills and attributes that it takes to be a successful athlete? How hard does he work? Is he a good teammate? Does he stay out all night drinking and doing drugs, or does he take his job seriously? Is he willing to learn from his coaches? How resilient is he in the face of adversity? When the pressure is greatest and the game is on the line, how well does he perform? Is he someone likely to be better over time or has he already peaked? I think that we would all agree that these kinds of questions are much more complicated than — and every bit as important as — simple statistical measures of performance, particularly when it comes to the rarefied world of professional sports. Imagine that you were looking at a seventeen-year-old Michael Jordan. He wasn't the tallest or the biggest basketball player, nor the best jumper. His statistics weren't the finest in the country. What set Michael Jordan apart from his peers was his attitude and motivation. And those qualities can't be measured with formal tests and statistics. They can be measured only by exercising judgment, by an expert with long years of experience, drawing on that big database in his or her unconscious and concluding, yes, they have it, or no, they don't. The very best and most successful basketball teams — like the best and most successful organizations of any kind — are the ones that understand how to combine rational analysis with instinctive judgment. The Getty wasn't wrong to bring in the lawyers and the geologists and the archeologists. They were wrong to rely *only* on that kind of expertise.

4. A Call to Action

In my first book, *The Tipping Point,* I tried to lay out a plan of action for people interested in creating social change. It wasn't quite a formula (because I think the world is much too mysterious for formulas). But it was intended as a kind of guidebook. *Blink* is clearly a different kind of book. It wasn't intended as a call to action in nearly the same way. I thought of it more as a simple adventure story — a journey into the wonders of our unconscious. But in the time since the book has come out, as I've talked to readers and revisited some of my ideas, I've come to believe that there is a social agenda in *Blink* as well.

The story I think back on the most is the one from the conclusion: the tale of blind auditions and Abbie Conant's confrontation with the Munich Philharmonic. I'm drawn to it for a very simple reason: the classical music world had a problem — *and they fixed it.* Before the advent of blind auditions, the percentage of women in major symphony orchestras in the United States was less than 5 percent. Today, twenty-five years later, it's close to 50 percent. This is not a trivial accomplishment. Suppose that back before the advent of screens, you and I had been on a committee charged with addressing the terrible problem of discrimination against women in major symphony orchestras. What would we have proposed? I think we would have talked about creating affirmative action programs for women in the music world. I think we would have talked about awareness programs for gender bias, and how to teach female musicians to be more assertive in making the case for their own ability. We would have had long discussions about social discrimination. I think, in other words, that our suggestions for change would have been fairly global and long-term. Think about what we would have been dealing with, after all. Orchestras are run by maestros, and maestros are powerful, brilliant, single-minded, highly entrenched men who run their organizations like their own private fiefdoms. It's not as if we can walk up to the maestro and say, "Maestro, you don't know me, and, to be honest, I don't know that much about classical music. But I really think the reason you aren't hiring women is that you are in the grip of some powerful, buried biases against women." I suspect, at the end of long days of meetings, we would probably have thrown up our hands and said that we would just have to wait until the current generation of maestros — with their ingrained biases against women — was replaced by a younger, and hopefully more open-minded, set of conductors.

But what happened instead? Experts in the classical music world tackled the problem by addressing the way in which the instinctive judgments in auditions were made. They didn't fixate on the person making the snap decision. They examined the context — the unconscious circumstances — in which the snap decision was being made. They put up screens. And that solved the problem then and there.

If I have any goal for *Blink*, it is that it will encourage this kind of practical problem solving. Let me give you an example. One of the striking characteristics of the criminal justice system in the United States is how much more likely blacks are to be arrested and convicted and imprisoned for crimes than whites are. I'm not talking here about racial differences in overall crime rates. What I'm talking about is this: if, for example, a white man and a black man are charged with the identical drug-related crime, the black man is far more likely than the white man to go to jail. How much more likely? Here is an excerpt from a recent report by the nonprofit group Human Rights Watch: "Nationwide, the rate of drug admissions to state prison for black men is thirteen times greater than the rate for white men. In ten states black men are sent to state prison on drug charges at rates that are 26 to 57 times greater than those of white men in the same state. In Illinois, for example, the state with the highest rate of black male drug offender admissions to prison, a black man is 57 times more likely to be sent to prison on drug charges than a white man."

These are extraordinary numbers. But I don't think that if you've read *Blink* you'll find them at all surprising. This is no different from what Ian Ayres found when he did his study of the way black men were treated by car salesmen in Chicago. I don't think the car salesmen in that study meant to discriminate against black men. But they did — overwhelmingly and punitively — because they were subject to the kind of biases that many of us carry around in the nether regions of our brains, which affect our behavior as much as the opinions that we knowingly hold. Put a black man inside the criminal justice system and the same thing happens. Justice is supposed to be blind. It isn't.

So, what should we do? Well, we can spend the next twenty years trying to address the fundamental problem of unconscious racism in our society. Or we can try, in an immediate and practical way, to fix the flawed snap decisions that distort the course of justice. What if the legal community took a page from the classical music world?

What if we put screens in the courtroom? We have a jury system in the Western world based on an idea that goes back to antiquity: that the accused has the right to confront his accusers and to be judged by a jury of his peers. Back then it was thought that for justice to be achieved, the jury, the accuser, and the accused all had to see one another. But now we know more: we know that what we see — particularly when it is the color of someone's skin, or gender, or age — does not always aid understanding. Sometimes we can make better judgments with less information. I think that the accused in a criminal trial shouldn't be in the courtroom. He or she should be in another room entirely, answering questions by e-mail or through the use of an intermediary. And I think that all evidence and testimony in a trial that tips the jury off to the age or race or gender of the defendant ought to be edited out.

I gave a talk at Harvard Law School a few months ago and laid out this idea to a group of some of the country's brightest young minds. I thought they would be skeptical. But they weren't. Even though many raised legitimate concerns about the practicality of the idea, or about just how much difference it would make in the end, there seemed to be little disagreement with the idea that we have to do *something* to reduce the shameful disparity in the way we treat people in the legal system based on the color of their skin. This is the real lesson of *Blink:* It is not enough simply to explore the hidden recesses of our unconscious. Once we know about how the mind works — and about the strengths and weaknesses of human judgment — it is our responsibility to act.

Notes

INTRODUCTION. THE STATUE THAT DIDN'T LOOK RIGHT

Margolis published his findings in a triumphant article in *Scientific American:* Stanley V. Margolis, "Authenticating Ancient Marble Sculpture," *Scientific American* 260, no. 6 (June 1989): 104–110.

The kouros story has been told in a number of places. The best account is by Thomas Hoving, in chapter 18 of *False Impressions: The Hunt for Big Time Art Fakes* (London: Andre Deutsch, 1996). The accounts of the art experts who saw the kouros in Athens are collected in *The Getty Kouros Colloquium: Athens, 25–27 May 1992* (Malibu: J. Paul Getty Museum and Athens: Nicholas P. Goulandris Foundation, Museum of Cycladic Art, 1993). See also Michael Kimmelman, "Absolutely Real? Absolutely Fake?" *New York Times,* August 4, 1991; Marion True, "A Kouros at the Getty Museum," *Burlington Magazine* 119, no. 1006 (January 1987): 3–11; George Ortiz, *Connoisseurship and Antiquity: Small Bronze Sculpture from the Ancient World* (Malibu: J. Paul Getty Museum, 1990), 275–278; and Robert Steven Bianchi, "Saga of the Getty Kouros," *Archaeology* 47, no. 3 (May/June 1994): 22–25.

The gambling experiment with the red and blue decks is described in Antoine Bechara, Hanna Damasio, Daniel Tranel, and Antonio R. Damasio, "Deciding Advantageously Before Knowing the Advantageous Strategy," *Science* 275 (February 1997): 1293–1295. This experiment is actually a wonderful way into a variety of fascinating topics.

For more, see Antonio Damasio's *Descartes' Error* (New York: HarperCollins, 1994), 212.

The ideas behind "fast and frugal" can be found in Gerd Gigerenzer, Peter M. Todd, and the ABC Research Group, *Simple Heuristics That Make Us Smart* (New York: Oxford University Press, 1999).

The person who has thought extensively about the adaptive unconscious and has written the most accessible account of the "computer" inside our mind is the psychologist Timothy Wilson. I am greatly indebted to his wonderful book *Strangers to Ourselves: Discovering the Adaptive Unconscious* (Cambridge, Mass.: Harvard University Press, 2002). Wilson also discusses, at some length, the Iowa gambling experiment.

On Ambady's research on professors, see Nalini Ambady and Robert Rosenthal, "Half a Minute: Predicting Teacher Evaluations from Thin Slices of Nonverbal Behavior and Physical Attractiveness," *Journal of Personality and Social Psychology* 64, no. 3 (1993): 431–441.

Chapter One.
The Theory of Thin Slices:
How a Little Bit of Knowledge
Goes a Long Way

John Gottman has written widely on marriage and relationships. For a summary, see www.gottman.com. For the thinnest slice, see Sybil Carrère and John Gottman, "Predicting Divorce Among Newlyweds from the First Three Minutes of a Marital Conflict Discussion," *Family Process* 38, no. 3 (1999): 293–301.

You can find more information on Nigel West at www.nigelwest.com.

On whether marriage counselors and psychologists can accurately judge the future of a marriage, see Rachel Ebling and Robert W. Levenson, "Who Are the Marital Experts?" *Journal of Marriage and Family* 65, no. 1 (February 2003): 130–142.

On the bedroom study, see Samuel D. Gosling, Sei Jin Ko, et al., "A Room with a Cue: Personality Judgments Based on Offices and Bedrooms," *Journal of Personality and Social Psychology* 82, no. 3 (2002): 379–398.

On the issue of malpractice lawsuits and physicians, see an interview with Jeffrey Allen and Alice Burkin by Berkeley Rice: "How Plaintiffs' Lawyers Pick Their Targets," *Medical Economics* (April 24, 2000); Wendy Levinson et al., "Physician-Patient Communication: The Relationship with Malpractice Claims Among Primary Care Physicians and Surgeons," *Journal of the American Medical Association* 277, no. 7 (1997): 553–559; and Nalini Ambady et al., "Surgeons' Tone of Voice: A Clue to Malpractice History," *Surgery* 132, no. 1 (2002): 5–9.

CHAPTER TWO. THE LOCKED DOOR:
THE SECRET LIFE OF SNAP DECISIONS

For Hoving on Berenson etc., see *False Impressions: The Hunt for Big Time Art Fakes* (London: Andre Deutsch, 1996), 19–20.

On the scrambled-sentence test, see Thomas K. Srull and Robert S. Wyer, "The Role of Category Accessibility in the Interpretation of Information About Persons: Some Determinants and Implications," *Journal of Personality and Social Psychology* 37 (1979): 1660–1672.

John Bargh's fascinating research can be found in John A. Bargh, Mark Chen, and Lara Burrows, "Automaticity of Social Behavior: Direct Effects of Trait Construct and Stereotype Activation on Action," *Journal of Personality and Social Psychology* 71, no. 2 (1996): 230–244.

On the Trivial Pursuit study, see Ap Dijksterhuis and Ad van Knippenberg, "The Relation Between Perception and Behavior, or How to Win a Game of Trivial Pursuit," *Journal of Personality and Social Psychology* 74, no. 4 (1998): 865–877.

The study on black and white test performance and race priming is presented in Claude Steele and Joshua Aronson's "Stereotype Threat and Intellectual Test Performance of African Americans," *Journal of Personality and Social Psychology* 69, no. 5 (1995): 797–811.

The gambling studies are included in Antonio Damasio's wonderful book *Descartes' Error: Emotion, Reason, and the Human Brain* (New York: HarperCollins, 1994), 193.

The human need to explain the inexplicable was described, most famously, by Richard Nisbett and Timothy Wilson in the 1970s. They concluded: "It is naturally preferable, from the standpoint of prediction and subjective feelings of control, to believe that we have such access. It is frightening to believe that no one has no more certain knowledge of the workings of one's own mind than would an outsider with intimate knowledge of one's history and of the stimuli present at the time the cognitive process occurred." See Richard E. Nisbett and Timothy D. Wilson, "Telling More Than We Can Know: Verbal Reports on Mental Processes," *Psychological Review* 84, no. 3 (1977): 231–259.

On the swinging rope experiment, see Norman R. F. Maier. "Reasoning in Humans: II. The Solution of a Problem and Its Appearance in Consciousness," *Journal of Comparative Psychology* 12 (1931): 181–194.

CHAPTER THREE.
THE WARREN HARDING ERROR: WHY WE
FALL FOR TALL, DARK, AND HANDSOME MEN

There are many excellent books on Warren Harding, including the following: Francis Russell, *The Shadow of Blooming Grove: Warren G.*

Harding in His Times (New York: McGraw-Hill, 1968); Mark Sullivan, *Our Times: The United States* 1900–1925, vol. 6, *The Twenties* (New York: Charles Scribner's Sons, 1935), 16; Harry M. Daugherty, *The Inside Story of the Harding Tragedy* (New York: Ayer, 1960); and Andrew Sinclair, *The Available Man: The Life Behind the Masks of Warren Gamaliel Harding* (New York: Macmillan, 1965).

For more on the IAT, see Anthony G. Greenwald, Debbie E. McGhee, and Jordan L. K. Schwartz, "Measuring Individual Differences in Implicit Cognition: The Implicit Association Test," *Journal of Personality and Social Psychology* 74, no. 6 (1998): 1464–1480.

For an excellent treatment of the height issue, see Nancy Etcoff, *Survival of the Prettiest: The Science of Beauty* (New York: Random House, 1999), 172.

The height-salary study can be found in Timothy A. Judge and Daniel M. Cable, "The Effect of Physical Height on Workplace Success and Income: Preliminary Test of a Theoretical Model," *Journal of Applied Psychology* 89, no. 3 (June 2004): 428–441.

A description of the Chicago car dealerships study is found in Ian Ayres, *Pervasive Prejudice? Unconventional Evidence of Race and Gender Discrimination* (Chicago: University of Chicago Press, 2001).

For proof that you can combat prejudice, see Nilanjana Dasgupta and Anthony G. Greenwald, "On the Malleability of Automatic Attitudes: Combating Automatic Prejudice with Images of Admired and Disliked Individuals," *Journal of Personality and Social Psychology* 81, no. 5 (2001): 800–814. A number of other studies have shown similar effects. Among them: Irene V. Blair et al., "Imagining Stereotypes Away: The Moderation of Implicit Stereotypes Through Mental Imagery," *Journal of Personality and Social Psychology* 81, no. 5 (2001): 828–841; and Brian S. Lowery and Curtis D. Hardin, "Social Influence Effects on Automatic Racial Prejudice," *Journal of Personality and Social Psychology* 81, no. 5 (2001): 842–855.

Chapter Four.
Paul Van Riper's Big Victory:
Creating Structure for Spontaneity

A good account of Blue Team's philosophy toward war fighting can be found in William A. Owens, *Lifting the Fog of War* (New York: Farrar, Straus, 2000), 11.

Klein's classic work on decision making is *Sources of Power* (Cambridge, Mass.: MIT Press, 1998).

On the rules of improv, see Keith Johnstone, *Impro: Improvisation and the Theatre* (New York: Theatre Arts Books, 1979).

On logic puzzles, see Chad S. Dodson, Marcia K. Johnson, and Jonathan W. Schooler, "The Verbal Overshadowing Effect: Why

Descriptions Impair Face Recognition," *Memory & Cognition* 25, no. 2 (1997): 129–139.

On verbal overshadowing, see Jonathan W. Schooler, Stellan Ohlsson, and Kevin Brooks, "Thoughts Beyond Words: When Language Overshadows Insight," *Journal of Experimental Psychology* 122, no. 2 (1993): 166–183.

The firefighter story and others are discussed in "The Power of Intuition," chap. 4 in Gary Klein's *Sources of Power* (Cambridge, Mass.: MIT Press, 1998).

For Reilly's research, see Brendan M. Reilly, Arthur T. Evans, Jeffrey J. Schaider, and Yue Wang, "Triage of Patients with Chest Pain in the Emergency Department: A Comparative Study of Physicians' Decisions," *American Journal of Medicine* 112 (2002): 95–103; and Brendan Reilly et al., "Impact of a Clinical Decision Rule on Hospital Triage of Patients with Suspected Acute Cardiac Ischemia in the Emergency Department," *Journal of the American Medical Association* 288 (2002): 342–350.

Goldman has written several papers on his algorithm. Among them are Lee Goldman et al., "A Computer-Derived Protocol to Aid in the Diagnosis of Emergency Room Patients with Acute Chest Pain," *New England Journal of Medicine* 307, no. 10 (1982): 588–596; and Lee Goldman et al., "Prediction of the Need for Intensive Care in Patients Who Come to Emergency Departments with Acute Chest Pain," *New England Journal of Medicine* 334, no. 23 (1996): 1498–1504.

On the consideration of gender and race, see Kevin Schulman et al., "Effect of Race and Sex on Physicians' Recommendations for Cardiac Catheterization," *New England Journal of Medicine* 340, no. 8 (1999): 618–626.

Oskamp's famous study is described in Stuart Oskamp, "Overconfidence in Case Study Judgments," *Journal of Consulting Psychology* 29, no. 3 (1965): 261–265.

CHAPTER FIVE.
KENNA'S DILEMMA: THE RIGHT — AND WRONG — WAY TO ASK PEOPLE WHAT THEY WANT

A lot has been written about the changing music industry. This article was helpful: Laura M. Holson, "With By-the-Numbers Radio, Requests Are a Dying Breed," *New York Times,* July 11, 2002.

Dick Morris's memoir is *Behind the Oval Office: Getting Reelected Against All Odds* (Los Angeles: Renaissance Books, 1999).

For the best telling of the Coke story, see Thomas Oliver, *The Real Coke, the Real Story* (New York: Random House, 1986).

For more on Cheskin, see Thomas Hine, *The Total Package: The Secret History and Hidden Meanings of Boxes, Bottles, Cans, and*

Other Persuasive Containers (New York: Little, Brown, 1995); and Louis Cheskin and L. B. Ward, "Indirect Approach to Market Reactions," *Harvard Business Review* (September 1948).

Sally Bedell [Smith]'s biography of Silverman is *Up the Tube: Prime-Time TV in the Silverman Years* (New York: Viking, 1981).

Civille and Heylmun's ways of tasting are further explained in Gail Vance Civille and Brenda G. Lyon, *Aroma and Flavor Lexicon for Sensory Evaluation* (West Conshohocken, Pa.: American Society for Testing and Materials, 1996); and Morten Meilgaard, Gail Vance Civille, and B. Thomas Carr, *Sensory Evaluation Techniques,* 3rd ed. (Boca Raton, Fla.: CRC Press, 1999).

For more on jam tasting, see Timothy Wilson and Jonathan Schooler, "Thinking Too Much: Introspection Can Reduce the Quality of Preferences and Decisions," *Journal of Personality and Social Psychology* 60, no. 2 (1991): 181–192; and "Strawberry Jams and Preserves," *Consumer Reports,* August 1985, 487–489.

CHAPTER SIX.
SEVEN SECONDS IN THE BRONX:
THE DELICATE ART OF MIND READING

For more on the mind readers, see Paul Ekman, *Telling Lies: Clues to Deceit in the Marketplace, Politics, and Marriage* (New York: Norton, 1995); Fritz Strack, "Inhibiting and Facilitating Conditions of the Human Smile: A Nonobtrusive Test of the Facial Feedback Hypothesis," *Journal of Personality and Social Psychology* 54, no. 5 (1988): 768–777; and Paul Ekman and Wallace V. Friesen, *Facial Action Coding System, parts 1 and 2* (San Francisco: Human Interaction Laboratory, Dept. of Psychiatry, University of California, 1978).

Klin has written a number of accounts of his research using *Who's Afraid of Virginia Woolf?* The most comprehensive is probably Ami Klin, Warren Jones, Robert Schultz, Fred Volkmar, and Donald Cohen, "Defining and Quantifying the Social Phenotype in Autism," *American Journal of Psychiatry* 159 (2002): 895–908.

On mind reading, see also Robert T. Schultz et al., "Abnormal Ventral Temporal Cortical Activity During Face Discrimination Among Individuals with Autism and Asperger's Syndrome," *Archives of General Psychiatry* 57 (April 2000).

Dave Grossman's wonderful video series is called *The Bulletproof Mind: Prevailing in Violent Encounters . . . and After.*

The stories of police officers firing their guns are taken from David Klinger's extraordinary book *Into the Kill Zone: A Cop's Eye View of Deadly Force* (San Francisco: Jossey-Bass, 2004).

A number of studies have explored racial bias and guns, including the following: B. Keith Payne, Alan J. Lambert, and Larry L. Jacoby,

"Best-Laid Plans: Effects of Goals on Accessibility Bias and Cognitive Control in Race-Based Misperceptions of Weapons," *Journal of Experimental Social Psychology* 38 (2002): 384–396; Alan J. Lambert, B. Keith Payne, Larry L. Jacoby, Lara M. Shaffer, et al., "Stereotypes as Dominant Responses: On the 'Social Facilitation' of Prejudice in Anticipated Public Contexts," *Journal of Personality and Social Psychology* 84, no. 2 (2003): 277–295; Keith Payne, "Prejudice and Perception: The Role of Automatic and Controlled Processes in Misperceiving a Weapon," *Journal of Personality and Social Psychology* 81, no. 2 (2001): 181–192; Anthony Greenwald, "Targets of Discrimination: Effects of Race on Responses to Weapons Holders," *Journal of Experimental Social Psychology* 39 (2003): 399–405; and Joshua Correll, Bernadette Park, Charles Judd, and Bernd Wittenbrink, "The Police Officer's Dilemma: Using Ethnicity to Disambiguate Potentially Hostile Individuals," *Journal of Personality and Social Psychology* 83 (2002): 1314–1329. This study is a videogame in which whites and blacks are presented in ambiguous positions and the player has to decide whether to shoot or not. Go to http://psych.colorado.edu/%7ejcorrell/tpod.html and try it. It's quite sobering.

On learning how to mind-read, see Nancy L. Etcoff, Paul Ekman, et al., "Lie Detection and Language Comprehension," *Nature* 405 (May 11, 2000).

On two-person patrols, see Carlene Wilson, *Research on One- and Two-Person Patrols: Distinguishing Fact from Fiction* (South Australia: Australasian Centre for Policing Research, 1991); and Scott H. Decker and Allen E. Wagner, "The Impact of Patrol Staffing on Police-Citizen Injuries and Dispositions," *Journal of Criminal Justice* 10 (1982): 375–382.

CONCLUSION.
LISTENING WITH YOUR EYES:
THE LESSONS OF *BLINK*

The best account of the Conant story is by Conant's husband, William Osborne, "You Sound like a Ladies Orchestra." It is available on their Website, www.osborne-conant.org/ladies.htm.

The following articles were particularly helpful on changes in the world of classical music: Evelyn Chadwick, "Of Music and Men," *The Strad* (December 1997): 1324–1329; Claudia Goldin and Cecilia Rouse, "Orchestrating Impartiality: The Impact of 'Blind' Auditions on Female Musicians," *American Economic Review* 90, no. 4 (September 2000): 715–741; and Bernard Holland, "The Fair, New World of Orchestra Auditions," *New York Times,* January 11, 1981.

Acknowledgments

A few years ago, before I began *Blink*, I grew my hair long. It used to be cut very short and conservatively. But I decided, on a whim, to let it grow wild, as it had been when I was a teenager. Immediately, in very small but significant ways, my life changed. I started getting speeding tickets — and I had never gotten any before. I started getting pulled out of airport security lines for special attention. And one day, as I was walking along Fourteenth Street in downtown Manhattan, a police van pulled up on the sidewalk, and three officers jumped out. They were looking, it turned out, for a rapist, and the rapist, they said, looked a lot like me. They pulled out the sketch and the description. I looked at it and pointed out to them as nicely as I could that, in fact, the rapist looked nothing at all like me. He was much taller and much heavier and about fifteen years younger (and, I added in a largely futile attempt at humor, not nearly as good-looking). All we had in common was a large head of curly hair. After twenty minutes or so, the officers finally agreed with me and let me go. On the grand scale of things, I realize, this was a trivial misunderstanding. African Americans in the United States suffer indignities far worse than this all the time. But what struck me was how even more subtle and absurd the stereotyping was in my case: this wasn't about something really obvious, such as skin color or age or height or weight. It was just about hair. Something about the first impression created by my hair derailed every other consideration in the hunt for the rapist. That episode on the street got me thinking about the weird power of first impressions. And that thinking led to *Blink* — so I suppose, before I thank anyone else, I should thank those three police officers.

Now come the real thanks. David Remnick, the editor of the *New Yorker,* very graciously and patiently let me disappear for a year while I was working on *Blink*. Everyone should have a boss as good and generous as David. Little, Brown, the publishing house that treated me like a prince with *The Tipping Point,* did the same this time around. Thank you, Michael Pietsch, Geoff Shandler, Heather Fain, and, most of all, Bill Phillips, who deftly and thoughtfully and cheerfully guided this manuscript from nonsense to sense. I am now leaning toward calling my firstborn Bill. A very long list of friends read the manuscript in various stages and gave me invaluable advice — Sarah Lyall, Robert McCrum, Bruce Headlam, Deborah Needleman, Jacob Weisberg, Zoe Rosenfeld, Charles Randolph, Jennifer Wachtell, Josh Liberson, Elaine Blair, and Tanya Simon. Emily Kroll did the CEO height study for me. Joshua Aronson and Jonathan Schooler generously gave me the benefit of their academic expertise. The wonderful staff at Savoy tolerated my long afternoons at the table by the window. Kathleen Lyon kept me happy and healthy. My favorite photographer in the world, Brooke Williams, took my author photo. Several people, though, deserve special thanks. Terry Martin and Henry Finder — as they did with *The Tipping Point* — wrote long and extraordinary critiques of the early drafts. I am blessed to have two friends of such brilliance. Suzy Hansen and the incomparable Pamela Marshall brought focus and clarity to the text and rescued me from embarrassment and error. As for Tina Bennett, I would suggest that she be appointed CEO of Microsoft or run for President or otherwise be assigned to bring her wit and intelligence and graciousness to bear on the world's problems — but then I wouldn't have an agent anymore. Finally, my mother and father, Joyce and Graham Gladwell, read this book as only parents can: with devotion, honesty, and love. Thank you.

Index